Congress and the Administrative State

Viewpoints
On American Politics

EDITOR: SAMUEL KRISLOV

American Legal Processes
WILLIAM MCLAUGHLAN

Congress and the Administrative State
LAWRENCE DODD AND RICHARD SCHOTT

From Social Issues to Public Policy
ROBERT EYESTONE

Congress and the Administrative State

Lawrence C. Dodd
Richard L. Schott

The University of Texas, Austin

JOHN WILEY AND SONS

New York   Chichester   Brisbane   Toronto

Library of Congress Cataloging in Publication Data:

Dodd, Lawrence C
    Congress and the administrative state.

    (Viewpoints on American politics)
    Includes index.
    1. United States—Congress.   2.   United States—
Executive departments.   3.   Administrative agencies—
United States.   4.   Legislative oversight—United States.
I.   Schott, Richard L., joint author.   II.   Title.

JK585.D6   328.73′07′456   79-14347
ISBN 0-471-21741-7

Printed in the United States of America

10 9 8 7 6 5 4 3 2 1

Preface

The idea for this book dates back to our early teaching careers. Each of us, working with the material that pertained to his specialization—Dodd, the Congress; Schott, the federal executive branch—became increasingly aware of the lack of serious studies that attempted to bridge these two institutions. It seemed to us that most if not virtually all scholars writing about Congress from the perspective of the federal bureaucracy treated it with a mixture of disdain and apprehension. Congress was a meddlesome child, ignorant of the requisites of good and efficient administration, one that interfered with accepted administrative processes solely on the basis of narrow, parochial, and partisan interests. For their part, scholars of Congress either ignored the bureaucracy or viewed federal agencies and their officials—in whose hands lay the power to implement (or subvert) much of congressional legislation—as recalcitrant, officious technicrats, insensitive to the legitimate representative functions of legislative bodies. There was, in short, a lack of empathy among students of the legislative culture for the dynamics of the bureaucratic culture, and vice versa.

Although historical treatments of both the executive branch and of Congress existed, little attention had been paid to the influence of the one on the other. This omission, we felt, seriously limited our understanding of the relationship between these institutions, of the historical interplay between the first branch of American government and the "fourth." Moreover, the lack of a recent assessment of the impact of the reform decade of the 1970s on Congress and on its oversight of the

v

bureaucracy gave added impetus to the need to examine this relationship.

Other concerns also sparked our interest in writing such a book. One was the development of the field of policy studies with its emphasis on policy as a continuum ranging from legislative proposals to administrative implementation. This perspective reinforced our commitment to study the interaction of Congress and the bureaucracy in various phases of the policy process.

Finally, the perennial issue of accountability needed to be reexamined. How responsive and truly democratic are the procedures by which these two institutions design and implement policies and programs? And how effective is congressional surveillance of the bureaucracy—whose norms of hierarchical authority and deference to expertise are often at loggerheads with democratic norms of equality, representation, and consensus? The search for the answers to these questions is a *leitmotif* of this book.

Our hope is to provide an historical, synthetic study of congressional-bureaucratic relations, one that is descriptive and analytic, retrospective and prospective. In so doing, we have drawn both from the existing literature in the field and from our personal experiences in Washington. Much of our discussion is meant as an exploratory attempt to lead the reader through the maze of congressional-bureaucratic relations and to trace some broad themes and supply insights. We do not claim to have provided a definitive treatment, but we do hope to stimulate debate over our major themes and to further research into this neglected area of American government.

The organization of the book has been guided by four central concerns. The first is our conviction that an analysis of congressional-bureaucratic relations should include more than simply oversight or congressional "control" of administration. Such an analysis must look more broadly at the historical development of each institution and its impact on the other—for the relationship depends in large measure on how each institution has developed, how it is organized, and where within it power resides. A corollary of Santayana's famous admonition is that those who are ignorant of the past may also be ignorant of the present. Scholars, we feel, need to take an increasingly historical approach to the study of these two institutions in order to understand better their development, their power structure, and their roles.

Thus, in Chapters 1 to 4, we examine the historical evolution of the Congress and the federal bureaucracy, what stages of development mark their evolution, and how the growth of one institution may have influenced the other. For the federal bureaucracy, we identify first a period of relative quiet lasting for most of the nineteenth century, then the beginning in the 1880s of three phases of rapid growth: one stretching from the 1880s to around 1920; another dating from the Depression to the early 1950s; and a third lasting from the 1960s to the present. These periods of growth, especially the second and third, have, we argue, not only posed challenges for the Congress but also helped trigger changes in its internal distribution of power and resources.

For the Congress, we have identified three basic stages of evolution: a period of party government, dominating the nineteenth century and the first decade of the twentieth; a period of committee government, lasting from the early 1900s through roughly the 1960s; and a third, subcommittee government, in whose heyday we now live. The evolution of Congress as a professional, institutionalized body has accomplished the latter two stages, as has a gradual downward drift of power to the subcommittees. An important and related theme is the recent democratization of Congress as well as attempts to strengthen the congressional leadership as a reaction to the dispersion of power typical of subcommittee government.

In Chapters 5 and 6, we turn to a consideration of congressional oversight of federal administration. Here we attempt to broaden the treatment of oversight beyond the existing, excessively narrow literature that grows largely out of the analysis of congressional committees. A comprehensive picture of congressional oversight must examine not only the work of committees and subcommittees but the total range of congressional activities affecting the bureaucracy. We thus examine not only committee activity and oversight devices but also individual members, staff, and the congressional support agencies—the General Accounting Office, the Congressional Budget Office, and others.

We devote considerable attention to an assessment of the impact of congressional oversight efforts on the bureaus and agencies themselves. Our aim here is to focus less on the oversight work of particular committees and more on oversight as perceived by the bureaucracy itself. Our analysis suggests that increased oversight *activity* on the part of Congress has not necessarily led to enhanced surveillance of policy implementation by the executive branch. Given the lack of coordination of oversight efforts, congressional influence on the bureaucracy may have actually decreased. We conclude that so long as Congress fails to solve the many problems inherent in subcommittee government and subsystem politics, efforts to strengthen oversight will be blunted, perhaps doomed to failure.

Our third concern follows from those above. What are the implications of recent reform efforts and the development of subcommittee government for the role of the bureaucracy in the policy process? This question, examined largely in Chapter 7, attempts to describe the current shape of policymaking and policy implementation in the administrative state. Here we discuss the contribution of the federal bureaucracy to public policy and the proliferation of political subsystems. We conclude that recent developments in congressional-bureaucratic relations may have encouraged greater subsystem complexity, increased autonomy at the bureau level, and resulted in a more insulated and less responsive policy process within the executive branch itself. This conclusion, though tentative, is our best judgment based on current literature and our analysis of congressional-bureaucratic dynamics.

Finally, given our pessimistic assessment of the current dilemmas facing congressional control of federal administration, we turn to examine ways in which this control might be improved. In this discussion, presented in the final chapter, we consider such approaches as reorganization of the federal bureaucracy, further reform of Congress, and constitutional revision. Our view is that the structure of the federal bureaucracy is not in itself a fundamental deterrent to effective congressional surveillance of administration. The problem, we believe, lies with the Congress and to an extent with the Constitution itself, which was written under assumptions about the nature of the legislative branch that are no longer valid.

In developing these four areas of concern, we have tried to present our analysis in a way that would be useful to both undergraduate and graduate students, to other scholars, and to the informed general reader. This book is intended both as a vehicle for teaching and as a scholarly synthesis that provides a broad, integrated treatment of congressional-bureaucratic relations previously lacking in the field. Only the reader, of course, is the final judge of the extent to which our efforts have succeeded.

We are indebted to several people for their advice and criticism. Our series editor, Samuel Krislov, and Wiley editor, Wayne Anderson, provided advice, encouragement, and patience during the book's gestation. And we have benefitted especially from the counsel of Morris Ogul and Emmette Redford. In addition, we wish to thank—for a variety of reasons—a number of individuals, among them Melissa P. Collie, Philip Diehl, Cheryl Dodd, Wiley Jordan, Dwight Kiel, David Landsidle, Thomas Mann, Bruce Oppenheimer, Sharon Park, John C. Pierce, Mary Ryan, Larry Schechter, and George Shipley.

Both of us have been stimulated, over the years, by teachers and colleagues who have sparked both our intellectual curiousity and our concern with the issues raised here. Yet each of us has one former professor to whom he is especially thankful. In Dodd's case, Isabelle Hunt, former Professor of Government at Midwestern State University, played a major role in introducing him to the excitement and joy of political analysis and in directing his attention to American national politics. She represents the very best in the tradition of the committed teacher who stimulates the imagination and the desire to learn.

Schott is indebted to the late Roscoe C. Martin of the Maxwell School, Syracuse University. A man of broad understanding, keen judgment, and compassion, Roscoe Martin encouraged students to separate the wheat from the chaff and to appreciate what was worthwhile among new currents of thought while respecting the contributions of the past. He approached his students not as a master but as a *primus inter pares,* and his constant emphasis on the democratic political environment surrounding administration stimulated a concern with the political processes and institutions that drive the bureaucracy. His legacy is evident in these pages.

To these two fine individuals and teachers we dedicate this book.

Austin, Texas   **Lawrence Dodd**
June, 1979   **Richard Schott**

Contents

Congress and the Administrative State

1
Introduction

A distinguishing feature of political life in twentieth century America has been the spectacular growth of the functions and services provided by our national government. Along with this growth has come the creation of a federal bureaucracy of great size, scope, and power—an "administrative state" composed of a multitude of federal departments, agencies, boards, and commissions. Few areas of our daily lives go untouched by a national bureaucracy that delivers our mail, regulates our drugs, our industry, and commerce; provides food stamps to the hungry and relief payments to the poor; subsidizes our education; helps ensure our national security; and also collects a part of our personal incomes to finance its activities. Due in part to the vast reservoir of information at its disposal and to its political muscle, this federal bureaucracy has emerged as a fourth branch of American national government. As such, it is engaged in struggle for control of public policy with the three branches created by the Constitution: the Congress, the executive, and the courts.

The ascendancy of this powerful and pervasive administrative state has not come by accident, nor by some deep and sinister bureaucratic conspiracy, but by the conscious choice (or series of choices) of the American people acting through their elected representatives. For it is the Congress that, in response to the needs and demands of the population, has given birth to our national administrative system. No federal department, agency, administration, or major federal program has ever been created without the express or implicit consent of Congress, nor may one be abolished without its approval.

1

The administrative state is, however, in many respects a prodigal child. Although born of congressional intent, it has taken on a life of its own and has matured to a point where its muscle and brawn can be turned against its creator. Over the past several decades, the federal bureaucracy has come to rival the president and the Congress, challenging both for hegemony in the national political system. Protected by civil service tenure, armed with the power to issue orders and rules that have the force of law, supported by strong clientele and interest groups, and possessing a wealth of information, knowledge, and technical expertise, it goes forth to battle its institutional rivals on equal, and sometimes superior, terms. And, though occasionally defeated, it rarely returns home repentant.

The modern federal bureaucracy is a formidable force not only in the execution of policy (its original task) but increasingly also in its formulation. Its agencies are staffed by specialists, career civil servants who have spent a lifetime immersed in the details of a particular program. Strong among their ranks are professionals and scientists whose special training has given them fresh insights into how a proposal might be improved or a new policy initiated. The expertise of these career bureaucrats, combined with the technical facilities for data collection and analysis that are at their disposal, allows them to bring to policy struggles an authority and knowledge that is difficult for members of Congress, presidents, or political appointees to match. These specialists, working through the political appointees that head their departments, or working directly with members of Congress and their staffs, can mold and constrain the legislative options open to both Congress and the president. In more cases than generally recognized, the germs of policy ideas emanating from the White House originate with these career officials.

The implementation of these policies is, among other things, a constant refinement of congressional intent as expressed in legislation. This refinement involves the formulation of rules and regulations, their application to specific programs and cases, and numerous administrative decisions interpreting their application—a translation into tangible programs of broad public policy guidelines laid down by the Congress. This process whereby law is distilled into administrative action, known as "sub-legislation," gives the bureaucracy a great deal of discretionary latitude. To the degree that an agency opposes congressional policy, this latitude can be exploited to undercut, even destroy, legislative intent. And to the degree an agency supports a policy, this latitude provides an aggressive agency the opportunity to aggrandize power by interpreting broadly its legislative mandate.

Presidents, Congress, and the Administrative State

The coming of age of the administrative state has not gone unnoticed by those whom it has challenged. With the growth of the bureaucracy, presidents have sought from Congress (and have been given) substantial power to coordinate and control the agencies of the executive branch. These include: (1) authorization of large-scale assistance to the president; (2) presidential power to control the bureaucracy and change executive branch structure; and (3) a relatively free hand in high level appointments. Among the mechanisms that Congress has provided presidents is the Executive Office of the President. This powerful organization consists of a group of personal advisors, staff offices, and advisory councils (among them the Office of Management and Budget, the National Security Council, the Council of Economic Advisors) designed to supply presidents not only with intelligence about what is happening in the depths of the administration, but also with public policy options and the organizational tools to coordinate both the formulation and execution of public policy. In addition to the Executive Office, Congress has given Presidents substantial budgetary powers, including the authority to formulate a unified national budget and to oversee its administration.

To help control the bureaucracy, Congress has given occupants of the Oval Office the right—subject to congressional approval—to reorganize executive branch structure. Rolling back the high-water mark of civil service domination of federal agencies reached in the 1950s, Congress has provided presidents with a second tier of political appointees serving in responsible policymaking positions below the secretary level. And Congress has traditionally accorded presidents wide latitude in the confirmation of those individuals who a president nominates to head the various federal departments, commissions, and agencies. In granting presidents this wide range of checks and controls over the federal bureaucracy, Congress has chosen to institutionalize the presidency as a counterweight to the administrative state. The Executive Office, a key feature of the "institutionalized presidency," is, like the federal bureaucracy, a creation of Congress.

Inevitably, many of the very devices that Congress has given presidents in an effort to strengthen their hand over the bureaucracy have led as well to the strengthening of the presidency vis-à-vis Congress, thus returning to haunt the Congress as ghosts of decisions past. For example, the authority to prepare a nation's budget carries with it the opportunity to manage the nation's pursestrings and thereby to determine programmatic priorities. The power of the purse, Madison writes in Federalist #58, provides the legislature "the most complete and effectual weapon with which any constitution can arm the immediate representatives of the people, for obtaining a redress of every grievance, and for carrying into effect every just and salutory measure." A Revolutionary War slogan captured the point a bit more succinctly: "No taxation without representation!" The power Congress has given presidents to prepare an executive budget from agency recommendations and to present it to Congress as basic policy exalts the presidency as the central budget office of our government. The president's role as chief budgetary officer undermines congressional control of the national pursestrings and limits thereby the ability of Congress to have an independent influence on public policy.

The power vis-à-vis Congress inherent in presidential formulation of the national budget is augmented by a second, presidential access to information. Information, the saying goes, is power. It provides the raw material from which to formulate, justify, and implement public policy. Through the institutional capability to collect, organize, and present information provided by the Executive Office, the president has attempted to centralize control of this resource. Moreover, presidents have moved in recent years to gain control of this information by expanded use of the claim of executive privilege and by restrictive classification of executive branch documents. This near-monopoly of information and the system of secrecy associated with it, Arthur Schlesinger, Jr., has argued, are key elements of the "imperial presidency." Restoring "constitutional comity" between Congress and the presidency and the "hope of democratic control" over policymaking, he suggests, rest at least in part on the "loosening of the executive monopoly of information."[1]

The emergence of the administrative state and numerous congressional grants of authority over it to the president have contributed to a dramatic shift in the constitutional balance of power in America. The intent of the founding fathers, as represented in the *Federalist Papers,* was to construct a representative government of limited powers, which would serve primarily to conduct foreign policy, provide for domestic tranquility and national security, and ensure the ease of commerce among separate states. Authority to act in the areas of foreign policy, national security, and interstate commerce, along with a limited number of other jurisdictional areas, was explicitly delegated to the national government, with all other powers reserved to the states or the people.

The goal of the founders was to construct a government with the ability to preserve the nation (and its existing structure of social and economic power) and to create an aura of civil liberties and democratic processes. But they also intended to limit the possibility that the national government might be used aggressively by a new majority to redirect or redistribute economic and social power. While delegating specific powers to the national government, therefore, the founders chose to separate governmental functions among three branches, the Congress, the presidency, and the courts, giving each specific checks against the others. Because the founders did not plan for (or desire) an

---

[1]Arthur Schlesinger, Jr., *The Imperial Presidency* (Boston: Houghton Mifflin, 1973), p. 317.

extensive national government, they did not foresee the emergence of a large bureaucracy and thus made no provisions concerning the constitutional role it would play. As an unanticipated national bureaucracy has grown, it has been drawn into the president's orbit and thereby "tilted" the balance of American politics toward the executive branch—a tilt sanctioned in congressional grants of authority.

It would be misleading, of course, to assert that the courts or Congress have been eclipsed. First, considerable tension remains between the president and the bureaucracy. This tension often enables Congress to find allies among bureaucratic agencies on certain issues. Second, Congress has developed and employed a variety of devices to help it stand guard over the conduct and behavior of administrative agencies, devices discussed extensively later. Third, the judiciary may provide a court of last resort. The Supreme Court, for example, may rule on the constitutionality of specific acts of the executive. By appeal to the courts, Congress was able to overturn the majority of attempts by the Nixon administration to impound funds appropriated by the legislature. The avenue of judicial appeal, however, is cumbersome and time-consuming. It forces the Congress into direct confrontation with the executive and heightens a struggle between institutions rather than promotes a mutual quest for consensus over national public policy.

The struggle for institutional power, and the ensuing decrease in constitutional comity, have produced a serious challenge to representative government in America. Representative government rests on the assumption that fundamental policy decisions will be made by elected representatives of the people. Within the entire executive apparatus of our national government, from the White House to the Washington agencies to the local post office, only the president and vice president are elected; all others are appointed by the president or his appointees or selected by merit system procedures. Presidents are limited by the 22nd Amendment to two elective terms, so that two-term presidents serve half of their tenure without the spectre of electoral accountability. In addition, the 25th Amendment provides the possibility that both a president and vice president can be installed by nonelective means: the elevations of Gerald Ford and Nelson Rockefeller are examples. There is, therefore, no set of individuals within the executive branch who necessarily derive their positions from election and who are continually subject to electoral accountability.

In our national government, Congress is the only truly elective branch. Only in the halls of Congress can citizens seeking political redress of their grievances be assured of finding government officials whose fate depends directly on the vote of the people. The historic shift in power toward the executive and away from Congress makes more serious the fact that critical policy decisions are made by administrative officials who may have never served in elective office, who are largely hidden from public view, and who gain their jobs through political appointment or technical expertise instead of direct popular mandate. As Sam Rayburn commented to Lyndon Johnson concerning President John Kennedy's cabinet appointees: "They may be every bit as intelligent as you say, but I'd feel a whole lot better about them if just one of them had run for sheriff once."[2]

Studying Executive–Legislative Relations

The growth of executive power at the expense of Congress and the threat to representative government that this growth implies have received considerable scholarly attention. Most analyses, however, tend to personalize the presidency and to treat the relationship of the executive to the legislative as if it were primarily or exclusively a relationship between president and Congress. Studies in the latter vein offer material that is often dramatic, in which the issues are clear-cut and the action exciting—as, for example, in a successful attempt by Congress to override a presidential veto—and the clash of institutions more visible. Such a perspective, however, tends to ignore the fact that the "executive" is much more than the presidency; the executive

[2]Quoted in David Halberstram, *The Best and the Brightest* (New York: Random House, 1969), p. 41.

is essentially two related but often conflicting institutions: the presidency and the bureaucracy. The increased power of the executive, in short, results from not only the emergence of an imperial presidency but also the emergence of the modern administrative state.

To comprehend fully the challenge to representative government, to assess the problems and potentials facing Congress as it attempts to reassert its independent role, to understand Congress in relation to the executive and vice versa, it is necessary to investigate the relationship between Congress and the administrative state. By this we mean, however, not necessarily the relationship between an agency and a congressional committee but instead the dynamic, changing impact that each institution has on the other. It is our basic thesis that both Congress and the administrative state have a significant influence on the other's organization and function. Just as Congress created the administrative state, the rise of the administrative state influenced the emergence of the modern Congress at the turn of the century. This modern Congress has encountered significant problems in performing its constitutional role, problems that have led to recurrent and wide-ranging reforms of Congress, particularly during the 1970s. These reforms have been designed in part to give Congress better leverage over the administrative state—they are reforms that have influenced how the administrative state is organized and how it functions.

The first section of this book is the story of the rise of the administrative state and how this rise influenced Congress. The second section is an extensive examination of the modern Congress and how that Congress is now reforming in an attempt to come to grips with an age of administrative policymaking. In the third section, we turn our attention back to the administrative state and try to assess the impact of the reformed Congress on it.

A central assumption of this book is that an understanding of the current struggle between the executive and legislative branches requires an examination of the ways each institution influences the organization and function of the other. It is critically important to understand how Congress attempts to perform its constitutional roles within the context of an administrative state. In theory, the bureaucracy is a servant of the people. It can produce good or ill, depending on the guidance and direction it receives from Congress and the efficacy of the safeguards placed on it. By understanding the problems the administrative state creates for Congress as an institution, how Congress has attempted to address these problems and gain control over the bureaucracy, the issues Congress faces in attempting to influence the bureaucracy, and the impact that congressional control of the bureacracy has on the administrative state, we can better assess the nature of our current institutional dilemma and the shape of its potential resolution.

Policy Formulation and Subsystem Politics

In approaching the study of congressional-bureaucratic relations, a first connection to examine is their *legislative* interaction in the formulation of policy. Although Congress is constitutionally the wellspring of law and legislation, it has long been recognized that in this complex modern age, it is no longer the sole source of those proposals that provide grist for the legislative mill. Indeed, the present century has witnessed the growing dependence of Congress on the stimulus and initiatives for legislation developed in the executive branch. These initiatives may come from the president as a part of his legislative program, and are transmitted to Congress with the State-of-the-Union message, the budget message, and occasional special messages concerning specific policy or program areas. The president thus helps set the legislative machine in motion, and a significant part of its yearly output of bills is a modification of such initiatives.

Yet it would be a mistake to suggest that we have moved from an era in which Congress proposed and the president disposed to one in which the reverse is true. In reality, the bureaucratic agencies, as well as the president, members of Congress, and major interest groups play significant roles in formulating and lobbying for legislation. Neither the bureaucracy, the president, nor the Congress is the sole arbiter of public policy. Nor is any one of them a monolithic entity. Power, influence, and authority in the federal government are diffused among and within the major institutions, and policy formulation reflects this pluralism. Much of the ongoing process of national policy determination actually takes place outside the glare of television klieg lights, outside the public view in small "whirlpools" or "subsystems" of government. The major actors in these isolated dramas are generally congressional subcommittees, an executive agency or bureau, and an interest group or groups that are affected by or benefit from a given policy.[3] Debates over the regulation of the fares and frills offered by the nation's airlines, for example, involve a triangle composed of the Civil Aeronautics Board (the federal regulatory agency), the House and Senate transportation (aviation) subcommittees of the respective Commerce committees, and the interest or pressure groups associated with the airline industry, chief among them the Air Transport Association.[4] It is in a subsystem such as this that much legislation in a particular policy area will be proposed, debated, drafted, and ratified.

Nearly every major program or policy of national government is at least partly formulated in one or more legislative subsystems. These subsystems, little groups of policy neighbors, are often in substantial agreement on the basic policy issues confronting them—an agreement that may not coincide with the majority views of the larger institutions of which they are a part. These subsystems tend to develop a momentum of their own, proceeding along policy lines that are mutually advantageous to the members of the subsystem until some outside crisis or force challenges their existing consensus (or threatens the balance of power among them). When this happens, the traditional triangle is broken, and the arena in which policy decisions are made shifts to other competing subsystems or into the larger institu-

[3] Among the first to identify and discuss the notion of the subsystem and its implications were Arthur Maass, *Muddy Waters—The Army Engineers and the Nation's Rivers* (Cambridge: Harvard University Press, 1951) and J. Lieper Freeman, *The Political Process* (New York: Random House, 1955).

[4] A discussion of the civil aviation subsystem may be found in Emmette S. Redford, "A Case Analysis of Congressional Activity: Civil Aviation, 1957–58," *Journal of Politics* (May, 1960), pp. 228–258.

tions of which the subsystem members are a part—the Congress, the presidency, the bureaucratic departments, and the public.

Much (perhaps too much) of the daily policymaking of national government takes place in or through these subsystems, an arena in which the agencies of the administrative state play a crucial role. The power of Congress or the majority of its members to control public policy and determine policy priorities depends very much on the ability of Congress to play a forceful role in subsystem politics, to control the behavior of its own members at the subsystem level, and to coordinate the decisions made in the different policy subsystems.

Policy Surveillance and Subsystem Politics

The second major relationship between Congress and the bureaucracy involves the surveillance and supervision by Congress of the execution of public policy and administration. Without the power to know how the executive branch is translating its policy directives into action, Congress cannot gauge the adequacy of policy or ascertain whether agency behavior is consistent with Congressional intent. Without the power to ensure that policies are actually implemented, the legislative power of Congress is meaningless. As Woodrow Wilson wrote in *Congressional Government,* "quite as important as legislation is vigilant oversight of administration":

> It is the proper duty of a representative body to look diligently into every affair of government and to talk much about what it sees. It is meant to be the eyes and the voice, and to embody the wisdom and the will of its constituents. Unless Congress have and use every means of acquainting itself with the acts and disposition of the administrative agents of the government, the country must be helpless to learn how it is being served.[5]

In his classic book, Wilson concludes that the "argument is not only that discussed and interrogated administration is the only pure and efficient administration, but, more than that, that the

---

[5]Woodrow Wilson, *Congressional Government* (Gloucester, Mass: Peter Smith, 1885, 1965), p. 195.

only really self-governing people is that people which discusses and interrogates its administration."[6]

As with legislative interaction, much of congressional surveillance and supervision of bureaucratic action occurs largely at the subsystem level. Although Congress has attempted, through the use of Government Operations committees in both houses, to establish some kind of central mechanism for investigating bureaucratic agencies to ascertain whether they are performing their given tasks, this attempt has been less than successful. One reason—related to the distribution of power among committees—appears to be a reluctance on the part of the Government Operations committees to intrude on the domain of the other standing committees. As a result, oversight responsibilites have fallen largely to the same committees and subcommittees involved originally in drafting legislation. To a large extent, therefore, the subsystems in which policy is initially formulated and funded are also the subsystems in which the implementation of policy is debated, investigated, and assessed.

The power of Congress to ensure that legislative intent is carried out by the bureaucracy depends on the quality of the resources and information that the subcommittees possess and on coordination among relevant subcommittees to ensure that the president, key agencies, or interested lobbies cannot play one subcommittee off against another. It depends further on the ability of Congress as a whole to break the subsystem triangle through other mechanisms when subcommittees cannot or will not perform the desired roles of policy surveillance and supervision. The critical nature of subsystem politics means that the ability of Congress to assert its policy roles and keep executive action in bounds depends on the success of Congress in organizing and disciplining itself.

The Central Questions

Congress must be able to surmount the barriers to representative government that the federal agencies may devise without destroying the effectiveness of the bureaucracy as an instrument

[6]*Ibid,* p. 198.

of governmental administration. Congress must be able to ensure that a national majority can act to formulate policy and to ensure that it is carried out—yet it must be able to guide and constrain both the president and the bureaucracy without hamstringing either.

This challenge raises a set of fundamental questions. Can Congress oversee the executive without reducing it, and government in general, to impotence? Is the problem ultimately one of finding the appropriate mechanisms of Congressional supervision and control, or does it lie elsewhere, for example, in congressional structure or constitutional system? Can representative government, within the current system of checks and balances, allow for legislative decisionmaking, supervision, and control while also ensuring that legislation will in fact be implemented? How can representative democracy, within the context of our constitution, be reconciled with the existence of the administrative state? Can the people rule through the representative institutions provided in the American constitutional system without destroying the ability of the government to govern?

The task confronting the authors (as well as the readers) of this book is to understand the dilemmas confronting congressional-administrative relations and at least to begin the search for their resolution. This book constitutes our own intellectual journey into the complicated maze of puzzles and paradoxes that constitute congressional-executive relations. Our study of congressional-executive branch relations focuses on Congress and the federal bureaucracy instead of on Congress and the president. In addition, it is a study that focuses on the broad sweep of the relationship, and particularly on the recent reforms of Congress and their likely impact on the administrative state.

Our concern with congressional-administrative relations is admittedly not unique in the literature of political science and public administration; several works have shared a similar focus. One study is that of Charles Hyneman, who in *Bureaucracy in a Democracy* (Harper & Row, 1950) analyzed the implications for modern government of the sudden growth of the federal bureaucracy during the New Deal and World War II periods. Hyneman's basic concern was the control of a sprawling administration; greater responsibility for oversight of federal administration on the part of the Congress and the president was his proposed solution. Another study with similar themes is that of Joseph Harris, who in *Congressional Control of Administration* (Brookings Institution, 1965) examined the various devices Congress has at its disposal in exercising its responsibilities for oversight of the bureaucracy. Harris, writing in the halcyon days of presidential initiative, concluded that Congress had, in some cases, gone too far, had pushed its control into areas more properly reserved for the Chief Executive and through means that injected too much arbitrary congressional "politics" into administration. Congress, Harris felt, had limited the ability of the President to take firm control and manage a bureaucratic mechanism rightfully his.

Both these works are now somewhat dated, and both carry a certain bias to their respective treatments of their themes. There are more recent treatments that provide some coverage of the congressional-executive relationship in certain functional areas. Among these are Aaron Wildavsky's discussion of the federal budgetary process, Harold Seidman's analysis of executive branch organization, Morris Ogul's analysis of congressional oversight of the bureaucracy in three substantive areas, and Morris Fiorina's analysis of the symbiotic relationship between Congress and the bureaucracy.[7]

Our hope is to provide the reader a broad historical perspective on the relationship between the two institutions and to place contemporary changes within each institution in the context of one's relationship with the other. In particular, we hope to shed some light on the problems that the rise of the administrative state have caused for Congress and thus identify more precisely the underlying dilemma that a large administrative state poses for representative government, particularly one based on a separation-of-powers system of government.

[7]Aaron Wildavsky, *The Politics of the Budgetary Process* (Boston: Little Brown, 1974); Harold Seidman, *Politics, Position and Power* (New York: Oxford, 1975); Morris Ogul, *Congress Oversees the Bureaucracy* (Pittsburgh: Pittsburgh University Press, 1976); Morris Fiorina, *Congress: Keystone to the Washington Establishment* (New Haven: Yale University Press, 1977).

We begin our study with a consideration of the rise of the federal bureaucracy to power and institutional permanence and its impact on Congress. We then turn to a consideration of the problems Congress has faced in policy formulation within the context of the administrative state, and how it has attempted in recent years to resolve them. Next, we focus on the way Congress attempts to influence executive implementation of legislation, the problems Congress has faced in overseeing the executive, and its recent attempts to reform oversight procedures. Then we assess the impact that Congress has made on the bureaucracy and policymaking within the administrative state. Finally, we review the problems for representative government that our analysis suggests and propose some possible solutions.

2
The Rise of the Administrative State

The Constitutional Setting

The scope and pervasiveness of the modern federal bureaucracy could hardly have been anticipated by the framers of the American constitution. Had the founding fathers been able to see the America of the 1970s through a crystal ball, they would likely have refused to believe their eyes. The political scene of late 18th century America was dominated by the three primary institutions—Congress, the president, the courts—the constitution had called into being. Its authors, more concerned with the balance of governmental power instead of how to administer it, made only passing reference to the structure of the executive branch.

They provided that the president could appoint, with the consent of the Senate, ambassadors, Supreme Court judges, and all other officials "whose appointments . . . shall be established by law;" and could require written opinions of the "principal officers in each of the Executive departments." Congress, for its part, could vest the power to appoint minor ("inferior") officials in the President, in the courts, "or in the Heads of Departments" (Art. II, Sec. II). But the constitution remained silent on the shape, scope, and size of federal executive organization. Nor did it spell out which branch was to have responsibility for the exercise of administrative power, an omission that has contributed to a continuing struggle between Congress and the executive branch over their respective roles in administration.[1]

The founding fathers did, however, make two additional provisions that clarified the respective roles of Congress and president vis-à-vis an executive bureaucracy. One was the constitutional proscription (Art. I, Sec. 6) that forbade members of Congress from concurrently holding federal executive office and thus made impossible the comingling of the executive and legislative estates typical of a parliamentary system. (Indeed, this provision represented a conscious aversion to the British model.) The second concerned the rights of a president to remove executive branch officials whose original appointments had been confirmed by the Senate. This "decision of 1789," implicit in legislation creating the first executive department, recognized broad, almost unlimited removal powers on the part of the president.[2]

That the constitution neglected the details of administrative organization did not mean that its authors had no experience with the problems of administration. They had seen the failure of the attempt by the national legislature during the Confederation period (1775–1789) to administer such affairs of state as war and foreign relations directly through its own committees or through joint boards. Also, the issues surrounding executive branch organization had been the subject of considerable debate during the constitutional convention. What had emerged was a general consensus that administrative departments, headed by a single official appointed by the president, would become the standard form of administrative organization.[3]

---

[1]So argued the constitutional scholar William F. Willoughby. See Lloyd M. Short, *The Development of National Administrative Organization in the United States* (Baltimore: Johns Hopkins Press, 1923) p. 2. An extended analysis of the constitutional role of the president as chief administrator may be found in Edward S. Corwin, *The President: Office and Powers, 1787–1957* (New York: New York University Press, 1957) pp. 69–118.

[2]Paul Van Riper, *History of the U.S. Civil Service* (New York: Harper & Row, 1958) pp. 14–15.

[3]Short, *op. cit.,* p. 88.

Early Beginnings

The creation of a rudimentary departmental structure was high on the agenda of the new Congress of the United States. By the end of its first year, 1789, it had established the first three departments: State, Treasury, and War. It provided each with a single top official, a secretary, appointed by the president and subordinate to him. Congress proved much more specific, however, in its treatment of the Treasury Department than in the other two. Whereas only a general indication of the duties of the secretaries of War and State were provided in the statutes creating these departments, the duties of the Treasury secretary were spelled out in detail, additional responsibilities given other Treasury officials (among them the comptroller and auditor), and the organizational structure of the Treasury Department specified.[4] Congress, which had traditionally kept a firm hand on financial administration during the early years of the Republic, was unwilling to give the president a free hand in the administration of Treasury. It insisted, then as now, in keeping a close watch on the structure and administration of financial organization. The establishment of two minor offices, those of the Attorney General and the Post Office in the same year (1789) and the creation of an additional department, that of the Navy in 1798, brought to a close the Federalist phase of federal executive branch organization.

The Jeffersonians, who captured the reigns of power from the Federalists in 1801 and held them until the election of Andrew Jackson in 1828, kept the administrative structure they inherited largely intact. Adhering to a more limited view of both the presidency and of federal administration, the Jeffersonians added little to federal administrative organization. True, a General Land Office was created in the Treasury Department to administer the sale of new public lands, and the War of 1812 brought in its wake reforms in the War and Navy Departments. But no major administrative initiatives were undertaken. The growth of federal officialdom reflected increases in established

[4]*Ibid.,* p. 100.

activities of the national government and its population rather than the assumption of new duties.

The size of the federal bureaucracy in these early years was small by the standards of today—3000 civil officials at the turn of the century, less than 20,000 by 1830. The State Department of 1800 consisted of the secretary of state, a chief clerk, seven ordinary clerks, and a messenger boy.[5] The attorney general, legal counsel to the president and his department heads, was expected to earn his living through private practice; not until 1818 did Congress grant him office space and a clerk. Although it was relatively small, the federal service of the Federalist and Jeffersonian eras was competent, generally free from corruption, and staffed at least at its upper levels by gentlemen of substantial character and public-mindedness. Direct presidential appointees came predominantly from the patrician elite—the landed gentry, such established professions as law, medicine, and the clergy—and to a lesser extent from the newly wealthy merchant classes. Presidential selection for high office was made largely on the basis of fitness of character (with a nod to geographical representation), as was Senatorial confirmation.

It would be a mistake, however, to characterize the early federal bureaucracy simply as administration by gentlemen. Although these elites did dominate the upper-level, presidential-appointee positions, the large majority of federal officeholders were drawn from the emerging middle class. They enjoyed a certain security of position and a kind of informal tenure in office, whereas the bulk of presidential appointees were replaced by a new incoming administration.[6] Thus the distinction between a relatively mobile cadre of "political" appointees and a relatively distinct and protected bureaucracy of civil officials was drawn early in the development of the American bureaucracy.

The scope of American executive branch organization that had been determined by the time of the election of Andrew Jackson endured for decades. From 1828 until after the Civil

[5]Leonard D. White, *The Federalists* (New York: Macmillan, 1948) pp. 123, 136.
[6]Frederick C. Mosher, *Democracy and the Public Service* (New York: Oxford University Press, 1968), pp. 55–60.

War, national government and its administration remained small, unpretentious, and limited to a few essential functions. Only one new department, Interior, emerged in this period, and it was formed largely to assume specific domestic functions of other departments (the Patent Office of State, for example) that had grown tired of them. Minor reorganizations were accomplished in the Post Office and in the Navy Department, and Congress made a tentative step in the direction of regulation by creating in the Treasury Department a Steamboat Inspection Service (1838) in response to fatal accidents caused by boiler explosions on steamboats. But initiatives for the expansion of federal administration on the part of either president or Congress were rare.

The slow pace of the development of national administration in this period reflected among other things the extreme reluctance of Congress to threaten its own hegemony in the constitutional system by expanding the executive branch. But it may also be traced to the impact of Jacksonian democracy and the main currents of nineteenth century political and social thought. For the most part of that century, America was a rural society that placed great value and emphasis on the individual, the family unit, on self-effort and self-sufficiency. American individualism, associated with and reinforced by a rugged pioneer spirit, relied on individual accomplishments and disdained, for the most part, collective or governmental action. Government was not to do for people what they should do for themselves.

Another strong current was democracy. The expansion of the suffrage brought the yeoman, the frontier pioneer, the homesteader, the commoner into the electoral arena. Congressional and executive branch politics changed from the patrician and genteel to a robust, hectic game of rough and tumble. Democratization of politics brought about the politicization of administration.

In addition to these basic beliefs and currents of thought, another factor severely limited the expansion of the functions of the national government. Deriving its impulse from the federal nature of American government, this was the reservation under the Constitution of the basic police powers to the states. For the most of the nineteenth century, the states, not the national government, were the primary jurisdictions for protecting the health and safety of Americans. Those programs of internal development and regulation that *were* undertaken—the regulation of banks, commerce, insurance; the building of canals and roads; support for primary and secondary education—were generally the province of state and to a lesser extent local governments rather than Washington. The states were the most powerful and active units of government; and aside from the basic national functions discussed earlier, there was little in the way of national policies and programs to be translated into executive branch growth.

These conditions influenced greatly the attitude of Congress toward national administration. The expansion of the federal bureaucracy in this period barely kept pace with the growth in population. Very few new administrative units were created by Congress, nor were existing agencies well funded. Appropriations were, with few exceptions, parsimonious. Departments and bureaus went directly to Congress with requests for funds, often to several (sometimes competing) committees. Neither the president nor Congress exercised what today would be called budgetary control over the bureaucracy, and congressional consideration of agency requests was both haphazard and picayune. With the exception of the military services, appropriations were often itemized to the last candle and quill pen, functions of personnel were spelled out in minute detail, and most offices limited to a strictly specified number of persons at precise salary figures. Little if any administrative discretion in the spending of appropriated funds was tolerated.[7]

The Democratization of Public Service

Beginning with the administration of Thomas Jefferson and gaining impetus under that of Andrew Jackson was a gradual broadening of the social base from which appointees to high

[7]Leonard D. White, *The Republican Era* (New York: Macmillian, 1958) pp. 54–57.

federal office were drawn. Jefferson's egalitarian beliefs led him to move from the "artificial" aristocracy of wealth and family position as the primary pool for executive appointments toward a "natural" aristocracy based on talent and virtue and developed through education. He rejected, as did Jackson, the nepotism that was a hallmark of Federalist appointments. Jackson carried the egalitarian impetus further by opposing the inheritance of offices and increasing the possibilities for broader participation through rotation in office; he placed considerable emphasis on equality of opportunity and broader access to federal employment.[8] Jackson differed from his predecessors, however, in his view of the requisites of federal officeholding. "The duties of all public offices," he opined, "are so plain and simple that men of intelligence may readily qualify themselves for their performance; and I can not but believe that more is lost by the long continuance of men in office than is generally gained by their experience."[9]

The elaboration and downward extension of these trends in Jackson's and succeeding administrations culminated in what came to be known as a "system" of spoils. Large numbers of federal officials (many more than those forming the political leadership cadre) came to owe their positions to the victorious party and to raw partisan influence. Sales of offices, graft, and kickbacks to the party's coffers became the order of the day. Thousands of federal employees were removed with a change of administration and replaced with loyal workers from the victorious party. The spoils system had become firmly entrenched by the time of the Civil War; Abraham Lincoln turned out of office nearly ninety percent of incumbents and is reported to have once written a letter dunning a patronage appointee who had reneged on the usual assessment.[10]

Part of the rationale behind the spoils system was the assumption that administration was kept close to the people by circulat-

---

[8]See Sidney H. Aronson, *Status and Kinship in the Higher Civil Service* (Cambridge: Harvard University Press, 1964) pp. 3–22.

[9]Quoted in Mosher, *op. cit.*, p. 62.

[10]Van Riper, *op. cit.*, pp. 43, 47.

ing citizens through its ranks—a notion of a kind of "peoples bureaucracy" somewhat similar in concept to the citizen army. But in practical terms, the patronage that the spoils made available was essential to the growth of strong national parties, for whom the graft and inefficiency it spawned was of slight concern. Moreover, it served not only the national party structure but the Congress as well, augmenting the power base of individual members. The Senate, as was its prerogative, gradually increased the number of executive positions subject to senatorial confirmation. Such expansion was coupled with the Senate's deference to the device of "senatorial courtesy," whereby an individual Senator could block confirmation of a nomination by registering a personal objection to the individual concerned, and thus increased the patronage base and attractiveness of Senate seats. Patronage over designating postmasters gradually fell to the House. Thus what was formally a presidential patronage system in reality became more of a fiefdom of Congress. Moreover, not a few defeated members of both houses pressed their claims for appointment to even minor administrative offices.[11]

Change and Administrative Growth: 1880–1920

By the third quarter of the nineteenth century, however, many of these previously dominant values, beliefs, and social institutions were in flux. An industrial revolution had begun to sound a death knell for the simple, agrarian economy on which the American constitution was predicated. Industrialization spawned large, impersonal cities, attracting hordes of menial laborers to factory floors and sweatshops. Large corporations, swelled by the success of monopolistic or oligopolistic practices, grew beyond the bounds of state regulation. An increasingly sophisticated technology brought complexity and interdependency to everyday life. A new wave of immigration, largely from Eastern

[11]*Ibid.*, pp. 48–49.

Europe, flooded the industrial cities—adding new elements to the melting pot and spurring the growth of organized labor. Available land in the western regions of the continent, which had provided a safety valve for previous generations of the frustrated and impoverished, began to dry up. By 1890, Frederick Turner argued, the "frontier" had vanished. These societal and economic transformations brought new pressures to bear on American social and political institutions, pushing in the process both Congress and the executive branch into a more corporate, more specialized, more complex "modern" era.

Although it is difficult, and perhaps presumptious, to place an exact date on the beginnings of the transformation of the national executive from the old to the modern, in retrospect the decade of the 1880s appears to be a watershed. Then, a variety of changes in executive branch organization and function began to emerge. The national government began to develop forward momentum and to take a more active role in American society and its economy—a momentum that was soon translated into a significant expansion of the executive branch. It is here that one perceives the dawn of the modern American administrative state, the onset of a first phase or cycle of bureaucratic growth that lasted until roughly 1920.

A lynchpin in the developing machinery of the bureaucratic state was the decay of the spoils system and the reform of the federal public service. While the spoils system had been designed in part to keep bureaucracy close to the people, it had led more to a corruption of the public trust than responsibility to it. Further, the onrush of technology and specialization had questioned the assumption that executive government and administration were simple tasks, appropriate for simple talents. Moreover, the burden the spoils system placed on newly elected presidents had become overwhelming. President James Garfield lamented, "The stream of callers . . . became a torrent and swept away my day. . . . I felt like crying out in the agony of my soul against the greed for office and its consumption of my time."[12] The spoils system ultimately consumed Garfield's life as well as

[12]Quoted in White, *Republican Era,* p. 94.

his time. It was his assassination at the hands of a frustrated office suplicant that gave final impetus to reform.

This reform found its earliest congressional expression in the passage of the Pendleton Act of 1883, creating the Civil Service Commission and introducing the merit system into the federal public service. The intent of the new civil service system was to take administration out of partisan politics. The hiring of federal officials was to be based on competence and ability, usually determined by examination, and appointments were to be nonpartisan. After a probationary period, an official gained tenure, permanence on the job, and could be removed only through specified procedures. Later, officials were severely limited in the extent to which they could take part in national electoral politics. The merit system took partisan politics out of the public service and eventually the public service out of the political arena. And it made administration a relatively secure career.

The introduction of civil service reform coincided historically with the beginning of substantial growth in the number of federal civil servants, a growth that itself reflected an expansion of federal executive functions. The number of civilian employees in the executive branch, estimated at 100,000 in 1881, had by 1900 more than doubled and by 1910 had nearly doubled again.[13] Although the percentage of officials covered under merit procedures during the early years of the merit system was small, by 1900 roughly fifty percent of federal civilian employees were under its umbrella.

A major side effect of the introduction of the merit system has been the creation of an institution, an administrative "estate" rather separate from both Congress and the president. Its emphasis on merit in hiring has promoted the development of a professional, specialized bureaucracy whose expertise cannot be matched either by president or Congress. Its emphasis on tenure and permanence in office has built into this bureaucracy an insensitivity toward and protection from the direct overhead political control of the president. We shall look later at some of

[13]U.S. Bureau of the Census, *Statistical History of the United States from Colonial Times to the Present* (Stamford, Conn.: Fairfield Publishers, 1965), p. 710.

the characteristics of this bureaucratic institution. Suffice it to say here that in establishing a merit system during what proved to be the initial stage of the growth of the modern federal bureaucracy, Congress gave birth to a creature it often finds difficult to control.

In addition to civil service reform, a new departure that did much to increase the scope of the federal government was the drive for regulation of business and industry. By late in the nineteenth century, large industrial combines in steel, oil, railroads, and other sectors had come to dominate much of the economic landscape. Large fortunes were amassed by owners of near-monopolies against which the ordinary consumer stood powerless. And as these combines spread beyond the bounds of state regulation, pressure mounted to use the muscle of the national government as a counterweight to their power. Public outcry against the excesses of unrestrained corporate power led to the substantial intervention of the national government in the economy, a significant violation of the dictates of *laissez faire*. The move against big industry and big business took two forms—industrial regulation, and the drive to break up or control monopoly and oligopoly known as "anti-trust." Congressional sanction for the government to weigh in against large combines came in the landmark Sherman Anti-Trust Act of 1890, the provisions of which were enforced by the Department of Justice. Expanded efforts to control monopoly came with the creation of the Federal Trade Commission (1914), which became an additional organizational locus for anti-trust enforcement.

Government regulation of particular industrial sectors began with the railroads, whose exploitation of the farmer by high freight rates had been particularly rapacious. As a partial check on their excesses, Congress in 1887 created the Interstate Commerce Commission (ICC), first in a series of major federal regulatory bodies. Powers given the Commission included issuing rules governing rail services and the setting of rates charged rail customers. Congress was reluctant to place such a powerful body directly under the president. It designated as the heads of the Commission a body of commissioners serving staggered terms for a period of time longer than the four-year presidential term, thus isolating the Commission from direct presidential control.

The ICC proved a relatively successful experiment in federal regulation, and became a model for subsequent regulatory bodies created in the next several decades. Among the more familiar agencies are the Board of Governors of the Federal Reserve System (1913) in the banking area; the Federal Trade Commission discussed above; and the Federal Power Commission (1920).

In addition to the anti-trust and regulatory movements, a further movement toward expansion of federal administrative agencies derived from the increasing specialization of society. The rise of societal groups and interests organized to pursue common concerns found vehicles for expression in the creation of executive branch departments as "representatives" of these interests. Whereas the original departments had been built around specific federal functions—the War Department for national defense, State for the conduct of foreign relations, and so on—the latter half of the nineteenth century witnessed the creation of certain offices, bureaus, and departments of the federal government around group interests. Farming, the largest occupation in its day, secured recognition with the establishment of a Department of Agriculture that gained full cabinet status in 1889. Education interests got a foothold with the creation of a Bureau of Education (1869) in the Interior Department, forerunner of the Office of Education. The emergence of organized labor, whose ranks were swelled by the industrial revolution, led to the creation of the Department of Labor in 1888. Not far behind were small business and commercial interests that helped secure the establishment of a Department of Commerce in 1903 (actually a joint Department of Commerce and Labor until 1913).

Also contributing to an expansion of federal functions in this period was the early movement toward conservation of America's natural resources, leading to the establishment of a Reclamation Service (1902) in the Interior Department, the Forest Service in 1905, and the beginnings of the national park system in 1916. Additional stimulus came from the spread of the federal

grant-in-aid device, whereby federal monies rather than federal
lands were made available to the states for specific purposes,
among them agricultural education (1900) and highway construction (1916). In the first two decades of the century, Congress increasingly turned to the use of the grant-in-aid device
and tightened federal administrative supervision over how such
monies were spent by the states. New supervisory functions in
highway construction, for example, were vested in a Bureau of
Public Roads, soon to become a powerful grant-disbursing
agency.[14]

A substantial impetus to administrative growth has traditionally been war. The nature of modern warfare seems almost
to predestine an increased role for the national government in
the economy and the society—accompanied by new wartime
agencies created by presidential executive orders under congressional grants of authority and incursions of the national
government into the private sector on a scale that would not be
tolerated in peacetime. World War I, following on the heels of
federal domestic expansion, was no exception. Numerous new
agencies were created almost overnight to coordinate the war
effort, to subsidize war industries, to build housing for wartime
workers, for the mobilization and recruitment of military and
civilian personnel, and to run the nation's railroads under governmental control.

The close of World War I marked the end of the first phase or
cycle of major growth of the federal bureaucracy, an era that
had witnessed unprecedented incursions of the federal government into areas of activity formerly the province of the states or
the private sector. The impact of national government activity in
the period 1880 to 1920 is graphically illustrated by the growth
of the federal bureaucracy relative to the American population.
The aggregate population of the United States little more than
doubled from 1880 to 1920, yet the number of federal executive
branch employees tripled from 1880 to 1910 and had increased
sixfold by 1920. The pattern of federal budget outlays is similar.

[14]See Arthur W. Macmahon, *Administering Federalism in a Democracy* (New York:
Oxford University Press, 1972) pp. 72–77.

National government expenditures as a percentage of the national wealth more than tripled in the same period.[15]

Often in the history of nations, a post-war period brings a mood of consolidation; a reaction against bigness, organization, the corporate; an emphasis on the individual rather than government or the state; a return to the privateness of life. America in the 1920s exhibited many of these reactions. After demobilization, the war agencies were for the most part abolished, the number of federal civil servants shrank (though not to pre-war levels), and the nation entered a period of "normalcy" with a return to an emphasis on the private sector. The business of government, as Calvin Coolidge laconically observed, was business. The "roaring twenties" may have captured the mood of the nation, but this mood did not penetrate to the corridors of national government.

For the administrative state, the 1920s was a decade of relative quiet, punctuated by modest growth in law enforcement (occasioned by the rapid rise of organized crime during Prohibition), the regulation of radio and of some farm and dairy products, by additions to the national park and forest systems, and the establishment of farm credit banks. It seemed as if the public and its polity were pausing to catch their breath before the turbulence of the Great Depression.

The Second Phase: 1933–1953

Then came the stock market crash of October 1929, the beginning of bank failures, and the onset of severe unemployment. The nation was soon plunged into an economic recession and the electorate repudiated the leadership of engineer–businessman Herbert Hoover for the liberal patrician Democrat Franklin Roosevelt, who promised a "New Deal." The election in 1932 of Roosevelt and substantial Democratic majorities in both houses of Congress ushered in a second, perhaps most intensive

[15]U.S. Bureau of the Census, *Historical Statistics of the United States, 1789–1945* (Washington: Government Printing Office, 1949), pp. 10, 26, 294–295, 299. (National wealth estimate for 1920 by extrapolation.)

period of national administrative growth in American history. Indeed, the expansion of the federal government in the New Deal period was, in terms of both its breadth and scope, so great as to be termed a near-revolution. It wrote into law the end of *laissez faire*.

During the New Deal, administrative agencies proliferated. A reorganized Farm Credit Administration (1933) restored solvency to bankrupt farmers' credit cooperatives and provided emergency loans. A Federal Deposit Insurance Corporation created in the same year insured the savings of depositors with the full faith and credit of the government. A Tennessee Valley Authority (1933) developed the resources of the Tennessee River valley, controlled its flooding, produced electricity and fertilizer—often in direct competition with the private sector—and was condemned on the right as state socialism. The Civilian Conservation Corps (1933) employed hundreds of thousands of youths who flocked to rural areas to restore cut-over timber lands. The Securities and Exchange Commission (1934) was created to bring order to the chaotic and turbulent securities market and its stock exchanges, and a Federal Power Commission was established (1935). The Works Progress Administration (1935) and related agencies made the federal government an employer of last resort by putting to work millions of the unemployed building bridges, airports, and schools, writing books and giving dramatic presentations, and, more prosaically, raking leaves.

Two important pieces of legislation in 1935 placed the national government foursquare in new areas of activity. A program of national social insurance, known as "social security," provided cash payments to those over 65 and retired and created a federal-state system of unemployment compensation and grants to the dependent aged, blind, and children—all funded by a tax on employers as well as participating employees. It was administered by a bureau that later formed the bulk of a new Federal Security Agency (1939). Another major piece of legislation, the National Labor Relations Act (1935), established the right of private sector employees to bargain collectively with their employers, and a National Labor Relations Board was instituted to supervise administration of the act.

A prominent feature of the growth of the federal bureaucracy during the New Deal—from under 600,000 in 1932 to over a million by 1940—was that much of it occurred outside the umbrella of the civil service. At the request of the president, Congress allowed him to by-pass civil service procedures in hiring personnel for a number of the new agencies. As a result, the percentage of employees covered under the merit system decreased from roughly 80 percent under Hoover to under 60 percent by the end of the decade. Having recruited to these new agencies officials who were loyal to his programs and policies (and having bolstered his political fortunes through this extended patronage), Roosevelt later took advantage of congressional authority to "blanket in" these officials under the coverage of civil service—often without merit exams. By the time the country entered World War II, nearly 85 percent of the bureaucracy was protected by civil service tenure.[16]

The expansion of the administrative state during the decade of the 1930s implied pronounced difficulties for presidential coordination and control (and for congressional oversight of administration). Given the scores of new administrative entities, no longer were a couple of secretaries and ad hoc advisors—the only presidential "staff" under previous administrations—sufficient to allow the president to shoulder effectively his responsibilities as chief executive. Response to the need for greater presidential staff support came in the creation by Congress of the Executive Office of the President (1939), including an expanded Bureau of the Budget brought in from Treasury, and the provision of a number of personal advisors to the president. Designed to help the president extend his control over the executive branch, the Executive Office, as we shall see, developed a bureaucratic life of its own.

Scarcely had the American public time to begin to digest the innovations of the New Deal and its spate of domestic initiatives when the nation was once again drawn into war. The demands made by World War II, a modern, nearly total war effort, were significantly greater than those of World War I. Administrative as well as strictly military resources had to be mustered quickly.

---

[16]Van Riper, *op. cit.,* pp. 320–347.

Rather than add to the burdens of existing agencies and departments, Roosevelt, acting under broad grants of congressional authority, created scores of new administrative agencies
and offices by executive order. Attached for the most part to the
newly created Executive Office of the President, these units became known collectively as the "war agencies."

Most of the war agencies came under the umbrella of the
Office of Emergency Management (OEM), responsible for the
direction of vast areas of the society and its economy. Perhaps
most famous (or infamous) among them was the Office of Price
Administration (1941), which set price ceilings on a wide variety
of goods and services and rationed such necessities as sugar,
gasoline, tires, and coffee. Also created were such entities as the
War Production Board (1942), charged with monitoring and
stimulating war-related industrial output, the War Manpower
Commission (1942), whose responsibilities included manpower
development for domestic production, and the War Labor
Board, which exercised control over wages and other labor benefits. Other war agencies—estimated at more than 140 by the
Bureau of the Budget—supervised such activities as civil defense, censorship, overseas information, conservation of
strategic materials, and a host of others.[17] Little of what traditionally had been considered the domain of the private sector
was not immediately or ultimately subject to national governmental regulation or coordination. Indeed, in this respect
World War II represented a high water mark—as did the
number of federal bureaucrats. The number of civilian federal
employees mushroomed from slightly over a million in 1940 to
3,800,000 in 1945.

Although the defeat of Germany and Japan brought a relatively rapid demobilization of America's military forces, the nation, in contrast to World War I, was not granted the luxury of a
rapid return to "normalcy." America could not afford, as it had
in the 1920s, to retreat and to turn inward, for at the war's close
it had emerged as a world power (and an atomic one at that) with

---

[17]A study of the war agencies may be found in U.S. Bureau of the Budget, *The
United States at War* (Washington: Government Printing Office, 1946).

substantially increased responsibilities overseas. As the only major nation able to buttress the war-torn nations of Western Europe, it felt compelled to help rebuild them as a counterweight to the expansionist tendencies of its recent ally, the Soviet Union. These new facts of national and international life, supported by a strong bipartisan foreign policy in the Congress, were translated into new programs and new components of a still-expanding administrative state.

An important initiative was the congressional decision to bring aid, through the Marshall plan, to the devastated economies of Western Europe, where billions of dollars were funneled by the Economic Cooperation Administration (1947). In view of the deepening cold war, the Central Intelligence Agency was created to develop intelligence on the new Soviet threat (and on the activities of allies) and—though this was not a part of its public charge—to carry out covert intelligence operations. The same year 1947, brought an initial reorganization of the military establishment, culminating in a new Department of Defense (1949) that brought under one (admittedly huge) roof the various armed services. As the cold war with Soviet Russia deepened by Soviet consolidations in Eastern Europe and threats against Berlin, a shooting war began in Korea in 1950. And the United States, which had brought the boys home quickly after World War II, was once again placed on a war footing. From 1950 to 1954, military conflict again engaged the nation's energy and attention.

At home, domestic initiatives reinforced this forward motion. The establishment of the National Science Foundation (1950) to support research and education in science marked the beginning of a greatly expanded federal involvement in scientific research and development. The new Department of Health, Education and Welfare (1952) brought together clusters of related agencies and programs. The U.S. Information Agency (1953), created to counter hostile propaganda from the Communist nations, was directed to "tell America's story" abroad.

The eventual return of the nation to a period of relative quiet, delayed from the mid-1940s by war and by a new internationalism that mitigated against a return to isolation, finally came by 1953 to 1954. The end of the Korean war marked the end of what will probably rank as the most important and most prolonged period of growth of the federal bureaucracy and the executive branch. During this second period of expansion from 1933 to 1953, the American population increased by only 30 percent; the number of employees in the executive branch, however, increased fourfold. In 1933, there was one federal civil servant for every 280 Americans; by 1953 there was one for every 80. Similar growth patterns may be seen in the role of the federal budget in the economy. While the gross national product (the nation's production of goods and services) grew by a factor of six in this period, the expenditures of the federal government grew at more than twice the rate of the national product—some 15 times.[18]

This period was also, as we shall see, of great importance to relationships between Congress and the executive. It is here that Congress began to become painfully aware of the challenge presented by the growth of administration and to speak for the first time seriously of the necessity for oversight of the administrative behemoth it had created. Growth of the executive during the war and congressional sentiment for reform appear to have gone hand in hand.

The Eisenhower years provided a brief pause—one interrupted significantly only by the flurry of reaction to the orbiting of Sputnik by the Soviet Union that produced the National Aeronautics and Space Administration (1958)—between the second and third periods of major administrative growth.

1961 to the Present

The third phase, in whose twilight we now live, was triggered by the election of John F. Kennedy and of substantial Democratic majorities in Congress, and expanded during the regime of Lyndon Johnson. Like others who have presided over the growth of the executive branch, Kennedy offered the electorate a sense of dynamism, forward movement, and a "new" pro-

[18]U.S. Bureau of the Census, *Statistical History,* pp. 7, 139, 710, 719.

gramme. For Theodore Roosevelt, it had been a "new nationalism"; for Woodrow Wilson, a "new freedom"; for Franklin Roosevelt, a "new deal"; for Kennedy, it was a "new frontier", a frontier pushed outward by the "great society" of his successor.

This third period, however, differs in important respects from the first two. Earlier periods of administrative growth generally reflected a pattern of expansion in the domestic activities of the federal government, followed and reinforced by a major military conflict or conflicts. In this third period, domestic expansion and foreign war (Vietnam) were pursued concurrently in a conscious policy of guns *and* butter. Indeed, the escalation of the Vietnam conflict and the expansion of domestic programs in the mid-1960s occurred simultaneously. A second difference regarding the earlier two periods may be seen in patterns of growth in the federal budget and the executive bureaucracy. In the period 1960 to date, growth in the federal bureaucracy has come either in proportion with the nation's increase in population (roughly 20 percent) or has lagged slightly behind. And while the increase in federal budgetary expenditures has been substantial (fourfold from 1960–1977), it has remained roughly proportional to the growth of the gross national product. Federal outlays as a percentage of GNP were 19 percent in 1960 and estimated at roughly 22 percent in 1977.[19]

How does one account for the fact that the political and administrative activism of this period does not appear to be reflected in statistics of growth of the federal bureaucracy and the federal budget? The answer is two-fold. First, a substantial shift has occurred in the proportion of the federal budget devoted to social and domestic programs as against that devoted to national defense. National defense expenditures have declined, those for domestic programs have increased. In 1960, national defense represented 49 percent of the federal budget; in 1965, 41 percent. After an upward trend during the height of the Vietnam War, by 1970 defense expenditures accounted for 40 percent

---

[19]U.S. Department of Commerce, *Statistical Abstract* (Washington: Government Printing Office, 1977), p. 248.

and by 1977, 25 percent. Human resource expenditures, on the other hand—those for education, manpower, health, income security, and the like—have increased. Thus, while the federal budget itself has increased, it has remained relatively constant as a proportion of GNP and has shifted from an emphasis on national defense toward domestic and human resources.[20]

Second, though the *federal* bureaucracy has grown only in proportion to the national population, state and local government employment—stimulated by federal domestic programs—has increased substantially. During this period, federal expenditures for domestic programs have increasingly been channelled to the states and localities, exemplified by funds for community development, education, law enforcement, and others. This "fiscal federalism" is graphically illustrated during the decade 1965 to 1975. While the federal budget grew little over two-and-a-half times, federal payments to state and local governments surged from 11 billion dollars to 53 billion dollars—nearly a five-fold increase. The grant-in-aid device linked to categorical funding, begun during the first phase of federal growth, has become a leitmotif of its third phase and has been augmented by an increased state role in the distribution of entitlement payments to individuals. Partly in response to this pattern of dispersion, state and local government employment has grown from about five and a half million in 1960 to nearly 12 million by 1974. Fiscal federalism, which has pushed expenditures outward and downward, in short, has been reflected in the growth of the state and local public service rather than in the federal bureaucracy.[21]

The details of new directions in federal government policy in the 1960s and 1970s is recent history. The themes of this period have included federal assistance to depressed geographical areas; commitment to a cleaner environment; massive support for vocational and for primary and secondary education; "economic opportunity" for the poor; housing and community ac-

[20]U.S. Department of Commerce, *Statistical Abstract* (Washington: Government Printing Office, 1976), p. 225.
[21]*Ibid.*, pp. 256, 272.

tion programs; federally supported medical insurance for the poor and the elderly; enforcement of legislation outlawing discrimination in accommodations, hiring, and voting; federal aid to local law enforcement and the criminal justice system; organization for voluntary action; the development of new energy resources and the conservation of existing ones; the promotion of consumer interests; and a host of others. Although the pace of administrative growth slowed during the Nixon period especially, and also in the Ford and Carter administrations, challenges by consumer protection, environment, and energy have continued to give impetus to the creation of new constituents of the administrative state. Granted, these expressions of federal growth have under recent Republican administrations come more as a reaction to crisis (especially in the energy area) than as executive initiatives for expansion of the federal domain.

The current period has witnessed the establishment of a number of new executive branch organizations. Three major departments, those of Housing and Urban Development (1965), Transportation (1966), and Energy (1978) have emerged. A number of significant independent agencies and commissions have been created, among them the Arms Control and Disarmament Agency (1961), the Peace Corps (1961), the Administrative Conference (1964), the Applachian Regional Commission (1965), the National Foundation on the Arts and Humanities (1965), the Law Enforcement Assistance Administration (1968) in the Department of Justice, the Environmental Protection Agency (1970), ACTION (1971), the Consumer Product Safety Commission (1972), the Community Services Administration (1974), and the Nuclear Regulatory Commission (1975). In addition, a score or more smaller organizational units have appeared. Though the pace of growth has slowed during the 1970s, it is still premature to suggest that this third era is at an end.

The result of nearly a century of relatively rapid expansion of the administrative state is an organizational landscape rich and diverse in form and function. One may presently count twelve major departments, a dozen major and a score of minor agencies of less than departmental status, nearly a dozen significant regulatory commissions, and numerous and assorted federal corporations, services, boards and foundations. A brief listing of the major units of the federal executive branch appears in Table 2-1.

Mechanisms of Presidential Control

Congress, of course, is the fountainhead from which these agencies flow. It determines their names, their structure, their personnel, their responsibilities, and their programs. And it has produced an executive structure that is as varied, as decentralized, as truncated, as pluralistic as Congress itself. Different agencies cater to different clientele and interest groups, are subject to varying degrees of presidential control, responsive to different political influences, responsible for different programs, influenced by different professional cultures, and conditioned by unique histories. This balkanization has produced an administrative structure extremely difficult to coordinate, direct, and control. Yet it is supposedly the servant of Congress, not its equal, and certainly not its master. To ensure that it retains at least a modicum of responsiveness to its creator, Congress has developed a number of methods and mechanisms for its control. Indeed, the history of bureaucratic growth, as we shall see, is intertwined with the history of congressional oversight. In its efforts to check the almost natural bureaucratic drive toward independence and autonomy, Congress has not only developed mechanisms that *it* employs, but has also given the president substantial statutory and procedural powers over federal administrative agencies. It is these presidential controls we examine here; those of Congress are the subject of a later chapter.

Control over Federal Personnel

Control of a bureaucracy implies control of its bureaucrats. The replacement of the spoils system with a merit system reduced the immediate power of both Congress and the president over the

Table 2-1.
Major Organizational Units of the Executive Branch

Departments	Independent Agencies	Boards and Commissions
Agriculture	ACTION	Civil Aeronautics Board
	Community Services Administration	Consumer Product Safety Commission
Commerce	Environmental Protection Agency	Equal Employment Opportunity Commission
Defense	Farm Credit Administration	
Energy	General Services Administration	Federal Communications Commission
Health, Education & Welfare	International Communication Agency	Federal Election Commission
	National Aeronautics and Space Administration	Federal Maritime Commission
Housing and Urban Development	National Foundation on the Arts and Humanities	Federal Power Commission
Interior	National Science Foundation	Federal Reserve System
	Small Business Administration	Federal Trade Commission
Justice	Tennessee Valley Authority	Interstate Commerce Commission
Labor	U.S. Arms Control and Disarmament Agency	Merit System Protection Board
State	U.S. Postal Service	National Labor Relations Board
Transportation	Veterans Administration	Nuclear Regulatory Commission
		Occupational Safety and Health Review Commission
Treasury		Securities and Exchange Commission

appointment and separation of public officials, although the president naturally maintained his constitutional power of removal over most political appointees. The patron of public employment was no longer the president and his party; this role was delegated to the Civil Service Commission (CSC). Congress did, however, provide the president with substantial authority over both the Commission and the merit system itself—authority that gained in importance with the expansion of the federal bureaucracy. Congress provided originally that the commissioners of the CSC be appointed by the president and, unlike the case with most other Commission appointments, that they serve at his pleasure. It gave the president, rather than the Commission, the power to issue regulations governing the exercise of merit system procedures. And it provided the president with the power to decide whether and when to extend ("blanket in") civil service coverage to groups and occupational categories previously outside its purvey. Congress has cooperated with the presidential impetus toward expansion of civil service coverage by allowing its extension to positions previously exempted by statute. Throughout most of its history, the CSC was (in contrast with other regulatory commissions) viewed as a "presidential" rather than a "congressional" agency.[22]

Congress has, however, also limited the powers of the president over the civil service. Although studies of federal executive organization (among them the Brownlow Committee in 1937 and the two Hoover Commissions in 1949 and 1955) have urged that the CSC be replaced by a personnel office in the immediate Executive Office of the President, Congress has proved reluctant to do so. Until quite recently, it remained opposed to any alteration of the commission form of personnel administration. In 1978, however, the Congress—responding to the initiative of President Carter and CSC Chairman Alan Campbell—agreed to separate the administrative and adjudicative functions of the Commission, abolishing it in the process. In its place were created a Merit System Protection Board and an Office of Per-

[22]Joseph P. Harris, *Congressional Control of Administration* (Washington: Brookings Institution, 1964), p. 171.

sonnel Management. The function of the Board is to enforce merit system principles and hear employee appeals, whereas the new Office of Personnel Management (OPM) assumed most of the administrative responsibilities—recruiting, testing, training, investigations, and the like—of the CSC. The Director of the OPM is appointed by the president, thus strengthening his control over federal personnel administration.[23]

Congress and its committees have developed a number of devices or informal customs that tend to undercut the influence of the President, the OPM, and department heads over individual civil servants. One such device has been the granting of statutory authority for program administration directly to an agency's bureau chief instead of its appointed political officials. Further, Congress may require a career official to consult it in advance or keep it informed of impending actions and issue "instructions" that may run counter to those of his superiors. It may forbid the transfer of a favorite civil servant (this is often the case with agency budget officers, who may have a special relationship with members of the relevant appropriations subcommittee) or extend his mandatory retirement date. And it may spell out in statutory detail the duties and procedures with which an official is charged. In short, though the civil service remains the province of the president and his appointed officials, it is subject to congressional intervention of various kinds.

Above and beyond the various powers over personnel that Congress has given the president is his constitutional authority to appoint those officials who hold the commanding heights of federal departments and agencies. By appointing persons who share his political philosophy, the argument runs, the president is assured that his policies and decisions will be carried down the hierarchical chain of command. Career bureaucrats are responsible to political appointees, who are responsible to the president, who is elected by the people; thus the bureaucracy itself is ultimately responsible, through this "overhead democracy," to the people's will. The president, in his role as chief adminis-

---

[23]The reorganization of the structure of federal personnel administration became effective in January 1979.

trator, acts on an electoral mandate that is translated into executive programs through political cadres responsive to his direction.

In theory at least, the power of political appointment, like the power of removal, is a strong check over the administrative state. The Congress, moreover, has traditionally given the president a relatively free hand in its confirmation of nominees. Few are subjected to thorough scrutiny; even fewer are rejected. The potential for control offered by the power of appointment, however, is seldom fulfilled. This results partly from the well-documented fact that Congress, by making certain career officials responsible directly to it, creates substantial gaps in the chain of command. And the alliances formed between congressional committees and executive bureaus, and between congressmen and bureaucrats, often run counter to overhead executive control.

Control over the Budget

As Congress has provided the president with substantial influence over the human resources of the administrative state, so has it granted him a share in the control of its financial resources. Although Congress has the constitutional responsibility for the purse strings, the president, under grants of congressional authority, has come to influence significantly the size of the purse and the use of its contents. The evolution of the national budget is much too detailed a story to be summarized here. By the first decade of the twentieth century, the federal coffers were shrinking and the costs of federal government growing rapidly. The resulting scarcity of resources led eventually to the creation of a national presidential budget and of a series of mechanisms for its formulation and execution.

Through the Budget and Accounting Act of 1921, the cornerstone of national budget legislation, Congress gave the president the right to formulate the budget and to direct its administration. It reserved for itself the authority to approve the budget through the appropriations process and to pass on the legality of expenditures through a congressional audit. Congressional enthusiasm for substantial presidential budgetary powers was not, it should be noted, unanimous. Speaker Joe Cannon, for one, warned that "when Congress consents to the Executive making the budget it will have surrendered the most important part of representative government, and put this country back where it was when the shot at Lexington was 'heard round the world.' "[24] But Cannon's was a minority view. Not only did Congress grant the president the power to formulate and administer the budget, but also provided him staff assistance in the exercise of this power.

More recently, Congress has attempted to recapture some of the authority in budgetary matters it has granted the president. The Congressional Budget and Impoundment Control Act of 1974, undoubtedly the most significant piece of budgetary legislation since 1921, provides Congress with an enhanced capacity to review the presidential budget and to assert its own fiscal priorities in budgetary formulation. And it severely limits the ability of the president to impound appropriated funds during the actual administration of the budget. The impact of its provisions on presidential power over the agencies—discussed in a later chapter—is substantial.

Presidential authority over budgetary formulation has emerged as an extremely powerful tool of executive control both vis-à-vis the Congress, for whom the annual budget proposal has traditionally set much of the agenda for the appropriations process, and vis-à-vis federal agencies, which may be penalized should they prove less than responsive to overhead executive direction. The budget bureau created in 1921 to assist the executive in budget preparation, and now named the Office of Management and Budget (OMB) to indicate better the range of its functions, has emerged as the presidential staff agency *par excellence*. Its duties have grown beyond assisting in budgetary formulation to include budget administration, the clearance of legislative proposals emanating from executive branch agencies,

[24]Quoted in Jesse Burkhead, *Government Budgeting* (New York: Wiley, 1956), p. 26.

coordination of broad government-wide programs, assistance in the formulation of the president's legislative program, and advice to the president on whether to veto bills proffered by Congress. It also conducts executive oversight of program management and administration, reviews executive branch organization, and assists in the career development and assignment of top-level officials. The OMB looms large in the political environment of federal agencies: a phone call from a relatively low level OMB staffer can send tremors of apprehension through a departmental assistant secretary. Indeed the role of OMB has grown so powerful that Congress recently required that its director, heretofore appointed solely at the pleasure of the president, henceforth be confirmed in office by the Senate.

The Executive Office of the President

The very existence of the Office of Management and Budget represents yet another of the devices given the president by Congress to help guide and monitor the sprawling federal bureaucracy. This device, the Executive Office of the President, is a group of policy-oriented staff agencies and councils under the president's immediate organizational umbrella. The provision of an expanded presidential staff capability was, as noted above, a direct response to the second wave of federal expansion during the New Deal period that demonstrated an acute need to give the chief executive the ability to supervise the multitude of new programs and agencies. The Executive Office emerged as a principal recommendation of the Brownlow Committee, a presidential committee of academicians called to evaluate the management capabilities and structure of the executive branch. The Committee in its 1937 report asked how it was "humanly possible" for the president "to know fully the affairs and problems of over 100 separate major agencies, to say nothing of being responsible for their general direction and coordination."[25]

[25]U.S. President's Committee on Administrative Management, *Report, With Special Studies* (Washington: Government Printing Office, 1937), p. 3.

The Committee's recommendation received congressional blessing in 1939, and the new office rapidly became a major executive resource for the management of World War II. Roosevelt used it as the locus for the "war agencies." Although these agencies were dissolved shortly after the end of the war, the post-war period saw the emergence of a number of permanent constituents of the Executive Office. The National Security Council (with its intelligence arm, the Central Intelligence Agency) was established in 1947 to integrate the analysis of foreign intelligence and to advise the president on national security policy and affairs. The Council of Economic Advisors was created in 1946 to provide expert advice on national economic policy. A relatively recent (but temporary) addition to the Executive Office was the Office of Economic Opportunity, established in 1964 by Lyndon Johnson to coordinate the poverty program. (Johnson was suspicious of the ability and willingness of the traditional bureaucracy, principally the Department of Health, Education and Welfare, to carry out the "war on poverty" with sufficient fervor). President Nixon in 1970 created a Domestic Council, made up of the cabinet officers of the domestic departments, as a kind of counterpart to the National Security Council. And Gerald Ford resuscitated the Office of Science and Technology abolished by his predecessor. Other constituents include the Councils on Environmental Quality and Wage and Price Stability and Offices of Telecommunications Policy and Drug Abuse Policy.

Not all components of the Executive Office, however, have become permanent fixtures. Some have been abolished or transferred because they were no longer seen as functions critical enough to deserve placement in the direct staff arm of the president. In some cases, creation of a unit in the Executive Office may be a stop-gap measure awaiting congressional creation of a new agency or bureau. And some constituents, such as the former Office of Consumer Affairs and the Office of Economic Opportunity, have fallen victim to presidential displeasure. Presently there are a dozen members of the Executive Office, either placed there by Congress or ratified after the fact through provision of congressional appropriations in support of presidential initiative. Congress, it should be noted, traditionally has been willing to grant the president considerable flexibility in determining the structure of much of the Executive Office.

In addition to these staff offices is a cadre of intimate, personal advisors and counsellors to the president known collectively as the White House Office (WHO). Though the use to which the members of the WHO are put depends largely on presidential style and organizational preference, several positions have emerged rather consistently over the past several decades.[26] Prime among them is the chief of staff, who helps organize the official work of the president—a kind of guardian of the White House gates. Others include the advisor for national security affairs, the congressional liaison officer, and the domestic advisor. In addition to these positions are persons involved in the personal affairs of the president (his physician, his attorney) or who ride herd on his political prospects and problems.

The members of the White House Office, extensions of the president's eyes and ears, were to be confidants with what Louis Brownlow once called a "passion for anonymity." And though most of these persons have remained anonymous, certain ones in the Nixon administration proved to have developed other passions as well—which, as we shall see, has led Congress to a greater scrutiny of the White House Office and the Executive Office as well.

The White House and Executive Offices have contributed greatly to the institutionalization of the presidency and have brought greater coherence to the president's oversight of the executive branch. But they have also served to buffer him from direct contact with an environment that may be sending messages different from those the president receives from his aides. Although George Reedy's argument that this institutionalization augurs the "twilight" of the presidency is probably overstated, there is a germ of truth in the charge.[27] For as the Executive

---

[26]An historical treatment of various presidential approaches to organizing the White House and Executive Offices may be found in Richard T. Johnson, *Managing the White House* (New York: Harper & Row, 1975).

[27]George Reedy, *The Twilight of the Presidency* (New York: World Publishing, 1970).

Office may have developed the president's ability to control and integrate the administrative state, it may also have reduced the quality and frequency of direct congressional contact with the president concerning its problems—leading Congress to take stronger steps to ensure its role in oversight of the executive agencies.

Control over Executive Branch Reorganization

A final arena in which Congress has granted the president powers to aid in his supervision of the executive branch is that of reorganization. Congress is the source of executive branch structure, but it has from time to time given the president certain leeway in adjusting that structure without resorting to formal legislation. Beginning in 1932, Congress has granted the president the right to make organizational consolidations and transfers among departments and agencies—subject to congressional approval. This approval is linked to the use of a "congressional veto," whereby the president announces an intended reorganization that goes into effect if neither house of Congress passes a simple resolution opposing it.

Presidential authority in reorganization has, however, been neither permanent nor comprehensive. It has been granted for brief periods of from two to four years, and has generally prohibited the president from tampering with departmental structure. Congress has also exempted from reorganization powers pet agencies such as the Corps of Engineers, which provide the pork barrel so dear to congressional hearts. In recent years, Congress has proved increasingly reluctant to grant more than limited reorganization authority to the president. As a result, any reorganization that is other than a minor adjustment must be introduced as legislation and run the full gamut of the congressional process.[28]

[28]See Herbert Emmerich, *Federal Organization and Administrative Management* (University, Alabama: University of Alabama Press, 1971) *passim;* Clifford L. Berg, "Lapse of Reorganization Authority," *Public Administration Review,* Vol. 35, No. 2 (March/April, 1975), pp. 195–199.

Congress has given the president these and other mechanisms for overseeing the bureaucracy partly because they are viewed as indispensable if the chief executive is to cope with the size and scope of federal administration. But they also reflect a growing awareness on the part of Congress that as the bureaucracy has taken on a life of its own, it has begun to claim a share in the formulation of policy as well as in its execution. Neither the political nor the civil service officialdom of agencies is neutral. Most top administrators are knee-deep in policy, often advocates and partisans for agency policies and for the constituents they serve (or even for those they regulate). Public administration, as one of its scholars observed decades ago, is almost inextricably entwined with policy and with politics. Administration is not a neutral mechanism; it is a political process, a major process of government.[29]

The Federal Personnel Structure: An Overview

The policy role of the federal bureaucracy is a complex one—to which we return in a later chapter. But this role is conditioned by the structure of the federal personnel system and by the political and bureaucratic cultures and subcultures from which it is formed. A passing acquaintanceship with this structure is essential to an understanding of the themes we develop further on.

The personnel structure of the federal executive branch may be viewed as an elongated isosceles triangle, with a narrow band of appointed political executives at its apex. The top level political cadre—the departmental secretaries, regulatory commissioners, agency administrators, and so on, most of them subject to senatorial confirmation—numbers around 600. Another 500 or so political executives form a kind of second tier of officials, named by department secretaries and agency administrators to high-level policymaking positions. They are designated "non-

---

[29]Paul Appleby, *Policy and Administration* (University, Alabama: University of Alabama Press, 1949).

career" executives. Below these two tiers of political officials work two and a half million civil officials covered under the merit system of the civil service and similar systems in the Foreign Service, the Public Health Service, and other parallel merit structures.

The top three grades of the civil service (the "supergrades") and their equivalents in other career systems number about 10,000 individuals—a nucleus of civil service executives serving under the smaller group of political appointees. These civil service executives exhibit certain characteristics that set them apart from their political bosses, so much so that they form a rather distinct culture. For the civil service executive, government is first of all a lifetime career. The authors of a comprehensive study of the careers of these executives outline the "typical" career pattern as follows:

> The new entrant entered the federal service well before age thirty with an advanced degree. . . . The work experience which he brings to his present job and which now exceeds twenty years was acquired largely within the federal service–and within the department by which he is now employed! Prior to entering the federal service, he had only incidental work experience–summer jobs, and perhaps a year or more in private business. . . . In short, the breadth of experience, the skills he has acquired, and the breadth of understanding he brings to his present assignment have all been developed on the job within the federal service.[30]

The executive cadres tend to enter government service at a relatively early age, to work in one or, at the most, two departments or agencies and in one occupational field, and to have been promoted with some regularity.[31]

High level federal service is a career relatively closed to penetration from the outside. The vast majority of top-level civil service executives are recruited from the career ranks below. During 1976 (the most recent year for which data is available), only seven percent of appointments were promotions from outside

[30]John J. Corson and R. Shale Paul, *Men Near the Top* (Baltimore: Johns Hopkins Press, 1966), pp. 106–107.

[31]David Stanley, *The Higher Civil Service* (Washington: Brookings Institution, 1964), pp. 22–38.

the same agency.[32] Indeed, the civil service at its upper ranks is probably second only to the military in its aversion to bringing in outsiders. It is virtually a closed career system.

As a group, these civil service executives are distinctly unrepresentative of the American population, in terms of their socioeconomic status and particularly in terms of their educational backgrounds. Over two-thirds hold at least a master's degree, nearly a quarter have a doctorate, and fewer than one in ten have not completed a college education.[33] The fields in which these executives were educated are largely those of science and the professions. Nearly a quarter took bachelor's degrees in engineering, a fifth in law, slightly under a fifth in biological and physical sciences, and one in nine in the social sciences. The number of those majoring in the humanities (typically associated with a "liberal" education) is less than 5 percent.[34]

The *political* executives, who hold appointive positions at the very top of the hierarchy, differ in many and significant respects from the civil service executives under them. An extremely important distinction is that of career. The civil service executive, as we have seen, is first and foremost a careerist—recruited to and reared within a lifetime career system. The political executive is a relative short-timer, an almost transitory figure on the scene. The top tier of political executives, those with direct presidential appointments, hold their positions for at most a few years before moving on. A study of these executives from the Franklin Roosevelt through the early Johnson administrations found that their median tenure in position was two years and four months. Commissioners of regulatory commissions (appointed usually to six year terms) had the greatest longevity, four and a half years. At the other end of the spectrum, the deputy administrators averaged a bare 19 months on the job. The implications of such short terms for high level political ap-

---

[32]U.S. Civil Service Commission, *Executive Personnel in the Federal Service* (Washington: Government Printing Office, 1977), p. 19.

[33]*Ibid.*, p. 38. See also K. J. Meier, "Representative Bureaucracy," *American Political Science Review*, Vol. 69, No. 2 (June, 1975), pp. 526–542.

[34]Stanley, *op. cit.*, p. 31.

pointees are drawn by the authors of the study: "These officials would probably be more valuable to the government if they served in more than one job and in more than one agency. . . . The trouble is that the typical political executive doesn't stay around long enough to do justice to even one job."[35] There is some indication that the amount of time these individuals stay in office has grown even shorter, as witness the revolving door political appointment system under the Nixon and Ford administrations.

In terms of longevity in office, political executives are certainly not careerists. Moreover, their employment before and after government service reflects a pattern far removed from that of the typical civil service executive. Nearly two-thirds of these executives had prinicipal occupations in the private sector before appointments to their government jobs—26 percent in private law practice, 24 percent in business and industry, and 15 percent in other private sector jobs. A little over a third listed principal occupations in the public sector, largely lower-level appointed political positions in the federal government. (A substantial proportion of those coming from the lower-level political appointee ranks themselves came originally from private sector pursuits.) And when they leave these positions, they by and large return to the same private professional and business pursuits in which they were previously engaged; fewer than one in five remained in the federal government at a lower-level job.[36] The top political executives are not, however, necessarily neophytes. The median executive, though staying in the position only a little over two years, had several years of prior administrative experience in the federal government—on the average five years of full-time federal employment.[37]

We have seen that the upper levels of the civil service are relatively closed to outsiders. What about the mobility of indi-

[35]David Stanley, Dean Mann and Jameson Doig, *Men Who Govern* (Washington: Brookings Institution, 1967), pp. 57, 60, 83. For a more recent study of federal executives, see Hugh Heclo, *A Government of Strangers* (Washington: Brookings Institution, 1977).

[36]*Ibid.*, pp. 31, 73.

[37]*Ibid.*, p. 56.

viduals from civil service to political appointee jobs? Top-level political appointee positions are not as a rule filled by former civil service careerists, nor is the civil service a fertile breeding ground for such positions. Of appointees to top political positions studied by Stanley, less than a fifth were former careerists in the civil service or parallel federal merit systems.[38] Even this proportion is overstated by the practice of the State Department of rotating high-ranking Foreign Serice officers in and out of Assistant Secretary positions.[39] Although civil service executives enter the public service through merit examination, the top political executives are recruited through personal, political, and professional ties, and often serve in noncareer executive assignments before being selected for the highest positions.

Political and civil service executives also differ in their age level and educational patterns. The average age of political executives is somewhat younger than their supergrade civil service subordinates. They are more likely to have attended a private (often Ivy League) college than the civil service executive. They usually, at the four-year degree level, have majored in the humanities and the behavioral sciences, whereas civil service executives major largely in the physical and biological sciences and in such applied fields as engineering. And political executives appear to have come generally from families with higher social and economic status than civil service executives.[40]

Political and civil service career executives also appear to have somewhat different personality characteristics. A research group using a thematic apperception test interviewed a sample of political and civil service executives. Though these two groups were often similar in some dimensions, they differed in others. The career civil servant, the test results suggested, "possesses loftly aspirations, the majority of which stem from external in-

[38]*Ibid.*, pp. 41–42.
[39]Dean Mann, *The Assistant Secretaries* (Washington: Brookings Institution, 1965) pp. 271–272; Stanley et al., *op. cit.,* p. 36.
[40]William L. Warner et al., *The American Federal Executive* (New Haven: Yale University Press, 1963), pp. 121, 326, 352, 371–372; Corson and Paul, *op. cit.,* p. 165; Stanley et al., *op. cit.,* pp. 126, 129.

fluences, from herioc figures or models, and from demands made upon him by the system and by his role as a career man." The political executive also had lofty aspirations, "but not to the same degree of | intensity or commitment. . . . Sometimes he is concerned with his ability to attain these high objectives. . . . Uncertainty, fear of failure, and doubt of capacity mark the political appointee to a much greater extent than the civil service career executive." The civil servant, they found, derives his or her ideals from "exemplary figures, [but] in considerable measure he internalizes these pressures so that they become an integral part of his being." The source of motivation for the political executive, on the other hand, "is more internal, flowing directly from fundamental personality characteristics."[41]

The differing career patterns and characteristics of these two groups, differences highlighted for the sake of comparison, influence both their loyalties and the way in which they approach their responsibilities. Career officials, with long tenure in an agency or bureau, often feel intensely loyal to their organization and to its programs and policies, and will often defend them against all comers. Political executives, with a much shorter agency exposure, tend to be loyal to other political officials above them, to the administration and *its* policies, to the president who appoints them. The political executive, who may spend the bulk of time in office just learning the ropes, is often something of a dilettante; civil service executives are generally experts in the agency's dynamics, inner life, policies, and programs. The civil service official is an organization person, rather narrow and provincial; the political executive, with a greater interest in the agency's political environment, rather broader and cosmopolitan. The career executive is wed to the agency and to furthering his or her mobility there; the political executive is often interested in moving on to other political assignments or ultimately returning to previous private sector pursuits. The personal ties of the political executive tend to run to others in the administration and its party; those of the career official run to the agency's clientele and, importantly, to congressional

[41]Warner, et al., *op. cit.,* pp. 195–197.

committee staffs and individual congressmen on the relevant
legislative and appropriations committees.

Although the political and civil service cultures are certainly
distinct, they are not polar opposites. Indeed, several factors
operate to blur the distinctions drawn above. One of these is the
political and party preferences of the administrative state. The
federal bureaucracy, including its upper reaches, is somewhat
left of center, basically liberal and Democratic. This results
partly because much of its recent growth has come during
periods of Democratic hegemony but also because of the identification of federal officials with the programs they administer
and their belief in the inherent worthiness of a "positive" role for
the federal government in American society—if not the expansion of that role.[42] When Democratic administrations are in
power, there is some potential for affinity between the views of
civil service executives and their political superiors. Republican
administrations, on the other hand, have usually been opposed
to the expansion of federal government programs, take a more
conservative view of its role, and tend thus to appoint political
officials who share this philosophy. This clash of values between
Republican administrations and a Democratic public service may
create a hostility between political and civil service officials that
borders on mutual contempt.

All modern presidents, of course, have complained about the
sluggishness of the bureaucracy and expressed frustration that
orders from the top often bog down or fail to be executed. But
the problem is especially acute with Republican presidents assuming leadership after extended periods of Democratic rule.
This was the case with Dwight Eisenhower and especially with
Richard Nixon. The Nixonian disenchantment with the federal
bureaucracy bordered on paranoia—and led among other

[42]Joel D. Aberbach and Bert A. Rockman, "Clashing Beliefs Within the Executive Branch: The Nixon Administration Bureaucracy," a paper prepared for
delivery at the annual meeting of the American Political Science Association,
Chicago, 1974.
[43]See Richard Nathan, *The Plot That Failed: Nixon and the Administrative Presidency*
(New York: Wiley, 1975).

things to an attempt to "take over" the career bureaucracy by placing trusted lieutenants in strategic positions in the departments and agencies and by moving to exercise tight political clearance over certain key civil service positions.[43]

A second thread of commonality between the civil service and political cultures is professionalism. A high percentage of top level civil servants come from training in the professions, especially law, engineering, and medicine. The overall number of political executives who are schooled as professionals, especially attorneys, is also substantial. Almost half of top political executives in one study held law degrees, and a fifth of those studied in another held four-year degrees in engineering.[44] The tendency toward professionalism on the part of both civil service and political executives is pronounced, and offers the possibility of special relationships based on common professional training. Although career and political officials may be divided by their political loyalties and jobs, they may relate on the basis of a common professional peer group. A civil service executive from an engineering background, for example, may be less suspicious of directions given by a political appointee who also holds an engineering degree. Authority derived from expertise may reenforce the authority derived from position.[45]

Furthermore, one must bear in mind that political appointees in a department or agency live much of their organizational life, short as it is, within the milieu of the civil service culture. They may well become socialized (at least sympathetic) to its norms, folkways, and values during their tenure. Knowledge of the problems and the programs of an agency may bring a growing identification with them on the part of the political executive. Constant interaction with the upper reaches of the career bureaucracy may blunt feelings of loyalty toward one's own political masters in the White House. Longer exposure to an

[44]U.S. Civil Service Commission, *op. cit.*, p. 45; Stanley, et al., *op. cit.*, p. 17; Warner, et al., *op. cit.*, p. 364.

[45]A recent treatment of this theme may be found in Frederick C. Mosher and Richard J. Stillman, eds., "A Symposium: The Professions in Government," *Public Administration Review*, Vol. 38, No. 2 (March/April, 1978), pp. 105–150.

agency may make the political appointee an agency ambassador *to* the president rather than a representative *of* him. Indeed, these pressures may well have been behind the rantings of
John Erlichman, major domo of the Nixon administration, who
though earlier boasting that when the White House said "jump,"
the cabinet officer asked only "how high?" later came to complain bitterly that these same officials had decided to "go off and
marry the natives."[46]

The strength of the socialization effect may be partly explained by the fact that the political executives are under greater
pressure to adapt to the department or agency than vice versa.
As one long-time observer of the Washington bureaucracy
suggests:

> There are likely to be daily reminders that they are merely temporary custo-
> dians and spokesmen for organizations with distinct and multi-dimensional
> personalities and deeply ingrained cultures and sub-cultures. . . . A depart-
> ment head's individual style must not do violence to the institutional mys-
> tique, and the words he speaks and the positions he advocates cannot ignore
> the precedents recorded in departmental archives.[47]

Granted these caveats to the distinctiveness of the civil service
and political cultures, what is their impact on congressional-
bureaucratic relationships? First, the inherent tensions between
civil service career executives and their political masters can (and
often do) lead to less than complete compliance with their instructions, to a weakening of crucial links in the chain of command extending from the White House downwards into the
depths of the bureaucracy. The ability of the president to orchestrate, to integrate the administrative state through the
power of political appointment—one of the chief executive's
primary control mechanisms—is often vitiated, as we shall see in
a later chapter, by a strongly entrenched career bureaucracy.
The effectiveness of the appointment power of the president is
insulated and blunted, the downward pressure of "overhead
democracy" weakened. And it is the appointment power on

[46]Quoted in Harold Seidman, *Politics, Position and Power* (New York: Oxford
University Press, 1975), p. 87.
[47]*Ibid.*, pp. 121–122.

which the president relies heavily in his competition with Congress for control of the administrative state. To the degree that this control is weakened, so is the potential for congressional inroads into presidential power increased.

Presidential authority over the vast federal bureaucracy is both challenged and supplemented by the oversight functions exercised by Congress. But the tenor and quality of Congress' influence over the bureaucracy is of a different kind and often of a different intent. This difference, above and beyond the influences flowing from the special constitutional and statutory relationships of Congress to administration, may be traced in no small measure to the institutional development of the Congress itself, to the unique drives of history that have formed and conditioned it. It is to these drives, and to their impact on the evolution of congressional-bureaucratic relationships, that we now turn.

3
Congress: The Rise of Committee Government

The emergence of American national government as economic regulator, social architect, and international power has altered fundamentally the operation and procedures of the United States Congress. Representatives and senators from the early 19th century, glancing into a crystal ball at today's Congress, would scarcely have believed their eyes. In 1802, the legislative branch consisted of 152 individuals: one vice president, 32 senators, 106 representatives, and 13 staff members. By the 1970s Congress contained one vice president, 100 senators, 435 representatives and well over 35,000 staff members.[1] The early nineteenth century Congress "ordinarily worked only after the harvest season and before spring planting."[2] Today, Congress conducts business the year around, with short recesses and the August vacation serving as breaks during which members often tour their constituencies or hold investigations outside Washington. One hundred and sixty years ago, members of Congress roomed together in boardinghouses, leaving their families back home during the short congressional sessions. The

---

[1]For information on congressional personnel in the early 1800s, see James Sterling Young, *The Washington Community, 1800–1825* (New York: Harcourt Brace Jovanovich, 1966), p. 31; for the 1970s, see Joint Committee on Reduction of Federal Expenditures, *Report on Federal Personnel and Pay* (Washington: U.S. Government Printing Office, March, 1973) p. 11.

[2]Young, *op. cit.* p. 28.

modern-day members of Congress buy homes in the Washington suburbs or Georgetown and take their families to Washington with them. Once elected, today's members, unlike their early nineteenth century counterparts, tend to develop congressional careers that often span twenty, thirty, forty years. Congress has become a full-fledged institution.

These changes have occurred with only a few constitutional amendments regarding the role of Congress. In Article I of the Constitution the founding fathers gave to Congress "all legislative power herein granted." Section 8 of Article I enumerated these powers as including the authority to lay and collect taxes (with revenue bills to originate in the House of Representatives), to regulate commerce with foreign nations and among the states, to declare war and raise armies, to control such activities as the postal service and coining money, and finally the power "to make all laws which shall be necessary and proper for carrying into Execution the foregoing Powers, and all other Powers vested by this Constitution in the Government of the United States." Article II, section 2, gave the Senate additional power: the responsibility, with two-thirds of the members present concurring, to give advice and consent to the president on treaties and nominations.

Today, as in 1789, Article I, section 8, and Article II, section 2, are the fundamental source of the authority of the U.S. Congress. The transformations that have occurred are in the relevance and significance of the constitutional powers Congress was granted. In the eighteenth and nineteenth centuries an agrarian lifestyle provided selfsufficient towns and farms while the oceans protected the nation from threat of foreign invasion. The amount of interstate commerce was small; concern with foreign policy was minimal. Within the context of its constitutional powers—the most significant of which were the regulation of interstate commerce and the direction of military and foreign policy—there was relatively little for Congress to do. When the industrial revolution later helped create an interdependent economy based on interstate and foreign commerce, it expanded the role of Congress by confronting it with social and economic problems that lay within its constitutional jurisdiction.

The industrial revolution also provided America (as well as other nations) the technical means with which to span the oceans and conquer far-off lands. With the development of international markets, America discovered the world, the world rediscovered America, and Congress discovered anew the significance of its constitutional power to raise and finance the military and to supervise foreign policy.

The Emergence of a Professionalized Congress

The increased power of the national government over the lives of the citizenry—and the critical role of Congress in directing national power—had a considerable reciprocal effect on Congress itself. So long as the national government was small, Congress could (and often did) itemize appropriations virtually to the last pencil per agency, encourage presidents to obtain congressional approval for administrative decisions large and small, and supervise the administrative agencies almost haphazardly, without the fear that serious administrative mistakes would go undiscovered. Members of Congress needed, or felt they needed, very little expertise in specific policy areas. In addition, so long as the role of the national government was minimal, Congress itself held out little attraction as a place in which politicians could influence national life and attain power. As Congress undertook in the late nineteenth century initiatives that created the administrative state, Congress became a center of national power. As a result, the institution itself began to change.

One significant change that occurred within Congress was professionalization. Congress ceased to be a waystation in the lives of lawyers, farmers, or entrepreneurs who were preoccupied with local politics and business, and became instead a career in its own right. This trend closely paralleled changes that were occurring in the federal bureaucracy. Between 1880 and 1910, as we noted in Chapter 2, congressional legislation resulted in the introduction of the merit system, a career service, and a doubling and tripling of the size of the federal bureaucracy. During this same period, members of Congress increasingly became willing to remain in Congress, attracted to career service by the growing significance of national government in the everyday lives of Americans and by the influential role that Congress potentially could exert in an industrialized America. These changes occurred first in the Senate.

In the early years of the Senate, senators "fled the capitol—not yet located in Washington—almost as fast as was humanly possible." In fact, "prior to the Civil War one just did not make a long term 'career' out of continuous Senate service, except perhaps as a fluke."[3] Most senators during this time averaged only three to four years service. Starting in the 1870s and 1880s, however, senators became increasingly attracted to Senate service by the expanding importance of tariff policy, monetary policy, race policy, and by the Senate's control of federal patronage. Around 1880, the average length of Senate service began to rise from four years, lengthening to over eight years by the early 1900s.[4]

Professionalization in the House followed the Senate pattern with a lag of about 15 years, with its slower development resulting from a more competitive electoral system. "What the early House lacked was not safe seats, but a desire and incentive to retain one's seat." In the late nineteenth century, while the increased significance of national government provided members the incentive to return to Washington, re-election had become more risky "because many congressional districts had highly competitive party systems."[5] The 1896 elections, however, solidified one-party control of most congressional districts so that incumbents desiring re-election could win and thereby develop a professional House career. Throughout the early nineteenth century and into the 1890s, 38 to 65 percent of all congressional seats went to nonincumbents. After the 1896 realignment, the level of nonincumbency declined so that by the first decade of

[3] H. Douglas Price, "Congress and the Evolution of Legislative "Professionalism," in Norman J. Ornstein, ed., *Congress in Change* (New York: Praeger Publishers, 1975), pp. 5–7.

[4] Randall B. Ripley, *Power in the Senate* (New York: St. Martin's Press, 1969), p. 43.

[5] Price, *op. cit.*, p. 9.

the twentieth century, it ranged between 23 and 31 percent.[6] By
the turn of the century, "political life demanded undivided attention, and only men willing to sustain the effort reaped the
rewards. Fame, prestige, and power were reserved for those who
diligently and persistently pursued them. . . . Government service left little opportunity for anything else. . . .[P]olitics was a
full-time profession."[7]

A full-time profession required professional assistance. As
members became attracted to long-term service, and as the work
of Congress became increasingly complex, the internal resources
of Congress were increased. Between 1880 and 1910, the housekeeping expenditures of the House of Representatives more
than doubled from approximately 2 million to over 5 million
dollars. In 1899 the Library of Congress began to expand and
develop the massive research holdings and facilities it offers today. In the early 1900s, Congress opened its first office building
and began regularly to appropriate funds for clerical staffs for
standing committees and for the legislators themselves. In 1914,
it established the Legislative Reference Service, an adjunct of the
Library of Congress designed to provide members of Congress
with research into legislative matters. The Office of Legislative
Counsel was created in 1918 to provide assistance to members in
drafting legislation. By the early 1910s, Congress had lost the
trappings of a part-time job that it had in the early nineteenth
century and had taken on the appearance of a professional
body, replete with staff and office space.

As the national government became more important in national life, and as Congress became more professional, patterns
of influence on members and of their behavior within Congress
changed. "In the 1870s, lobbying for the first time became a vital
element in government," though the lobbyists' activities at first
were "careless and haphazard." In the late nineteenth century,
"congressional legislation became even more pertinent to a multitude of economic interests. . . . Tariff and currency rather than

---

[6]Morris P. Fiorina, David W. Rohde, and Peter Wissel, "Historical Change in
House Turnover" in Ornstein, *op. cit.*, pp. 29–31.
[7]David J. Rothman, *Politics and Power* (New York: Atheneum, 1969), p. 137.

the railroad policies now attracted the (lobbying) agents to Washington, and their numbers and importance swelled visibly." The lobbyists "supplied information that only representatives of particular organizations could gather. Helping members of Congress to understand the increasingly technical legislation that came before the chamber, lobbyists became the experts in an era of specialization."[8] And while members of Congress came to rely increasingly on lobbyists, constituents frustrated by the growing bureaucracy turned to their elected representatives for assistance. Around the turn of the century there occurred "a significant increase in what might be called the purely personal duties of Congressmen, who became, indeed, almost the special agents in Washington of their constituents. They came to be called upon, more and more, to attend to innumerable matters unrelated to their legislative function, to obtain passports . . . , report on claims against the government, to do the errands of influential persons in their congressional districts."[9]

The creation of the new office buildings and the provision of office space perceptibly altered congressional life:

> *In the time of Reed [the 1880s] few [members] were influential enough to have assigned to them offices in the Capitol, and only the committee chairmen were adequately housed. The average member's office was under his hat and one would find him dictating his correspondence to his stenographer in the corridors outside the House chambers, or in some quiet nook behind a sheltering bit of bronze or marble in Statuary Hall. The conditions at that time imposed some hardships upon members, but they had the effect, at least, of keeping them always close to the House when it was in session.*

The new arrangements, with members having private offices in "a building some little distance from the Capitol" were different. When members' presence was required, "they would be summoned by electric signals," elements of a modernized Congress:

> *The real business was transacted by a comparatively small number of men in actual attendance upon the session, the others rushing in from time to time to answer the rollcalls, and then darting out again to hurry back to their offices*

[8]*Ibid.*, pp. 191−220.
[9]George Rothwell Brown, *The Leadership of Congress* (Indianapolis: Bobbs-Merrill, 1922), pp. 249−250.

*there to remain until another occasion to vote might arise. Under this system
. . . the average member suffered in the Congress from a lack of familiarity
with the intricate details of the business of legislation."* [10]

Along with these general changes in Congress, differences
between the House and Senate began to emerge and solidify. An
important difference was size. Prior to the Civil War, conflict
over the extension of slavery constrained rapid expansion westward. With slavery destroyed, with the railroads available as a
new mode of transportation, and with western markets and resources to be exploited, the nation admitted twelve new states
between 1867 and 1912. As a result of the addition of new states,
the Senate increased in size from 72 to 96. The growth of the
nation westward, together with the swelling of urban centers in
the east through immigration, doubled, tripled, quadrupled the
nation's population. In an effort to keep up with increasing
population and the admission of the new states, the House of
Representatives increased the number of congressional seats
from 243 in 1860 to 435 in 1913. Since 1915, the size of the
House has remained fixed, with minor exceptions. Members of
the House determined that it was better to increase the number
of people being represented per member than to increase the
number of representatives indefinitely, thereby further crowd-
ing the House and making it even less flexible and more impersonal.

The increase in the size of the Senate did not alter that body
dramatically nor destroy the intimacy that could exist between
members. The Senate maintained its tradition of informality. It
did, however, create the cloture rule (Rule 22) in 1917, providing that debate in the Senate could be closed on an issue if
two-thirds of the senators present so voted—thus providing a
means to end filibusters. In the House, by contrast, the House
Rules Committee, for example, emerged as a powerful entity in
the scheduling and regulation of debate on legislation. Under
the new constraints, most legislation was limited to only nominal
debate and most bills were not open to significant amendments.
The considerable size differential between the two houses, and

[10]*Ibid.,* pp. 250–251.

the passage of the House beyond the threshold at which informal, intimate relations between members could be maintained, cast upon the House a curse of formality and procedural rigidity that the Senate escaped.

Constitutional differences between the two chambers reinforced the contrasts between them. In the early years of the Republic, the Senate had been "an honorific nothing."[11] (The nation then considered the House of Representatives the more prestigious chamber, owing to direct popular election of its members.) But the Senate did have the constitutional power to approve executive nominations and treaties. In the late nineteenth and early twentieth centuries, the expanding scope of the bureaucracy at home and the power of the nation abroad meant that approval of executive nominations and consent to treaties increased the prestige of the Senate. Its position in relation to the House thus improved. The House still held significant status, however, due to the increasing importance of tariffs, monetary policy, and the regulation of interstate commerce. (The Constitution specifies that the House must be the initiator of all revenue legislation, giving it the opportunity to set the nation's agenda in this critical area.) The preeminence of the House in fiscal matters, and the great importance this gave the House, is illustrated by the fact that two chairmen of the House committee that wrote revenue legislation, Ways and Means, moved from that position to the presidency itself (Garfield and McKinley). By the first decade of the twentieth century, the Senate had developed a specialized and significant role as overseer of the president's nominations and treaties. Because of its special constitutional role in revenue legislation, the House had emerged as the legislative guardian of the nation's pursestrings.

The Rise of Committee Government

The moves toward a more professionalized Congress and toward clear distinctions between the House and Senate was accompanied by an important institutional change—a major al-

[11]Price, *op. cit.*, p. 6.

teration in the congressional power structure. During most of the nineteenth century (and certainly by the end of the century) power in Congress had become concentrated in the hands of a relatively few individuals—normally the Speaker and his lieutenants in the House of Representatives, the majority party leader and his supporters in the Senate. These majority party leaders in each house had the responsibility for organizing committees, for appointing committee members and chairmen, and for ensuring the passage of the majority party's legislation through the committees and the house.

While the work of Congress occurred largely within congressional committees, the party leaders molded, coordinated, and influenced substantially the work of the committees. In addition, the party leaders, particularly the Speaker, possessed considerable discretionary power with respect to parliamentary procedure during floor debate and passage. The power of the party leaders helped ensure that the policies of the majority party would be enacted. They formed an identifiable group of individuals who could be held responsible for the overall development of public policy. In this party leadership system, the average members of Congress normally played minor roles. Woodrow Wilson, describing this system in 1884, observed that "all men of independent spirit chafe under the arbitrary restraint of such a system," and he concluded that "they let it stand because they can devise nothing better."[12]

The rise of a "professional" Congress is linked to the decline of the strong role of party leaders in Congress. Once a large number of members became attracted to long-term congressional service in the House, and once the party system began to stabilize and ensure safe seats to representatives, members of the House moved to attack the concentration of power in the Speaker's hands. In 1910, in one of the greatest political upheavals of congressional history, insurgent (progressive) Repub-

[12]*Woodrow Wilson, Congressional Government* (Cleveland: World Publishing, 1956 [1885]), p. 87; on the Speakership see also Lauros G. McConachie, *Congressional Committees* (New York: Thomas Y. Crowell, 1898), pp. 51–55; George B. Galloway, *History of the House of Representatives* (New York: Thomas Y. Crowell, 1962), pp. 101–106.

licans who were unhappy with the policies and arbitrariness of their Republican colleague, Speaker Joseph Cannon, united with the House Democrats to strip the speakership of most of its power. Prior to the insurgent movement, the Speaker had served as presiding officer and, simultaneously, controlled committee appointments, the Rules Committee, private and minor House business, the Special Calendar, and the party caucus. After the insurgency, while Cannon remained Speaker, the office itself was stripped of all major duties except the constitutional role of Presiding Officer; that role itself was narrowed, however, by the passage of rules limiting the Speaker's discretionary parliamentary prerogatives.[13]

A similar though less dramatic reduction in the role of party leadership occurred in the Senate. Historically, the Senate as an institution has never made party leadership easy or natural. Its smaller size makes the necessity of formal rules (and a leader to enforce them) less pressing than in the House. Because each Senator serves a "sovereign state," and because there are so few senators, each possesses a visibility and symbolic status that augurs against following a leader. In addition, no formal elected position exists in the Senate analogous to the House Speakership in stature or potential parliamentary power. The Constitution provides that there shall be a Speaker of the House who shall serve as its Presiding Officer and be selected by the House; this provision allows a majority party to place its party leader in the Speaker's chair and give the leader strong parliamentary power. Senators, by contrast, do not have the option of selecting an individual to preside over them; the Constitution gives that responsibility to the vice president. A majority party in the Senate thus lacks the option of placing its party leader in the position of Presiding Officer and investing in that position great parliamentary power. The constitutional structure of the Senate seems inherently biased against the possibility of strong party leadership on the part of a single individual.

[13]Kenneth W. Hechler, *Insurgency: Personalities and Politics of the Taft Era* (New York: Columbia University Press, 1940), pp. 27–82; see also Joseph Cooper and David Brady, "Organizational Theory and Congressional Structure," 1973 APSA Paper, pp. 52–61.

In the late nineteenth century the bias against party leadership in the Senate was briefly overcome. At that time, the state legislatures of most states selected the state's senators. Because senators controlled federal patronage in the state through a system called senatorial courtesy—a significant power considering the increase in patronage positions that occurred after the Civil War—state party organizations attempted to control Senate seats by controlling state legislatures and thus nominations to the Senate. Once in the Senate, senators tended to follow the national party's policy positions as a way of solidifying their support by the national party and thus their hold over patronage dispersed by it. In other words, the selection of senators by state legislatures, the control of state legislatures by state party organizations, the control of federal patronage by senators, and the existence of widespread federal patronage to be dispersed—all these factors together with the existence of experienced, capable party leaders in the Senate combined to develop in the late nineteenth century Senate a period of strong party leadership, a leadership expressed through caucus rather than individual rule. Whereas "Senators in the 1870s usually performed their tasks without party superintendence," by 1900

> all this had changed. The party caucus and its chieftains determined who would sit on which committees and looked after the business calendar in detail. Members were forced to seek their favors or remain without influence in the chamber. At the same time, both organizations imposed unprecedented discipline on roll calls. The Senate never achieved the standard set in the House of Commons; yet by 1900 the parties exercised key powers over the chamber's proceedings.[14]

The same progressive revolt that helped topple the speakership in the House also destroyed the underpinnings of party government in the Senate. First, opponents of the "spoils system" that helped create the incentives for cooperation within the party caucus moved to create the merit system in the federal bureaucracy. In the early years this reform did little to reduce the patronage power of senators because the merit system coverage spread only gradually. After the turn of the century, how-

[14]Rothman, *op. cit.*, p. 4.

ever, the merit system began to reduce significantly the patronage of Senators. Simultaneously, the reformers struggled to create an elected Senate. The move toward electing Senators came first at the state level as a number of states instituted popular elections. The nation as a whole instituted popular election of Senators with the Seventeenth Amendment, approved in 1913. In 1922, George Rothman Brown concluded, "This constitutional reform, making the Senator responsible to the people, accentuated his individualism . . . It had a tendency to undermine party solidarity . . . The Senator came to think more in terms of himself and his re-election, nearly always an impelling motive, and less in terms of party."[15]

By the third decade of the twentieth century, the progressive movement had destroyed the two bulwarks of party government in the Senate: a widespread patronage system and selection of Senators by party organizations in the state legislatures. In the late nineteenth century, senators had cooperated with state party organizations to gain their nominations and had worked closely with Senate party leaders to ensure control of patronage; senators in the twentieth century began to build personal campaign machines that were independent of state parties and to cast Senate votes that were consistent with their electoral security or personal preferences rather than the party platform. With the growing independence of individual Senators, party leaders in the Senate lost control of Senate deliberations and the cohesive party caucuses vanished. By the early 1920s, in the Senate as well as the House, the old order of party government had become a mere shadow of its former self.[16]

A new order emerged after 1910 and came to dominate both the House and the Senate in the twentieth century—*committee government*. While committees had existed throughout the nineteenth century as the place where hearings were held and legislation drafted, they had normally served as arms of the elected party leadership. After the party leaders were stripped of power (and after a short flirtation with caucus rule in the

[15]Brown, *op. cit.*, pp. 257–258.
[16]Rothman, *op. cit.*, p. 90; Brown, *op. cit.*, pp. 195–197, 275.

House) committee members, particularly the chairmen, moved rapidly to assert their prerogatives as the masters of legislation. Each committee became largely autonomous in its own area of jurisdiction. The committees and their leaders held their hearings and wrote legislation behind closed doors. Because the party leadership could not threaten their committee assignments, and because they were largely hidden from public view, committee members, particularly the chairs, were relatively free to follow their own heads rather than look to central leaders or the party for advice. As one observer wrote in 1922:

> *Too many captains are as much of a nuisance as a superfluity of cooks. Under the old regime a single chef had presided over the pot, and the broth was always piping hot, although perhaps not flavored to a universal taste. Under the new regime every one wished to be putting his spoon in. Every committee chairman was a captain.*[17]

Committee government rested on one central factor: the seniority system. It was assumed, first, that a member of Congress had a right to maintain a committee assignment once the assignment was made initially; the party leaders no longer had the power to discipline and retract an assignment. Second, as Lindsay Rogers observed in 1926, "appointments to legislative committees rarely depart from the rule of seniority and the result is—particularly in the relatively small Senate—a disproportionate number of choice committee assignments for members with long congressional service."[18] Third, leadership of a committee went, in an ironclad application of seniority, to the member of the majority party who had established the longest continuous service as a party member on the particular committee. These three informal rules constituted the seniority system. Together they provided a replacement for the discretionary power that strong party leaders had exercised in constituting committees and redrawing their membership from session to session. Responsibility to enforce these rules (rules that were really unwritten norms) and to exercise the limited discretion

---

[17]*Ibid.*, p. 244
[18]Lindsay Rogers, *The American Senate* (New York: Alfred A. Knopf, 1976) p. 109.

allowed by them was given, naturally, to a committee—the Committee on Committees established by the party caucuses in each house.

Committee Government and the Power of Congress

The rise of committee government was a reaction to the emerging power of the federal government, and to the administrative state that Congress was creating. Members of Congress were attracted by congressional service in the late nineteenth and early twentieth century by the vast increases in national powers. Service in Congress seemed to offer an accessible way in which to gain the political power with which to help mold public policy and direct the administrative state. Once in Congress, however, members found power so intensely concentrated that they actually could do little to influence congressional decisions. The solution was to disperse congressional power to the already existing congressional committees, thereby giving each member of Congress a better opportunity to influence some area of public policy and gain some degree of power.

So long as most members of Congress had not been interested in congressional careers and had stayed in Congress for relatively short periods of time, there had existed little incentive to disperse congressional power. After all, lacking a large proportion of senior members and a norm of seniority, selection of committee members and leaders would have been chaotic without strong party leaders to perform the task. With the rise of a professionalized Congress, however, seniority became available as an automatic and easily applied norm to follow in determining committee assignments and leaders. Most members were interested in congressional service and congressional power. Committee government thus offered an attractive alternative to party government, an alternative through which individual members of Congress could hope to gain power and influence.

Committee government and the seniority system also had several fundamental attributes to recommend them as efficient, rational procedures for organizing and conducting congressional business. By the early twentieth century, Congress confronted problems that, by nineteenth century standards, were enormous in their scope and complexity. Congress needed some system of specialized advice in the numerous policy areas facing it—access to experts who knew the legislative history of a policy, had studied intensely the policy options, and could make seasoned, reliable recommendations to the whole body. In addition, Congress confronted an administrative state whose programs and agencies increased seemingly with every session of Congress. Somehow Congress had to oversee these programs and agencies to ensure that they were operating in a fashion consistent with congressional intent.

Committee government and the seniority system offered solutions to both problems. The seniority system provided a replacement for strong party leaders and thus freed committee members to plan long-term careers within particular committees without fear of removal by an arbitrary leader. A long-term committee career offered members the opportunity not only to develop policy specialization but also to review particular agencies and programs for years and decades after the initial authorizing legislation was passed. Committee government thus provided a mechanism whereby the members of Congress, divided among the various committees, could be their own expert advisers and thus would not have to rely totally on lobbyists or outside specialists for information. Simply put, the new order appeared to provide a natural structure within which to supervise and control the emerging administrative state.

The rise of committee government, however, was not an unmixed blessing. In 1893, Speaker of the House, Thomas Reed had warned that:

The Speaker of the House holds an office of dignity and honor, of vast power and influence. . . . No factional or party malice ought ever to strive to diminish his standing or lessen his esteem in the eyes of Members or the world. Whoever at any time, whether for purposes of censure or rebuke or from any other motive, attempts to lower the prestige of that office, by just so much lowers the prestige of the House itself, whose servant and exponent the Speaker is. No attack, whether open or covert, can be made upon that great office without leaving to the future a legacy of disorder and bad government. [19]

The fall of the Speaker of the House symbolized the decline of party government in Congress, and Reed's comments are a prescient forecast of the consequences of that decline. The committee system whose governance replaced party leadership was "archaic," "crying for reform," and "fortified by selfish interests." The standing committees, which by the early twenties numbered as high as 60 in the House, "were imperfectly coordinated with the bureaus and departments of the executive branch." In addition, the country found that the magic replacement for party leadership, the seniority rule, was not a totally flawless tool. Brown, reflecting on the 1910s and early 1920s, observed:

> *the seniority rule, generally adherred to, was responsible for the fact that in a number of cases important chairmanships were held by men who were incompetent. Often the best minds could not be utilized by the party because of the system which accorded rank and power to those who had earned their places by long service rather than good service. It was inevitable that there should be embarrassments. Party policies were jeopardized and programs upset at the most inopportune times.* [20]

Disorder was further aggravated by the structure of the committee system. Five basic types of committees existed in the House and the Senate after the decline of party government. The vast majority of committees in both houses were *authorization* committees—committees whose bills initially created the policies and agencies of the federal government (subject, as with all committee legislation, to approval by both houses). As the name implies, bills from these committees authorized the existence of an agency and program, specified the responsibilities and powers, and often proposed the funding level that the program and agency should receive. In some cases, authorization committees could also appropriate funds.

Appropriations, however, were generally the province of a second set of committees, the House and Senate *Appropriations*

[19]Quoted in Brown, *op. cit.*, pp. 106–107.
[20]*Ibid.*, pp. 248–249.

Committees (one in each chamber). The Appropriations Committee approved the funds an agency and program would receive; without appropriations, no agency or program could be implemented, no matter how widespread the support for its authorizing legislation had been. A third set of committees were the *revenue* committees—the House Ways and Means Committee and the Senate Finance Committee. These committees established the procedures to raise the funds to meet the expenses generated by the authorization and appropriations committees. A fourth set of committees, the internal *housekeeping* committees, had the responsibility to take care of day-to-day affairs of Congress itself, such as overseeing the staff resources or office space. A fifth type of committee—*internal regulation*—existed only in the House of Representatives—the House Rules Committee. The role of the Rules Committee was to schedule bills for floor debate and to specify the rules and procedures under which particular bills would be debated.

This committee structure posed a number of liabilities for congressional government. First there was the problem of *leadership*. Under the old system, the Speaker of the House and the majority leader of the Senate possessed real authority and could articulate forcefully the policy positions of the majority of Congress. In conflict with the president or executive agencies, the party leaders of Congress spoke as the embodiment of Congress and could present coherent, highly publicized, authoritative statements of congressional sentiment. With the demise of party government, no one person or group could speak persuasively for Congress. Power was dispersed among hundreds of committees, subcommittees, special committees, and joint committees. Numerous members came to hold authority in a given policy area, making it difficult for the press or the public to identify a single congressional spokesman in that area. Lacking an easily identifiable legislative leader in a given area, Congress found it difficult to provide unified policy leadership to the nation.

Closely related to the lack of leadership was a second problem, that of *accountability* and *responsibility*. Under the old regime of Speaker power in the House and caucus government in the Senate, the strong power of party leaders usually assured the passage of legislation that enjoyed the support of the majority party and was a part of its programme. Party government admittedly had its problems, but under party government the country had a reasonable expectation that the majority party could at least legislate and afterwards could be held accountable for the legislation that it passed or failed to pass. Under party government, if a committee refused to respond to the majority party's program, that majority—acting through the leadership—could discipline the committee members and ensure a floor vote on legislation.

Under the new order, party leaders did not possess the power to discipline committee members who blocked party legislation. A committee's members, operating without accountability to a majority within either the House or the Senate, could stop any legislation that fell within the committee's jurisdiction, no matter how widespread the support for the legislation in the Congress or the country. As Lindsay Rogers observed in the 1920s, "The degree of control that each committee may have over the business of the House becomes of great importance, for the House, as a whole, may be completely bound by the accident of the personnel of a committee."[21]

Of all congressional committees, the House Rules Committee presented the greatest potential problem of responsibility. Under the old regime, the Speaker controlled the Rules Committee and could thus neutralize its ability to block the majority party's programs. The Speaker could also use the Rules Committee to block minor legislation that he did not want (a factor that helped lead to the revolt against Speaker Cannon). Nevertheless, the control of the Rules Committee by the Speaker assured that the committee would not stop the major legislation supported by the House majority, at least as long as the majority party was relatively cohesive and selected a Speaker who reflected its dominant stance on major policy issues.

Under the new system, this guarantee did not exist. The Rules Committee, as all other committees, was largely autonomous. The seniority rule applied to it as absolutely as to any other committee. Members of Congress feared that to challenge the

[21]Rogers, *op. cit.*, p. 131.

seniority rule as it applied to the Rules Committee—and seek to discipline its members for blocking key legislation—might undermine the seniority rule across all committees, a result that would threaten their own vested interests within their own committees. As a result, the Rules Committee had the power to act as a dictator of the House and to ignore the wishes of the House majority or national sentiment. The Rules Committee could simply refuse to schedule key legislation and thus kill it.

A third liability of committee government was its *insulation* from the nation at large. The insulation of the committees resulted from three factors. First, committees held most hearings and mark-ups (that is, committee votes on bills and amendments) in closed door sessions, where the public and the press could not observe their deliberations. Second, the number of committees, subcommittees, special committees, and joint committees totalled around 270 by the 1930s (around 80 of which were standing committees). Observers seeking to follow congressional action were confronted with a complex array of activity. Third, serious jurisdictional disputes existed among the committees, often throwing them into extensive conflict and struggle with one another, confusing observers who were concerned with policy deliberations. While the committees wasted a fair amount of time and effort both fighting among themselves for control over policy domains and fighting for the time of their members (all of whom had numerous committee assignments), the press and the public-at-large tended to view Congress as a mysterious, ineffectual relic of the nineteenth century. By closing its committee doors, creating a multiplicity of committees, and confusing jurisdictional lines, Congress isolated itself from the nation. Out of sight and often out of mind, Congress lost the country's attention and respect and often became an object of scorn and derision.

As Congress declined in prestige, and the executive branch emerged as the dominant, aggressive branch of American government, a fourth problem emerged: *administrative oversight.* Nowhere within the committee system structure was there a set of permanent "oversight" committees with broad powers and resources to investigate and monitor the conduct of administration and the execution of legislative policies. The investigations that did occur took place either in special committees established for specific investigation or in the permanent standing legislative committees. Temporary committees provided an unsatisfactory mechanism for oversight; they were formed, after all, only after a problem gained sufficient notoriety to warrant a special investigation, and thus could not themselves uncover the unseen problems that precipitated the investigation. The standing committees, likewise, were limited in their capacity for oversight. Because legislative committees were composed of members who had helped create the agencies and programs that fell under their existing committee jurisdiction and were thus often in sympathy with them, they often lacked the will to supervise or investigate. The better part of discretion was to leave the agencies largely to their own devices, lest the glare of publicity and the discovery of shortcomings force Congress to de-authorize a pet program, casting aspersions on those who originally drafted the legislation.

The logical solution—creation of permanent oversight committees—seemed politically infeasible. Members of Congress had vested interests in the existing committee structure. To establish a new committee devoted exclusively to oversight and possessing broad investigatory powers would threaten the existing committee system. First, such a committee would by its nature interfere with the substantive jurisdiction of the legislative committees by investigating agencies whose programs fell within their jurisdiction. Just as legislative committee members were themselves unwilling to investigate most bureaus because they might uncover practices best left unseen, they did not want an all-powerful oversight committee uncovering practices and program inadequacies that might undermine "their" agencies. A second factor was that a new and powerful oversight committee might well overshadow other existing committees in the quest for publicity, public attention, and the consequent ability to influence public policy. With a broad mandate to roam the administrative state in search of indiscretions and program inadequacies, the oversight committee could select the juicy topics for its own review, leaving to the other committees the less stimulating responsibility of legislating solutions to the problems it uncovered. The Congress had no intention of unleashing such a committee, particularly since most members knew they would not be on it. Thus, as Congress expanded the administrative state through the creation of new agencies and programs, it at the same time shied away from restructuring the committee system in a manner conducive to effective congressional oversight of administration.

Finally, nowhere within the committee arrangement did there exist procedures for *coordination* to ensure that the decisions of the authorization, appropriations, and revenue committees had some reasonable relationship to one another. Nowhere was there a budget committee to examine the relationship of revenues to expenditures. The committees of Congress made authorization, appropriations, and revenue decisions without any system to coordinate the three processes and establish an overall goal, or set of policy priorities, that would guide these three processes. In the age of strong party leadership, party leaders had played a significant role in policy and fiscal coordination. In their absence, a congressional vacuum existed. Members of Congress were loathe to fill this vacuum with a new authority—a Budget Committee or a chief congressional budget officer—to perform the coordination role. The power to coordinate would carry with it the power to set priorities, to guide the legislative program, and thereby to threaten the power of the individual committees and their leaders. Having consolidated power within committees by curtailing the power of party leaders, members of Congress were unwilling to give up some of this hard-won congressional power to a new congressional leader. They chose, therefore, to maintain the system of decentralized congressional power in which each member could hope to be a king of a committee's domain.

Congress did take a partial step toward greater coordination in the Budget and Accounting Act of 1921 establishing a national budget. Rather than placing the entire budgetary process in Congress, however, the act divided budgetary power between Congress and the executive. Formulation of the national budget and its actual administration became the responsibility of the president; approval of the proposed budget through appropriations and the audit of budget expenditures remained the province of Congress.

The 1921 budget reforms were not without beneficial aspects from the congressional perspective. The House of Representatives and, to a lesser extent the Senate, increased the power of the appropriations committees alone to write appropriations legislation. This change allowed the appropriations committees to gain overall control of the appropriations process, uniting in them responsibility that had formerly been shared with some authorizing committees. In the years following 1921, some observers argued that the 1921 changes had actually increased Congress's control of the purse, with the beneficial consequences of the unified appropriations process more than offsetting any loss of budget formulation power to the executive. One observer wrote that "since the inaugurating of a budget system (1921) and the concentration of the estimates in the hands of a single committee of the House and Senate, Congress has been much more efficient in controlling expenditures."[22] Another commented, "In creating a single Committee on Appropriations the House had not weakened itself, but had very much strengthened itself. . . . Many of the advocates of budgetary reform had conceived of the budget as an executive institution. The House calmly ignored this view of it, and established and used the budget as an institution of the legislative branch of the government, under the broad grant of the Constitution."[23]

In reality, however, the outcome was quite different. The failure of the presidents of the 1920s to use the new budget as an instrument of policy formulation and coordination—a failure explained by the passive view of national government and executive power held by the Republican presidents of the 1920s—lulled Congress into believing it was in control, into accepting decentralized committee government not only as a means of satisfying personal power drives but also as a workable system of congressional government. By the time the power of

[22]*Ibid.,* pp. 193–194.
[23]Brown, *op. cit.,* pp. 231–232.

the national budget under a strong president and aggressive bureaucracy became evident in the 1930s, committee government was deeply entrenched in the culture and operation of both the House and the Senate.

The Great Depression confronted committee government with challenges it was unprepared to meet. The structure of Congress had created a situation of congressional immobilism in which the institution itself seemed incapable of self-generated innovation or activism. It took the overwhelming landslide of Roosevelt's first election and the environment of crisis to break Congress out of its malaise. Even this breakthrough, however, lasted for a relatively short time, with the intransigence built into the congressional structure ultimately reasserting its dominance. In the middle and late 1930s, at a time when liberals controlled a majority of Congress, the seniority rule allowed conservatives to capture control of the Rules Committee in the House; thereafter, legislation that survived the warfare within and among the legislative committees faced a potent roadblock when its supporters attempted to schedule it for floor debate. In the Senate, a conservative coalition had formed by the late 1930s and utilized filibusters as its weapon of delay and deadlock.[24] Facing such immobilism within Congress, liberal activists began to turn to the executive for leadership:

> *Still functioning for the most part with the machinery and facilities inherited from . . . simpler days . . . , its calendars and committees became increasingly congested, its councils confused, and its members bewildered and harassed by multiplying technical problems and local pressures. It was only natural, under these conditions, for Congress to place greater reliance upon the President and his well-staffed agencies for guidance and to delegate responsibility for policy-making, economic regulation, and social adjustment to a host of federal commissions, bureaus, and agencies.*[25]

Important here, once again, was the budget. In 1945, George

---

[24]For an excellent history of this era see James T. Patterson, *Congressional Conservatisim and The New Deal* (Lexington, Kentucky: University of Kentucky Press, 1967).

[25]George B. Galloway, *Congress At The Crossroads* (New York: Thomas Y. Crowell, 1946), p. 53.

Galloway observed, "There is no mechanism in either house for taking an overall view of federal finances. Receipts and expenditures are considered by separate committees in each chamber. Spending programs are split up among a dozen different subcommittees. There is no attempt to impose a ceiling on total appropriations or to keep expenditures within the limits of income."[26] In order to exercise fiscal planning, congressional committees turned again to the executive, with many committees refusing to consider legislation that had not been cleared by the Bureau of the Budget. The tendency to defer to the executive in coordination of the budget, the increased reliance on the administration for initial policy proposals, and the use of personnel of administrative agencies for staff assistance in the congressional committees led to accusations by members of Congress that the executive branch was usurping the legislative function: "As a legislative body Congress is being reduced, they fear, to a 'rubber stamp,' permitted only to review and ratify or veto executive proposals. Departmental suggestions are entirely proper and valuable, some members concede, but Congress should draft its own laws in its own language."[27] Despite such protestations, however, Congress remained poorly organized to draft legislation. In 1945 the legislative drafting service of Congress employed only 12 lawyers on a budget of $90,000 per year, while the solicitor's office in *one* executive department, Agriculture, employed 204 lawyers and spent $1.6 million per year.

Problems with policy implementation exacerbated those of policymaking. In creating the administrative state to regulate social and economic activity, Congress gave to the administrative agencies and commissions the power to issue rules and regulations that would spell out in specific detail and concrete application the general principles of the legislation passed by Congress. Congress enacted broadly worded laws that outlined general policy goals; the agencies translated them into specific interpretations, regulations, and rules. In the process of interpretation, the agencies exercised considerable discretionary power. By the

[26]*Ibid.*, p. 254.
[27]*Ibid.*, pp. 7–8.

mid 1940s this procedure of delegating powers was returning to haunt Congress. As Galloway wrote in that year: "Congressmen generally recognize the need for delegating legislative powers as a means of reducing their workload and of taking care of technical matters beyond the competence of Congress. But they believe that the great growth of administrative lawmaking has become a menace to the constitutional function of Congress as the legislative branch of the national government." Unfortunately, Congress lacked sufficient resources to supervise and control these agencies in their exercise of discretionary authority. "Despite the variety of weapons in the armory of congressional oversight of delegated authority, these methods of inspection and review have proved inadequate, especially under the emergency conditions of the past decade . . . . Abuse of the rule-making power evidently calls for more than piece-meal investigations of individual complaints."[28]

The uncoordinated structure of committee government, forcing piecemeal oversight, played a major role in the position of Congress vis-à-vis the administrative state. Although the decentralization of the committee system allowed for specialized attention to individual agencies by specific committees or subcommittees, decentralization, unsupplemented by mechanisms of committee coordination, left Congress open to cooptation and misdirection by the bureaucratic agencies. When agency heads testified before Congress, they knew that no necessary relationship existed among any of the appropriations and authorizations committees, or even among the subcommittees within a standing committee, much less among special, temporary, or joint committees. The jurisdictional disputes among many committees, and the shared jurisdiction of authorization and appropriations committees over single agencies, meant that an agency would have four, six, eight, or more committees concerned with it— committees whose members might disagree violently over the proper direction of the agency. This proliferation of committees and lack of coordination among them allowed a politically astute agency head to play committees off against one another, seeking

[28]*Ibid.* pp. 242–243.

support and protection from sympathetic committees. Even if a majority of the members of Congress were enraged by agency behavior, the chaotic, uncoordinated nature of committee government meant that the agency could often find support among some key authorization or appropriation committee or subcommittee—support sufficient to stymie or considerably delay efforts by the majority to discipline the agency. In addition, the autonomous nature of committees, the closed nature of committee hearings, and the multiplicity of committees also meant that agencies could fashion their testimony to fit the biases of each particular committee without the fear that the heads of different committees, in a joint leadership meeting, would uncover the deceptions and discrepancies in testimony or promises.

Finally, and perhaps most importantly, the dispersed, uncoordinated nature of committee government undermined oversight of the bureaucracy because of the growth of subsystem politics—a form of politics in which the executive branch eroded the authority of Congress as an institution not by ignoring or overpowering it, but rather by seducing the individual members that comprised it. In the early and middle nineteenth century, major public policy was made primarily at a systemic level in the national government. The key actors were the leaders of Congress, the President, and cabinet officials. The lobby did not really grow up until the late nineteenth century and there were few lobbyists on Capital Hill. In the late nineteenth century, the number of major policy issues confronting the country increased dramatically, reducing the opportunity for major system-level actors to dominate debate, policymaking, and policy implementation. Numerous agencies were created at the subcabinet level to administer policy; several committees and subcommittees gained authority to help draft and oversee policy, and many lobbyists were drawn to Washington to try to influence policy.

The natural inclination of the individuals at the subsystem level was to seek as much autonomy from individuals at the system level as possible and also as much personal power as possible. In the search for autonomy and personal power, subsystem actors turned to each other for support and assistance.

Members of congressional committees who wanted power and influence looked to cooperation with lobbyists and bureaucratic agencies as a way of developing power and prestige. Bureaucratic personnel turned to the committee members and lobbyists. Lobbyists turned to the committee members and the agencies. In the process, sweetheart relationships developed wherein the various actors in a policy subsystem exchanged favors for each other as a way of developing avenues of personal influence. The impact of subsystem politics for the power of Congress as compared with the bureaucracy was considerable and largely negative.

To a very great extent, subsystem politics produced influence and prestige for individual members of Congress largely because these members became strong supporters of agencies and programs—supporters usually unwilling to conduct rigorous, objective, independent investigations into the activities of friendly agency personnnel or into programs that benefited friendly lobbyists. The ability of Congress to conduct serious oversight was hindered by the fact that the individuals on whom Congress relied to undertake oversight activities were coopted by a system of special relationships with agencies and interest groups. Unfortunately, because these relationships existed at an insulated, subsystem level, and because of the nature of seniority and committee power, the public was largely unaware of the existence of such relationships and had little means whereby to alter them. Thus, members of Congress could not really be held accountable individually for actions that undermined the power and prestige of the institution itself.

Consequently, Congress faced a crisis. As the subtitle of Galloway's classic book indicated, Congress was at a crossroads. The administrative state had come to pose a significant threat to the legislative powers of Congress and to the ability of Congress to supervise policy implementation. The threat derived in part from the aggrandizing motives of presidents and bureaucrats; the seriousous of the threat, however, resulted from the nature of Congress itself. On the one hand, committee government provided a rational, intelligent mechanism through which members of Congress could develop personal expertise and specialize in the creation and oversight of policies and agencies in specific jurisdictional areas; committees also provided a mechanism through which members seeking to influence policymaking could feel that they would have a direct impact on at least some policy decisions. Committee government thus served the personal ambitions of representatives and senators, providing each person an opportunity to share congressional power. From the perspective of the member of Congress, committee government served his or her immediate interest. The failure of committee government came in its impact on the interests and external power of Congress as an institution. Members and committees of Congress were so preoccupied with guarding their prerogatives in relation to one another that they failed to guard the prerogatives of the institution itself in relation to the executive branch.

The internal chaos of Congress, the numerous obstacles to majority action, the need to rely on agency or presidential guidance—all could be traced in large part to the proliferation of autonomous committees and the lack of strong internal party leadership. Members of Congress refused to create over them a congressional party leader or central congressional committee that could coordinate the authorization, appropriations, and revenue decisions; it seemed less a threat to each member simply to allow the executive branch for such coordination. This solution ensured that no one individual or group within Congress would become dictator of the budget and, thereby, direct public policy. No similar safeguard protected Congress against executive cooptation of the power of the purse. Members of Congress, operating in a late nineteenth century mindset that viewed Congress as *necessarily* supreme,[29] had failed to see that the executive branch was just as capable of threatening the prerogatives of congressional committees and committee members as were fellow members of Congress. Oversight proved difficult if not impossible because each committee jealously guarded its own pet

---

[29]This perspective is reflected clearly in *Congressional Government* by Woodrow Wilson. Wilson's was probably the most influential book in shaping popular conceptions of Congress in the years when the early twentieth century members of Congress were growing to adulthood.

policies and would often neither investigate them nor allow an
"outside" committee to do so. Executive agencies thus often went
largely unchecked and were able to substantially widen their
discretionary authority at the expense of Congress as an institution.

The 1946 Legislative Reorganization Act

The growing imbalance between Congress and the executive
deeply disturbed many members of Congress, who recognized
that responsibility for congressional weakness lay partly with the
internal structure of Congress. At the very time George Galloway was drafting his own critique (1945), a Joint Committee on
Congressional Organization was investigating the source of congressional malaise and drafting a Legislative Reorganization Act.
After considerable deliberation, the House and the Senate approved a modified version of their proposals in the summer of
1946. For the first time since the progressive insurgency shattered the old regime of party government and left the Congress
in disarray, Congress attempted to put its own house in order.

The 1946 Reorganization Act attempted first and foremost to
"modernize" and "streamline" the structure of committee government.[30] To accomplish these ends, the act reduced the total
number of standing committees from 33 to 15 in the Senate and
from 48 to 19 in the House of Representatives. The Congress
accomplished this reduction of the number of committees by
dropping minor, largely inactive committees and by merging
committees with related functions. The new system of committees created a structure in each house that roughly paralleled
that of the other house. The act attempted to specify more
clearly the boundaries of each committee to help reduce jurisdictional disputes among them. The act also reduced the number of
committees on which legislators could serve from ten to two in

---

[30]For summary discussions of the act see George B. Galloway, "The Operation of
the Legislative Reorganization Act of 1946," *APSR*, Vol. 45 (March, 1951), pp.
41–68; Charles W. Shull, "The Legislative Reorganization Act of 1946" *Temple
Law Review* (Jan., 1947), pp. 375–395.

the Senate and from five to one in the House (with specified exceptions in each case). The report of the Joint Committee, though not the act itself, recommended abandoning or reducing the use of special committees. As part of the modernization process, the act authorized each standing committee to hire professional staff members, setting a limit of four on all standing committees except the Appropriations Committees, on which no staff ceiling was placed. The act also regularized committee procedures with regard to periodic meeting days, the keeping of records, the reporting of approved measures, the presence of a committee quorum as a condition for committee action, and the conduct of hearings.

The second major objective of the act was to ensure greater congressional oversight of administration. It directed the standing committees to exercise "continuous watchfulness" over the implementation of law by the administrative agencies under each committee's jurisdiction. The provision gave to the committees, for the first time in a systematic legislative act, the explicit responsibility to oversee agencies, thereby removing any doubt as to their role in surveillance of the bureaucracy. By specifying that the existing standing committees, instead of new "oversight committees," would conduct such surveillance, the act created a three way division of labor in the performance of the oversight function: (1) the Appropriations Committees would exercise financial control before expenditures through scrutiny of agency budget requests; (2) the Expenditures Committees (later the Government Operations Committees) would review administrative structure and procedure; (3) the authorization committees would review the implementation and operation of programs, renew them when necessary, and assess the need for statutory amendments. The authors of the act assumed that the major obstacles to oversight previously had been the lack of an explicit legislative mandate for the committees to conduct oversight.

The Congress also moved to regain the power of the purse. The act authorized the House and Senate Appropriations Committees, the House Ways and Means Committee, and the Senate Finance Committee to meet at the beginning of each regular session of Congress as a Joint Committee on the Budget.

The Congress gave to this joint committee the responsibility to formulate and report to the respective houses by February 15 a "congressional budget" for the coming year that would include estimated overall federal receipts and expenditures. Depending on whether the receipts exceeded or fell short of expenditures, the members of the committee would recommend a reduction or increase in the public debt. The act provided no specific mechanism to enforce the congressional budget, and the size of the joint committee made it unworkable. The creators of the act assumed, mistakenly, that the party leadership would ensure its success.

As a means whereby the party leaders could exert greater control over Congress and coordination among its elements, the Joint Committee on Congressional Organization recommended the creation of party policy committees in each house. They intended these committees "to plan the legislative program, coordinate and guide committee activity, focus party leadership, and strengthen party responsibility and accountability."[31] The House balked at the creation of these committees, however, and the final act omitted them—though the Senate later created its own version. The House parties continued their informal "Steering Committees" that roughly paralleled the Senate policy committee but lacked a staff. Although the original Joint Committee contemplated membership on the policy committee by all committee chairmen, neither the Senate party policy committees nor the House party steering committees were composed of them.

Aside from the foregoing actions, the act instituted other changes. Members of Congress were provided greater personal staff assistance, and the financing of the Legislative Reference Service was increased. The act also attempted to regulate lobbying by requiring lobbyists to register and file financial statements with the Secretary of the Senate or the Clerk of the House. A final accomplishment of the act, "and one which probably sweetened the pill of its passage,"[32] was a provision that raised

---

[31]Galloway, "The Operation of the Legislative Reorganization Act of 1946," p. 51.

[32]*Ibid.*, p. 67.

congressional salaries by 25 percent and created for members of Congress an optional retirement program.

These reorganization efforts represented an attempt by many members of Congress to reconstitute congressional government along lines more amenable to coherent policy formulation and aggressive policy surveillance. In the hearings, witnesses repeatedly identified many of the elements of congressional deadlock: proliferation of committees and subcommittees; lack of procedures to regulate and coordinate committee action; and inadequate congressional resources. The act itself forced some painful sacrifices on the part of members of Congress, requiring them to give up cherished committee assignments, to surrender leadership positions on committees or subcommittees that were abolished, and to create a new status hierarchy with a smaller number of leadership positions for which to compete. The act did little, however, to alter the fundamental rules that underlay committee government. Writing in 1949, James MacGregor Burns argued that a "frank appraisal of congressional reform fully justifies Representative Kefauver's complaint that it has been largely a matter of 'patchwork, improvisation, and tinkering.' "[33] Among the elements of the congressional system that Burns found untouched were the seniority rule, the unrepresentative nature of some of the committees, the power of the Rules Committee, and the filibuster.

After several years had elapsed to allow a clearer evaluation of the act's consequences, the changes did not seem to have altered fundamentally the operation of Congress. First, the act did nothing really to strengthen party government, to increase the power of party leaders to coordinate committee behavior or provide a coherent party program. Second, and closely related, the act failed to provide a realistic mechanism for congressional coordination of the budget. Although the act created a new Joint Committee on the Budget composed of the existing appropriations and revenue committees, it was a committee too large to afford serious committee deliberations. The act gave no

[33]James MacGregor Burns, *Congress on Trial: The Legislative Process and the Administrative State* (New York: Gordian Press, Inc., 1949, 1966) p. 134.

real attention to meshing the fiscal year with the realities of congressional life, gave the Joint Committee very little staff assistance, and provided no weapons that the Joint Committee could employ in enforcing adherence to a congressional budget. Since there was no strong party leadership to enforce the congressional budget, the legislative committees had no immediate incentives to encourage their adherence to the budgetary ceilings of the Joint Committee (and many political reasons to ignore the ceiling). Writing in 1951, Galloway found that "the greatest failure to reorganization has been in the field of more effective fiscal control. In practice, many of the fiscal reforms embodied in the act have been virtually ignored or have failed to work. Attempts to carry out the legislative budget provisions during 1947–1949 proved abortive; in 1950 this section was ignored and it now appears to be a dead letter."[34]

The success of the Legislative Reorganization Act in the area of oversight was not markedly more pronounced. In the second session of the 81st Congress (1949–1950), for example, only "ten standing and five special committees of Congress were carrying on special investigations of matters which involved some oversight of executive activities." Galloway concluded after analysis of committee oversight efforts that "This feature of the act has met with only partial success to date. Many standing committees have been too heavily burdened with their legislative duties and limited staffs to keep very close watch upon the executive agencies within their jurisdictions."[35] As to the attempt at streamlining, the act did reduce the number of committees, clarify jurisdictions, and eliminate many special committees and subcommittees. No effective prohibition was placed on the creation of new special committees or subcommittees, however, nor were joint committees dropped as a form of congressional organization.

Of all the areas affected by the act, the one with the most significant results by the early 1950s was congressional staffing. Five years after its passage, the provisions of the act had pro-

---

[34]Galloway, "The Operation of the Legislative Reorganization Act of 1946," pp. 65, 62.
[35]*Ibid.*, p. 59.

duced an increase from 11 to 28 persons in the Office of Legislative Counsel, an increase from 66 to 156 in the Legislative Reference Service, and an increase from 356 to 673 in the staff members of committees, with a dramatic rise in the proportion of staffers who were professionals rather than clerks. Some congressional observers found even these increases insufficient to allow Congress to keep up with the growing administrative state.

In the final analysis, the 1946 Reorganization Act did not replace the old order of committee government with a new order of congressional rule; the Reorganization Act refurbished the old order and removed some of its most glaring shortcomings, but in the end left committee government intact and strengthened. While the act reduced the number of committees, no serious effort was made to provide coordination among the committees or to reduce their autonomy. The new committees, by virtue of broader jurisdictions and increased staff resources, were actually stronger and more potent forces than before. Because the new committees were stronger entities, committee chairs—whose prerogatives had not been significantly reduced—emerged as even more powerful figures. The small number of chairmanships made possession of any chair an extremely valued possession—even more because it was the chairs who normally controlled the new committee staff allowances, created and dissolved the new subcommittees, named subcommittee chairs, referred legislation to subcommittees, controlled parliamentary procedure during committee hearings and debate, managed committee legislation when it reached the floor, and selected the committee members who would serve on the conference committees that existed to resolve House–Senate differences on legislation. Since committee seniority remained the norm by which committee chairs (though not subcommittee chairs) were selected, the committee leaders of each policy area remained largely a function of the accident of personnel, longevity, and electoral security. After 1946, with the clarification of jurisdictional lines, there existed even less opportunity for party leadership to bypass an obstinate committee chair by maneuvering a bill into a committee chaired by a more responsive member.

The post-war system of committee government thus possessed virtually all the fundamental problems of the prior era. Congress had really addressed only the problems of committee proliferation and committee resources. The 1946 Reorganization Act, moreover, contributed to the *isolation* of most members from congressional power. In streamlining the committee system the 1946 Act left a relatively small number of positions that carried with them real power and status. Only 19 committee chairs existed in the House and 15 in the Senate. Some subcommittee chairs were available, of course, but they were named by the individuals who chaired the full committees. In addition, the individuals who chaired the full committees often chaired one or more subcommittees, thus limiting even further the spread of leadership positions among members of Congress.

Committee Government and Subsystem Politics

The small number of leadership positions confronted Congress with a dilemma. One of the primary justifications for a decentralized system of congressional committees and subcommittees is that it in theory allows for greater access to power by a wider range of individuals, thus increasing the opportunity for innovative ideas to be developed and pressed by many members of Congress, particularly the less senior. A primary drawback of committee government is that its decentralization makes coherent, coordinated "institutional" policymaking difficult. The post-war system of committee government suffered substantially from this latter limitation. Moreover, while the number of committee chairpersons was small enough to allow informal coordination, they each protected jealously their own prerogatives and did not readily seek the coordination that their small numbers would have allowed. Indeed, precisely because of their powerful prerogatives and the small number of the committee chairs, the primary asset of decentralization—wider access—was not achieved either.

After the 1946 Act, most members of Congress did not have access to positions of power and authority. Power was so concentrated in the hands of a few committee chairs that the average member of Congress, while possibly a relatively senior member of a programmatic majority, could be stymied in most efforts at activism or innovation by an obstinate committee chair. The modified structure did not really disperse power very widely nor offer most members a piece of the congressional pie. On the other hand, power was not concentrated in an elected leadership that could carry out the wishes of a majority of the members of Congress or be accountable to it. No centralized system existed to guide fiscal policy, establish policy coherence, or remove conflict in the activities of committees. No clear, powerful, coherent leadership existed to represent the congressional majority in conflicts with the executive branch or to present the policy positions of "the Congress" to the American people.

The leadership that did exist, particularly the Speakership of Sam Rayburn in the House and the majority leadership of Lyndon Johnson in the Senate, was an accommodative, brokerage leadership, a leadership dedicated in most cases not to leading but to mediating conflict and to facilitating the passage of committee legislation.[36] The nature of this leadership, and the structure of committee government, was conditioned by the political context of the post-war years, a context influenced in large part by the 1946 congressional elections. In 1946, northern Republicans achieved a widespread defeat of their Democratic opponents in the congressional elections, thus removing many northern liberals who had reached moderate to high levels of senior-

---

[36]On the leadership of the era, see Richard Bolling, *Power in the House* (New York: Capricorn Books, 1968, 1974), pp. 159–203; Randall B. Ripley, *Power in the Senate* (New York: St. Martin's Press, 1969), pp. 83–108, 159–186; Robert L. Peabody, *Leadership in Congress* (Boston: Little, Brown, 1976), pp. 27–65, 321–357; Ralph K. Huitt, "Democratic Party Leadership in the Senate," *APSR* Vol. 55 (1961); Harry McPherson, *A Political Education* (Boston: Little, Brown, 1972), pp. 11–155; Rowland Evans and Robert Novak, *Lyndon B. Johnson: The Exercise of Power*, (New York: New American Library, 1966), pp. 50–194; and Donald R. Matthews, *U.S. Senators and Their World* (New York: Vintage Books, 1960), pp. 118–146. For an excellent comparison of the success of party leadership in the late nineteenth century to that of these post-war years, see David W. Brady, "Congressional Leadership: Then and Now" in Robert L. Peabody and Nelson W. Polsby, *New Perspectives on the House of Representatives* (Chicago: Rand McNally, 1977), pp. 389–408.

ity; in the South, with its one party system, similar reversals did not occur. This election was significant in two major ways. First, it meant that as the nation entered the post-war years, it was the southern conservatives, not northern liberals, who possessed the greatest seniority among Democrats. When the Democrats controlled Congress, as they did for most of the post-war era, positions of power within the congressional party went to southern conservatives. Second, the 1946 election heralded the dawn of an era of divided government—an era in which, more often than not, the party possessing a congressional majority did not also occupy the White House.

In the 14 years before 1946, an era of domestic and foreign crisis, the Democrats had controlled Congress and the presidency. Congressional Democrats had become accustomed to following presidential leadership. This was particularly true for liberal activists who saw strong presidential leadership as the only means by which to break the deadlock inherent in the congressional committee structure. In the 14 years following 1946, by contrast, the same party controlled both branches for six years, whereas different parties controlled the two branches for eight years. The assumption that the executive would necessarily provide coherent leadership for the majority party in Congress ceased to be held, especially after Eisenhower brought his passive conception of presidential power to the White House. The age of liberal activism was gone. Conservatives controlled congressional committees: rural Republicans in Republican years, southern Democrats in Democratic years. And no longer could an activist president be counted on to offer means to overcome congressional conservatism. The President himself, in the Eisenhower years, was a passive, conservative figure.

Divided government and brokerage leadership in Congress—when combined with the changes of the Legislative Reorganization Act—altered the role of committees. In the Roosevelt years the autonomy of congressional committees had lessened as they came to rely on executive guidance, while in the new era committees ceased to rely as heavily on direction from the White House and became more nearly autonomous decisionmaking, or decisionblocking, entities. Because of the rela-

tively small number of committees, because members were restricted in the number of committees on which they could serve,
and because committee membership was relatively stable, committees began to take on very clearly the appearance of enduring, self-contained social systems. From the 1920s through the
1940s, committee life was chaotic; regularized patterns of behavior were difficult to identify. By the 1950s, political scientists
began to notice in extensive detail the special "personalities" and
group life of different committees. They found that committees
differed in the goals that motivated members and in the decision
rules operating within committees. Success within Congress depended on success in one's committees; committee success depended on adherence to a committee's norms and its orienta-
tions.[37]

The reliance on committee government resulted in a solidification of a major form of bureaucratic legislative interaction—
subsystem politics. Subsystem politics, as noted previously, refers
to the existence of a triangular relationship between three elements in American national politics: bureaucratic agencies,
interest groups, and congressional committees. Subsystem politics first emerged as a significant factor in the late nineteenth
century, when interest groups, bureaucratic agencies, and congressional committees found allies with one another in their respective attempts to determine public policy. In the 1930s, subsystem politics was already a very pervasive phenomenon. Griffith wrote at that time of subsystems or "whirlpools" in which

[37]Ralph K. Huitt, "The Congressional Committee: A Case Study" *APSR* Vol. 48
(June, 1954); Matthews, *U.S. Senators and Their World,* pp. 147–175; Charles
O. Toves, "The Agriculture Committee and the Problem of Representation"
APSR, Vol. 55 (June, 1961); James A. Robinson, *The House Rules Committee*
(Indianapolis, Bobbs-Merrill, 1963); Richard F. Fenno, Jr., *The Power of the
Purse: Appropriations Politics in Congress* (Boston: Little, Brown, 1966); Bruce F.
Norton, "The Committee on Banking and Currency as a Legislative Subsystem
of the House of Representatives" (Syracuse University, 1970), unpublished
dissertation; John Mauley, *The Politics of Finance* (Boston: Little, Brown, 1970);
Lawrence C. Dodd, "Committee Integration in the Senate" *Journal of Politics*
(Nov., 1972); David E. Price, *Who Makes the Laws?* (Cambridge, Mass.:
Schenkman Publishing, 1972); and Richard F. Fenno, *Congress in Committees*
(Boston: Little. Brown, 1973).

much policymaking occurred.[38] But with the institutionalization of committee government in the late 1940s—that is, with the creation of autonomous, clearly distinct committees composed of a relatively stable membership—subsystem politics came to the fore. Each committee operated in its own policy domain usually without presidential or majority leadership intervention. Committees, buttressed by subsystem allies, could move to impose their policy views in particular areas of policymaking, protect key agencies or interest groups, and isolate their policy areas from attack by other members of Congress or interest groups that might oppose them.[39]

The glue that held the system of committee government together was a set of overarching norms or folkways—behavior patterns into which new congressional recruits were socialized. Donald Matthews, exploring the world of the U.S. Senator in the middle 1950s, identified several of these norms. "The first rule of Senate behavior, and the one most widely recognized off the Hill," Matthews wrote, "is that new members are expected to serve a proper apprenticeship." Hand-in-hand with apprenticeship went two additional norms: a willingness to do legislative work and a willingness to specialize. The former norm rationalized the legislature as a body in which members engaged in "detailed, dull, politically unrewarding" work (the work of committees) instead of as a forum of debate and broad policy deliberation more typical of party government. The norm of specialization rationalized committees as a legitimate form of organization and focus of attention: "According to the folkways of the Senate, a senator should not try to know something about every bill that comes before the chamber or try to be active on a wide variety of measures. Rather, he ought to specialize, to focus his energy and attention on the relatively few matters that come before his committee or that directly and immediately affect his state."

[38]Ernest S. Griffith, *The Impasse of Democracy* (New York: Harrison-Hilton Books, 1939).
[39]See J. Leiper Freeman, *The Political Process: Executive Bureau—Legislative Committee Relations* (New York, Random House, 1955); Douglass Cater, *Power in Washington* (New York: Vintage Books, 1964), pp. 17–22, 25.

The conflict that would seem inherent in a system of committee government—conflict generated by a decentralized committee structure, unresponsive committee leaders, and often unrepresentative committee composition—was diffused by norms of courtesy, reciprocity, and institutional patriotism. A special emphasis on courtesy served to deny an intense opposition the major sword they might use against committee power—aggressive, sustained attack based on moral principle and a questioning of motive. Reciprocity, a willingness to return favors, helped guarantee majority votes on the floor for committee legislation that might actually be supported only by a congressional minority. Institutional patriotism exalted above all conflicts a commitment to maintain the prestige of the institution itself—and thus glorify its structure, committee government. Tying all of these folkways together, of course, was the ultimate norm: seniority.[40]

The late 1940s to the early 1960s were for Congress a golden age of committee government. Congressional power—the legislative authority to make the decisive choices on public policy decisions—rested largely within the full committees of Congress. Each committee possessed relatively clear jurisdiction over a specified policy area, an area that could not be easily encroached on by other committees or groups within Congress. Each committee possessed a staff to develop information independently from the executive branch and a budget to finance committee operations. When lobbyists or executive agencies wished to influence the direction of public policy within Congress, they normally turned their attention first to the standing committees and to their chairmen. The party leadership of Congress, while not powerless, served primarily to aid committees in the passage of committee legislation. The authority of Congress to regulate interstate commerce, to supervise the conduct of foreign and military policy, to oversee the bureaucracy, to control the nation's pursestrings—all these powers were exercised not by Congress as a whole or by some centralized body within Congress but rather by its disparate committees.

[40]Matthews, *U.S. Senators and their World,* pp. 92–117.

During this golden era, the increasing interdependence of American economic and social policy, and the growing involvement of the country in an international world order, created a complex political situation. Individuals and groups in American society who favored a certain policy in the areas of economic, social, or international relations normally had to seek adoption of that policy at the national level. Here citizens faced two primary groups of actors who were critical to their success. Legislators in Congress approved the authorizing legislation that legitimated a policy and established its requisite administrative apparatus; they also appropriated and raised the money necessary to execute policy and oversaw its implementation by the executive. After the progressive insurgency, the key legislative actors were those individuals at the committee level who dominated a committee's policymaking apparatus. A second group of actors, officials in the executive branch, implemented the policy.

The policy implementation process often entailed considerable elaboration of the general policy guidelines established by Congress. In administering programs, executive officials often would have authority to make decisions that could have substantive consequences for a given policy and the interests of affected groups. As administrative responsibilities and the size of the bureaucracy grew, these key decisions of policy implementation occurred increasingly at lower administrative levels and were made by civil servants or second-echelon political appointees. To be successful in many policy areas, interested groups of citizens had to focus considerable attention not solely on the president or congressional party leaders but on actors at the subsystem or subgovernmental level—on congressional committees and bureaucratic agencies.

Power in Washington by midcentury derived to a large extent from an ability to influence subsystem politics. In order for citizens to have power, they had to organize concrete demonstrations of their policy concern. They had to make clear to legislators and executive officials the resources that they could use to help their friends and punish their adversaries. Citizens had to enter the subsystem arena and support their policy commitments with information, with persuasive arguments, and with pressure.

Individuals affected by an existing policy were largely unimportant politically if they were unorganized and undirected, if they remained latent rather than manifest groups. A group's power and success depended on the leverage that it had within the policy subsystem relevant to its interests.[41]

In the executive branch, both the bureaucracy and the president shared authority. The president had power because of his statutory ability to influence the civil service and to reorganize the bureaucracy; his dominance of the Bureau of the Budget (later the Office of Management and Budget), which gave him some budgetary leverage over agencies and programs; his ability to appoint key political officials; and his ability, as president, to gain media exposure and to set policy directions for the nation.[42] The agencies, on the other hand, had power for an equally impressive array of reasons. Their numbers were so great that a president or his staff could not easily control or monitor them all. The merit system and the statutory authority of independent regulatory commissions made much of the civil service semi-autonomous vis-à-vis both the president and Congress. Finally, their presence on the frontlines of policy implementation gave bureaucrats a day-to-day freedom in policymaking that both the Congress and the president found hard to circumscribe or oversee.[43]

Within Congress, power in Washington was measured largely

[41]Studies of interest group politics in the early post-war years include David B. Truman, *The Governmental Process* (New York: Knopf, 1951); Stephen K. Bailey, *Congress Makes a Law* (New York: Columbia University Press, 1949); Bertram M. Gross, *The Legislative Struggle* (New York: McGraw-Hill, 1953); J. Leiper Freeman, *The Political Process* (New York: Random House, 1955); Douglass Cater, *Power in Washington* (New York: Random House, 1964).

[42]Studies of presidential leadership for this era include Richard E. Neustadt, *Presidential Power: The Politics of Leadership* (New York: John Wiley, 1960); Clinton Rossiter, *The American Presidency* (New York: New American Library, 1956); Bruce Miroff, *Pragmatic Illusions: The Presidential Politics of John F. Kennedy* (New York: David McKay, 1976).

[43]Peter Woll, *American Bureaucracy* (New York: W. W. Norton, 1963, 1977). Richard E. Neustadt, "Politicians and Bureaucrats" in *The Congress and America's Future*, David B. Truman, ed., (Englewood Cliffs, N.J.: Prentice-Hall, 1965).

in terms of the number of important policy areas and interests an individual legislator could influence, control, or protect through legislation or through successful personal intervention in the bureaucratic decisionmaking process. The party leaders in Congress possessed little formal authority as leaders that would aid them in exercising such power. To the extent that they had power, it came through their personal skills as brokers among committees and factions. Real power within Congress to regulate or protect derived from a member's position in the committee structure and from her or his skill at activating the authority implicit in that position. Because the 1946 Act had tightened and streamlined committee jurisdictions and had reduced the number of available committee or subcommittee positions, the number of such positions within the national network of policy subsystems was relatively small.

The congressional side of subsystem politics and national policymaking was dominated by those members of Congress who chaired key committees, particularly the "power" committees and the broader policy committees.[44] Within this group, the most powerful legislators were those who possessed the political acumen and sensitivity requisite to the subtle exercise of power, individuals such as Wilbur Mills.[45] The rewards derived from such positions within a subsystem network were numerous: access to considerable financial support in reelection campaigns from satisfied interest group members in the subsystems; status and deference from key political actors within Congress and within the general Washington community; and the personal

[44]See James MacGregor Burns, *Congress on Trial* (New York: Harper & Row, 1949); Samuel P. Huntington, "Congressional Responses to the Twentieth Century," Richard F. Fenno, "The Internal Distribution of Influence: The House," and Ralph K. Huitt, "The Internal Distribution of Influence: The Senate" in Truman, ed., *The Congress and America's Future.*

[45]For a portrait of Mills and his influence, see John F. Manley, "The House Committee on Ways and Means: Conflict Management in a Congressional Committee," *APSR,* LIX (December, 1965), pp. 927–939. For numerous examples of the role of the skill and personality of committee chairs in legislation, see David Price, *Who Makes The Law?* (Cambridge, Mass.: Schenkman Publishing Co., 1972).

knowledge that one could help mold key public policy in areas of personal constitutency interest.

Figure 3-1 demonstrates a simplified pattern of subsystem politics as it might have appeared in a policy area such as commerce in the 1950s. In this policy area, assuming that there were three subpolicy domains (such as oil imports, shipping subsidies, and patents), there normally would arise powerful organized groups connected with or influenced by a particular program in each subpolicy domain: the oil companies with respect to oil imports, the shipping lines with respect to maritime affairs, and patent lawyers with respect to patent policy. Each group would focus attention on the bureau within the Commerce Department concerned with its subpolicy domain. In addition, each group, as well as each bureau, would concern itself with the congressional committee having jurisdiction. With the tightening of committee jurisdictions that occurred after the 1946 Reorganization Act,

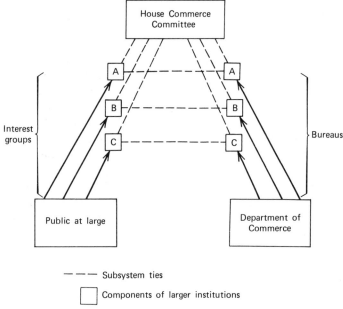

Figure 3-1. A typical subsystem model.

when the interest groups or bureaus were concerned with authorization legislation, they would all focus on the same authorizing committee: Commerce. In addition, assuming that the Commerce Committee remained relatively centralized after the 1946 Act and was chaired by a skillful politician, all three interest groups and all three bureaus would direct the bulk of their attention to the committee chairperson.

Within this admittedly simplified conception of subsystem politics, the congressional party leaders and the average members of Congress had only limited ability to control committee chairs; they could not discipline chairpeople by removing them because to do so would be to undermine the norm of seniority that held the system of committee government together, a system that most members believed preferable to its predecessor, party government. They could not easily move against legislation proposed by the committee chairs because the average members feared the consequences that might accrue if a powerful chair chose to retaliate. And control of committee chairs in subsystem politics was difficult because much of their influence over subsystem policy occurred not through legislation but through informal, interpersonal relations with members of interest groups and agencies.

Power within Congress in relation to a particular policy domain rested in the hands of key committee chairs. Because there are two houses of Congress, and because the two houses each have separate authorization and appropriation committees, four congressional committees normally had jurisdiction over legislation in the policy area. And in those policy areas where taxing power was significant, the two revenue committees were involved. Power thus rested in the hands of four or possibly six relatively autonomous chairpersons who might or might not be in agreement and who exercised power from very different legislative perspectives and in very different constituency and committee environments.[46]

[46]On the differential nature of committee environments, see Price, *Who Makes The Law?*, and Richard F. Fenno, *Congressmen in Committees* (Boston: Little, Brown, 1973).

The system of subsystem politics that emerged under these conditions was rather clearly one of mutual assistance. The *legislators* helped the interest groups by fashioning legislation that benefited them and by encouraging agencies to cut red tape and make favorable decisions in those cases where they had discretion. The legislators helped the agencies by approving and often expanding their budgets (including pay and personnel benefits) and by giving them power and status. The *agency personnel* helped interest groups by supporting their policy requests. They helped legislators by giving them some of the credit for producing decisions favorable to the interest group, and by processing casework for the legislators. Finally, the *interest groups* helped both the legislators and the bureaucrats by wining and dining them, lavishing benefits on them, giving them occasional insider information about investments, and, in the case of legislators, providing them with the financial support necessary to re-election.

Aside from being a mutual self-help arrangement, subsystem politics possessed several other clear characteristics. First, because organization and money were among the key elements binding the disparate actors together, subsystem politics in the 1950s had a conservative cast. Groups without visible organization, clearcut and easily specified interests, and large amounts of money were largely ignored. This conservative bias was reinforced by the fact that most powerful committee chairs in the 1950s tended to be conservative southern Democrats. Their conservative orientation also was reinforced because the key personnel within the agencies and the committee system, as well as the interest groups, changed very slowly, keeping a particular network of friendships and relationships intact for decades. In addition, because it existed at a subsystem level rather than at a systemic or institutional level—that is, it engaged bureaucrats, individual interest groups and committee chairs rather than the more widely known president and party leaders—subsystem politics often lacked national visibility. This tendency toward insulated politics was reinforced by the large number of subsystems that emerged as the national government grew—a phenomenon one observer has called "creeping pluralism."[47] Finally, because they tended to be dominated by powerful financial groups and insulated from public view, decisions made within the subsystem arena often were unresponsive to the majority sentiments of the national electorate.

At the height of its power, however, committee government had within it the seeds of its own undoing. Because it lacked centralized leadership, committee government possessed no means to represent "Congress" to the nation nor to present the country a coherent justification of the decisions made by the various committees. In cases where a battle for public opinion might arise between Congress and the executive, Congress lacked the ability to develop and articulate an institutional position. Second, because each committee was autonomous within Congress and because its members were protected by seniority, it was difficult if not impossible to hold any particular committee accountable to the majority views of Congress or the American public. Committee government often could generate decisions (or "nondecisions") quite out-of-step with the sentiment of Congress or the people. Congress was open to the charge that it was unresponsive to public sentiment, that it was an irrelevant relic of the past.

Third, there was the problem of administrative oversight. Committee government relied largely on authorizing and appropriating committees to conduct oversight of executive agencies or programs, which meant that many agencies and programs would go unexamined and that agency power vis-à-vis Congress would increase. Fourth, because committee government did not provide a central committee to coordinate the budget, it created a system in which considerable discrepancies could and did exist between authorizations, appropriations, and revenues. The inability of committee government to provide fiscal discipline allowed executive usurpation of Congress's power over purse. Finally, the post-war system of committee government concentrated power in the full committees and in their chairs. Most members of Congress possessed little author-

[47]J. Leiper Freeman, *The Political Process,* p. 5.

ity or power to influence decisionmaking, and many were quite unhappy with the distribution of power, particularly liberal Democrats who worked under the shadow of more conservative but senior southern Democrats.

Fifty years after the fall of Cannon, committee government was clearly ensconced within Congress. Power was spread among committees and committee chairs, distributed more widely than it would have been under centralized party government. And members of Congress were protected by seniority from arbitrary interference in their committee careers. Yet all was not well. In an effort to streamline the committee system, Congress had reduced dramatically the number of members who could benefit directly and immediately from committee government. The rejuvenated system of committee government possessed most of the problems—lack of leadership, coordination, and accountability—that originally had undermined the power of Congress in relation to the executive. Most members of Congress had sacrificed a fair degree of personal power to committee chairs and the full committees only to face once again the same internal structural problems that had allowed the executive to threaten congressional power. Underneath the facade of committee government, there were rumblings of discontent and calls for reform. Members wanted both a wider distribution of power and, simultaneously, a stronger institution. Congress appeared ripe for the creation of a new order of congressional government.

4
Congress:
The New Policy Process

The subsystem politics that grew up in the first half of the twentieth century and reached maturity after World War II was a natural consequence of the rise of the administrative state in a political system based on separation of powers wherein legislative authority was exercised by congressional committees. It was quite understandable, after all, that politicians seeking political power through elective office would unite with those powerful financial forces that could help guarantee their election and reelection. And it was predictable that the quest for power would entail attempts to control the bureaucracy, whose day-to-day actions constituted the exercise of governmental power. Suceess in subsystem politics could thus serve both the drive for reelection and the quest within Congress for personal power.

Despite its obvious advantages for the individual member, subsystem politics in the late 1940s and early 1950s confronted the member with three dilemmas. First, the 1946 Legislative Reorganization Act had limited severely the number of positions within Congress that members could use to gain access to and power within subsystem politics. Thus the number of members of Congress who could gain reelection and power through extensive subsystem activity was rather small. Secondly, most incumbent members in the late 1940s and early 1950s, particularly liberal northerners who lacked committee chairs or subcommittee chairs, faced highly competitive elections, whereas the southern Democrats who had positions of committee leadership also possessed safe seats. This situation, which existed in both the

House and the Senate, gave the "disadvantaged" members a strong incentive to create more positions of power within Congress so that they too might benefit from subsystem politics and gain electoral security.

Finally, subsystem politics in the 1950s increasingly faced a problem of institutional responsiveness. Congress—particularly the Democratic party—was becoming liberal and desirous of new policy directions while the Democratic committee chairs who dominated subsystem politics continued to be conservative. Policy activists committed to liberal legislation and convinced that a moderate-to-liberal majority existed in Congress thus had an incentive to increase the responsiveness of Congress to liberal legislation by constraining the power of committee chairs and by dispersing committee power more widely. Calls for reform were consequently heard again in the mid and late 1950s.

The efforts to make Congress a more responsive institution opened a pandora's box of reform far more serious than envisioned by most of the early reformers. The spread of power to more members would bring problems of coordination and leadership that reformers would have to address after they were successful in "democratizing" the Congress. Thus, the frustration of liberals in the 1950s set in motion a series of events that led in the 1960s and 1970s to a fundamental restructuring of congressional organization and procedure and to a new congressional policy process.

This chapter focuses first on the efforts to make Congress more accountable and open, discusses the problems that these efforts caused, and considers the reforms designed to provide for more coordination and strengthened leadership within Congress. Finally, we discuss the effects of these reforms on the policy process in Congress.

Accountability, Insulation, and the Dispersion of Power

In the early postwar years, committee chairs were safely ensconced in their positions. Slowly but surely, however, skirmishes began to occur between committee and subcommittee chairs, between committee chairs and committee members, and

between committee chairs and the party leadership. The subcommittee chairs wanted greater autonomy and control of their
own subcommittees. Committee members wanted faster, fairer,
and more favorable action on their committee legislation as well
as the creation of a greater number of subcommittee chair positions. And the party leadership wanted more responsiveness by
committees to the national program being espoused by the national party—a program that was more liberal than many chairpersons and one whose complexity could not be handled easily
by 20 or so committees operating in full committee session.[1]

Significant skirmishes with committee chairs began after the
1954 congressional elections that returned Democrats to majority party status in Congress and arrayed them against a Republican president. For the first time in over 20 years Democrats
controlled Congress but not the presidency. Democratic legislators thus were free to use leadership positions in committees
and subcommittees not simply to support a president's program,
as was normally the case under united government, but to push
their personal programs and claim credit for their success.

When the 1958 elections solidified Democratic control of
Congress and produced a clear liberal majority in the Democratic party caucuses, the struggles over power began in earnest.
The general theme of the struggles was a call for a more democratic Congress—one that was responsive to all elements with it
and accountable to its "real" majority.[2] To most of the "dispossessed" legislators, democratizing Congress meant cutting congressional power into more pieces and dispersing it more widely
and evenly. Reformers also sought a more open Congress—
openness in meetings being a primary way to publicize legislation that was blocked by conservative chairpersons and to force
procedural fairness on committee chairs. These moves toward
responsiveness and openness came in three waves.

The first wave in the dispersion of power came in the form of

[1]See James Mac Gregor Burns, *The Deadlock of Democracy* (Englewood Cliffs, N.J.:
Prentice-Hall, 1963); James L. Sundquist, *Politics and Policy* (Washington, D.C.:
Brookings Institution, 1968).
[2]See Richard Bolling, *House Out of Order* (New York: Dutton, 1965); Joseph
Clark, *Congress: The Sapless Branch* (New York: Harper & Row, 1964).

greater reliance on existing subcommittees to conduct committee business. Because of the smaller size of the Senate and the greater stature of its members, the Senate has never been as hierarchical as the House, nor has committee power been as concentrated in committee chairs. For this reason, the Senate relied on subcommittees from the outset of the post-war years, and this first wave was not prominent in the Senate. But in the House, even control of committee hearings was concentrated in the hands of full committee chairs. Calls for greater reliance on subcommittees thus had a great import in the House.

Figure 4-1 presents data from a study by Dodd and Shipley that demonstrates rather clearly the growth in reliance on subcommittees in the House.[3] The figures in this chart indicate the increasing percentage of committee hearings held in subcommittee rather than in full committee in the early post-war years from 1947 to 1954. (The figures exclude the Appropriations Committee, which was decentralized throughout the period.) Although between 60 and 65 percent of all Senate hearings were held in subcommittee, only between 20 and 30 percent of all House hearings were held in subcommittee. Starting in the 84th Congress (1955) the figures jump to 50 percent in the House, increasing to 60 percent by the 88th Congress and to 70 percent by the 89th Congress. In approximately twenty years the proportional use of subcommittees to conduct committee hearings thus doubled in the House, which joined the Senate in predominant reliance on subcommittees.

The message to committee chairpersons during this first stage of power dispersion was simple: utilize the subcommittees that already exist. In utilizing subcommittees, committee chairs gave up some control of legislation by letting hearings and initial

[3]See Lawrence C. Dodd and George Shipley, "Patterns of Committee Surveillance in the House of Representatives, 1947–1970," paper presented at the 1975 American Political Science Association Convention, Sept. 2–5, 1975; For more extensive presentation on the dispersion of committee surveillance in the House and Senate, see George W. Shipley, *Patterns of Committee Surveillance in the House of Representatives* (Doctoral Dissertation, The University of Texas, Austin, 1976); Philip Diehl, *Patters of Committee Surveillance in the Senate* (Masters Report, The University of Texas, Austin, 1976).

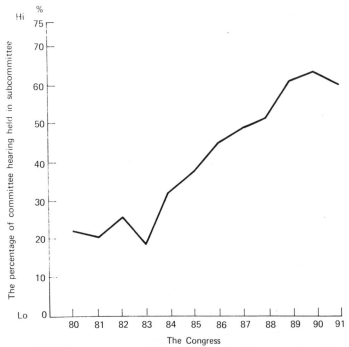

Figure 4-1. The percentage of House authorization committee hearings held in subcommittee, 1947–1970. *Source:* Lawrence C. Dodd and George Shipley, "Patterns of Committee Surveillance in the House of Representatives, 1947–70," a paper presented at the 1975 American Political Science Association Convention, September 2–5, 1975, p. 18.

drafting or markup of legislation occur in a subcommittee often headed by someone other than the committee chair. This move served both to spread authority more widely and provided Congress with the capacity to review a broader range of subjects more intensively by using more and smaller groups to conduct business. As subcommittees came to carry greater legislative responsibility, more members had an opportunity to attain positions that could carry some degree of authority. Despite these benefits, the first wave of power dispersion—encouraging committee chairs to utilize existing subcommittees—was limited in its impact. It did nothing about the reductions in subcommittee positions that occurred as a result of the 1946 Legislative Reorganization Act.

The second stage in power dispersion entailed moves to increase the number of subcommittees and thus the number of subcommittee chairs. These moves were fought out, often in very subtle ways, largely on a committee-by-committee basis throughout the 1950s and 1960s. Enlargement often came when a sitting committee chair died, resigned, or was defeated at the polls, and the new chair, in order to gain support within the committee, would "democratize" the committee somewhat by creating new subcommittees. In such cases, however, committee chairs normally maintained control of subcommittee staffs, appointments of subcommittee chairs, and most of the key prerogatives that would allow them to influence the general direction of subcommittee action.

In both the House and the Senate, the number of subcommittees grew. In the House in the early and middle 1950s, the number fluctuated between 80 and 85; by the middle 1970s, it had grown to approximately 140. In the Senate, the number increased from around 110 in the 1950s to 140 in the 1970s.[4] As a result of this expansion, more members of Congress could aspire to a subcommittee or committee chair. And those members who chaired a subcommittee gained a vested interest in protecting the existence, autonomy, and authority of subcommittees. But the committee chairs still held the upper hand, for they controlled the prerogatives that could be used to discipline subcommittee members and subcommittee chairs. This created an anomaly: committee workloads were decentralized, but con-

[4]The House data comes from Lawrence C. Dodd and Bruce I. Oppenheimer, "The House in Transition" in *Congress Reconsidered,* Lawrence C. Dodd and Bruce I. Oppenheimer, eds. (New York: Praeger, 1977), p. 37; the Senate data comes from Norman J. Ornstein, Robert L. Peabody, and David W. Rhode, "The Changing Senate: From the 1950s to the 1970s; in *Congress Reconsidered,* p. 15; on the subcommittee reforms generally, see Norman J. Ornstein "Causes and Consequences of Congressional Change: Subcommittee Reforms in the House of Representatives, 1970–1973" in *Congress in Change,* Norman J. Ornstein, ed. (New York: Praeger, 1975), pp. 39–47.

trol over committee resources and committee power remained
largely centralized in the hands of the chairs.

Starting in the late 1950s and continuing in the 1960s and the
1970s was a third stage. This was the move toward dispersed
power by formalizing the autonomy and authority of subcommittees and ensuring their responsiveness not to committee
chairs but to the full standing committee. This move toward an
"institutionalization" of subcommittee government occurred
particularly in the House of Representatives, largely as a result
of the efforts of liberal Democrats, sometimes in coalition with
Republicans. The effort to institutionalize subcommittee government brought with it moves to constrain committee chairs,
eventually leading to modifications in the norm of committee
seniority that grew up in the early twentieth century. Because of
the complicated nature of this third stage, and because the nature of power dispersion efforts differed between the House
and the Senate, it is discussed separately for the two chambers.

DECENTRALIZING REFORM IN THE HOUSE
By the 86th Congress, liberals made up a majority of the House
Democratic Caucus, though not a majority of the House itself.[5]
But the liberal contingent in the House Democratic caucus
lacked seniority, and was denied the leadership positions that
their numbers in the party would seemingly justify. Moreover,
the seniority norm applied to committee chairs but not to subcommittee ones. So even if liberals had seniority at the subcommittee level, the committee chair could deny them the chair of a
desired subcommittee. And if for some reason a liberal gained a
subcommittee chair, the standing committee chairperson could
still place significant constraints on the liberal by utilizing the
enormous resources and discretionary power of the chair's position.

Realizing their disadvantaged position, liberal Democrats in
the late 1950s decided that the best solution was to unite in an

[5]See Lawrence C. Dodd and Bruce I. Oppenheimer, "The House in Transition"
in *Congress Reconsidered,* Dodd and Oppenheimer, eds. (New York: Praeger,
1977), p. 23.

organization that could utilize their numbers as a weapon to achieve their reformist, programmatic, and power goals. Thus, in 1958, the liberal Democrats created the House Democratic Study Group (DSG), a liberal coterie within the House Democratic caucus devoted to decentralizing reform.[6] In assessing their predicament in the House, the members of the DSG came to realize that part of the power of committee chairs resulted from the formal rules of the House. Yet much of the power of committee chairs was more informal and traditional—power that resulted from the norm of seniority and the weakness of the party caucus. Liberal efforts to weaken the hold of conservative chairpeople and disperse power more widely were thus directed both at the formal rules of the House and at reform of the party caucus.[7]

Throughout much of the 1960s, liberals in the DSG worked for formal changes in House rules. In this effort, they often formed alliances with another group of outsiders—House Republicans. Their joint efforts produced the 1970 Legislative Reorganization Act, which reformed parliamentary procedure both at the committee and the House floor level. The changes at the committee level served to constrain the authority of committee chairs by making it more difficult for them to rush legislation through an unsupportive committee or to bottle up legislation within a committee that actually supported it. The changes in floor procedure also limited the ability of committee chairs to push legislation through a floor vote without prior notice, de-

---

[6]On the Democratic Study Group, see Mark F. Ferber, "The Formation of the Democratic Study Group," in Nelson W. Polsby, ed., *Congressional Behavior* (New York: Random House, 1971), pp. 249–67; and Arthur G. Stevens, Jr., Arthur H. Miller, and Thomas E. Mann, "Mobilization of Liberal Strength in the House, 1955–1970: The Democratic Study Group," *APSR,* 68 (1974: 667–681).

[7]See Dodd and Oppenheimer, "The House in Transition" in *Congress Reconsidered* for a similar discussion; see also Norman J. Ornstein and David W. Rhode, "Congressional Reform and Political Parties in the U.S. House of Representatives" in Jeff Fishel and David Broder, eds., *Parties and Elections in an Anti-Party Age* (Bloomington: Indiana University Press, forthcoming); David W. Rohde, "Committee Reform in the House of Representatives and the Subcommittee Bill of Rights," *The Annals,* 411 (January, 1974), pp. 39–47.

bate, or amendment. As committee chairs lost the opportunity to arbitrarily control committee or floor deliberations in their jurisdictional area, they were forced to work more closely with their liberal Democratic colleagues. This situation gave the liberals increased leverage over the committee chairs both within committee and on the floor.

As the rules changes approached adoption after a decade of liberal effort, the DSG shifted its attention to the second underpinning of the power of committee chairs—the quiescent party caucus. The liberals realized that rules changes were a necessary but not sufficient condition of liberal ascendancy. Formal changes in House rules could not alter the distribution of committee and subcommittee chairs since these positions derived from the majority party and were based on committee seniority. Nor could such changes ensure the procedural protection of House liberals or Republicans, since the only real way to enforce them was through discipline of committee chairpeople within the majority party; without mechanisms of party discipline, no way existed to make congressional leaders abide by the changes. The liberals thus focused on reform within the Democratic party—starting with a revitalization of the Democratic party caucus.

Throughout most of the twentieth century, the Democratic party caucus (that is, the organization of all House Democrats) had been largely dormant. At the beginning of the 91st Congress in January 1969, DSG members together with then Majority Leader Carl Albert were strong enough to convince Speaker John McCormick to support the activation of the caucus. The result was a party rule stating that a caucus meeting could be held each month if 50 members demanded the meeting in writing; a petition to the chair of the caucus would outline the proposed agenda.

The creation of the new party rule opened the caucus to reform-oriented Democrats and brought it to the fore as an instrument of change in the House. In March 1970, these liberals proposed the creation of a Democratic caucus committee to study reform. The caucus approved and Representative Julia Butler Hansen (D-Washington) became chairwoman of the committee. Operating through the Hansen Committee, liberal members were able to bring a series of reforms to the Democratic caucus. A first set of reforms (Hansen I) were implemented in the 92nd Congress. At the beginning of the 93rd Congress, in January 1973, the Hansen committee produced a second wave of reforms (Hansen II). In 1974 the Hansen committee, reacting to propositions of a committee headed by Congressman Richard Bolling (D-Mo.), produced a set of reforms focussing primarily on committee jurisdictions (Hansen III).[8]

The first result of the Hansen reforms was to spread power from committees and committee chairs to subcommittees and subcommittee chairs. By the end of the Hansen reform era, all committees composed of more than fifteen members were required to have at least four subcommittees. This rule institutionalized subcommittees as mandatory elements of virtually all standing House committees. Further, the power to select subcommittee chairs was taken away from the chairpersons of committees and placed in the Democratic membership of each standing committee. In addition, a member of a committee could chair only one subcommittee of that committee, limiting the ability of a committee chair or senior committee members to dominate the subcommittees. Each committee member was given the right to at least one "choice" subcommittee assignment, and subcommittees were provided fixed jurisdiction, authorization to meet and hold hearings on their own, adequate budgets, and staff selected by subcommittee chairs. These new rules of the Democratic caucus clearly nurtured the preeminence of subcommittees over committees.

The Hansen reforms also hastened the decline of committee government and the rise of subcommittee government by a second major reform effort—the democratization of the process whereby committee chairpeople were chosen. As noted earlier, the House had followed seniority for sixty years in selecting its

---

[8]The reforms associated with the Bolling Committee and the third Hansen reform effort are discussed more extensively in Chapter 7; see also Roger H. Davidson and Walter J. Oleszek, *Congress Against Itself* (Bloomington: Indiana University Press, 1977).

committee chairs. Seniority was a norm—an unwritten rule. The norm of seniority, however, was reinforced by rules that existed in each party for selecting the party's ranking members on each committee. In the case of the Democratic party, the Democratic Committee on Committees made nominations of ranking committee members (and committee chairs during periods of Democratic majorities). The Democratic Committee on Committees was composed of all House Democrats on the Ways and Means Committee, and it always followed committee seniority in making these nominations. It then presented the nominations to the caucus as a slate that the caucus, by open ballot, either voted up or down in its entirety; no way existed to single out one nominee and defeat her or him. It was politically impractical to vote an entire slate down, since the nominating power for the second slate would rest with the Committee on Committees, and that slate, as well as any further slates, might still contain the objectionable nominee or nominees, with the Committee on Committees removing the more "favored" candidates. In the end, the caucus, worn down by sheer exhaustion, might accept a final slate that was even worse than the initial one. Thus initial slates were nearly always ratified pro forma.

The second Hansén reforms moved decisively to change the method of selecting committee chairs and to strengthen the power of the party leadership. The method of voting on chair nominations was changed to virtually guarantee secret ballots on each committee chair nomination; under the new rules each nomination by the Committee on Committees would be voted on automatically and, if so demanded by 20 percent of the members, by secret ballot. The Hansen reforms expanded the Democratic Committee on Committees to include not only Ways and Means Democrats but the Speaker, Majority Leader, and Caucus Chairperson, with the Speaker rather than the Ways and Means chairperson to chair the Committee on Committees. And they created a new Democratic Steering and Policy Committee chaired by the Speaker and composed of 24 members; the role of the new committee was to direct the party's legislative strategy.

The reforms also increased the role of party caucuses by

mandating Congress to return in December of each election year, beginning in 1974, to organize the next Congress in advance. (Normally the caucuses had met only after the beginning of Congress.) This change allowed caucuses more time to conduct organizational business and thus increased the utility of the caucus to party reformers and activists. In the process, the reform spread power more widely among members of Congress.

By late 1974, as a result of the Hansen reforms, a decentralized House had emerged. The House moved to solidify this new structure by additional reforms and by the disciplining of committee chairs. By January 1975, the Democratic caucus had stripped Ways and Means Democrats of their role as the Committee on Committees, giving that power to the Steering and Policy Committee. This change meant that the power to nominate committee members and committee chairs no longer rested with Ways and Means Democrats but with the members of the Democratic Steering Committee. Further, the caucus adopted a rule that allowed nominations for committee chairpersons to be made from the floor of the caucus meetings in second-round votes where an initial Steering and Policy Committee nomination had been defeated. And the caucus adopted a rule requiring nominees for chairs of the Appropriations subcommittees to be approved by the same procedures that applied to nominees for chairs of other standing committees; this rule change seemed in order since Appropriations subcommittees are in many cases more powerful than authorizing committees.

In 1975 there were serious attacks on the renomination of sitting committee chairmen and a defeat of three of them. The defeat of these three men came not for ideological reasons *per se* but, at least according to an analysis of voting by Glenn Parker, because they had been arbitrary in their use of power.[9] These defeats marked the first clear-cut and premeditated violation of seniority by the party caucus since the progressive era and symbolized the end of the age of committee chairs.

[9]Glenn R. Parker, "The Evaluation of House Committee Leaders," a paper presented at the 1977 Annual Meeting of the Midwest Political Science Association, Chicago, April 21–23, 1977.

In January 1977, at the beginning of the 95th Congress, the House Democratic Caucus again signaled its willingness to discipline chairpeople, but this time turned its attention to a subcommittee chair and removed Robert Sikes (D-Fla.) from his chair on the House Appropriations Committee. And in moves to further spread power, the caucus provided: (1) no member could serve as a chair of more than one subcommittee; and (2) that the chairperson of a standing committee could not serve as subcommittee chair on another committee except in certain limited circumstances.

It is hard to know whether the attempt to institutionalize subcommittee government has played itself out. But it is difficult to envision further decentralizing reforms that will alter committee power so decisively as did the changes of 1970–1976. These reforms of the 1970s, built on the informal changes within committees that occurred throughout the 1960s, have created a House in which seniority is weakened and committee chairs are no longer the dominant political powers. The committee system today is more "open" to a wide range of influences than ever in congressional history. The openness of the committee system is reinforced, moreover, by the fact that during the Hansen era (though not as a part of the Hansen reforms) the House voted to require all committee sessions to be open to the public, except in certain specified and quite limited conditions.

POWER DEVOLUTION IN THE SENATE

The Senate is a very different institution from the House. The first and most obvious difference is size. Because the House is composed of 435 members, most members tend to lack independent visibility and national stature. Prestige, authority, and power in the House derive from gaining a "power position"—a chair of a committee or subcommittee. Without such a chair, most Representatives lack sources of influence and visibility. In the Senate, where there are only 100 members, each senator can hope to gain and maintain national prominence and even run for president. This prominence is reinforced by the fact that senators represent states, by their service in six year terms instead of two, and by the preeminence of the Senate in foreign policy. Their smaller number, longer electoral tenure, and higher symbolic status give senators independent stature and authority. The individual senator is less reliant on the committee system and organizational structure for power and authority. By the very nature of the Senate as an institution, power rests more naturally in the hands of senators as individuals.

Because the Senate is a much less hierarchical institution than the House, and an institution much less prone to centralizing tendencies, the term decentralization is in many ways a misnomer when applied to the Senate. It is much more appropriate to say that power in the Senate is *devolved* among individual members. Members differ in their power resources and the extent of their personal authority. But all members have real power as separate, autonomous actors, irrespective of their position in the committee system. The threat always exists that any senator can undertake a serious filibuster, gain media exposure to raise a major policy question, run for president, and eclipse their formerly more powerful Senate colleagues. And because there are so many policy areas and so few senators, the opportunity exists for a new and hardworking senator to gain expertise in some policy area and speak authoritatively.[10]

The differences between the House and Senate are seen clearly in the contrasts in the struggle over power. Because rules, procedures, and committee positions largely define power in the House, the House seems to spend much of its time engaged in elaborate organizational maneuvers over rules, procedures, and committee structure and prerogatives. These struggles take years and even decades, since House members who lack organizational power have to organize elaborate reform groups and attack numerous procedural hurdles before altering power relations significantly. In the Senate, where power relations are defined more by informal norms and relations among a small body of individuals who are often on a first name basis, many power shifts come more informally, and are fought less bitterly. This is

[10]See Jeffrey Pressman, *House vs. Senate* (New Haven, Conn.: Yale University Press, 1966).

not to suggest that there are no procedural or organizational reform struggles in the Senate, nor that there will not be intense battles. Nevertheless, as a review of internal politics in the last 20 years in the Senate will indicate, they are less dramatic.

In the late 1940s, after the 1946 Legislative Reorganization Act and the rise of the Conservative Coalition, senators varied in their power resources. But owing to the nonhierarchical and devolved nature of the Senate power structure, senators were never as "unequal" as representatives. Subcommittee chairs did maintain greater autonomy and hold hearings more often than counterparts in the House. Yet the Senate was run by an inner circle of Southern and conservative senators who were "more equal" than their Northern and liberal counterparts. The dominance of the inner circle or Senate "Club" was maintained because the Southern conservatives had the greatest seniority among Democrats, by the fact that they had the greatest knowledge, information, and expertise about Senate operations, and because they were sufficiently numerous that they could unite with Republican conservatives on key votes at the committee and floor level and enforce their own policy views. It was also maintained by the existence of the norm of apprenticeship.

Starting in the late 1950s, the Senate, like the House, began to undergo membership change. The Democrats began to gain a decisive edge in Senate membership while Southern Democratic senators began to decline in number, giving way to the rising tide of Republicanism in the South. The numerical significance of these shifts can be seen by a contrast between the 85th and 94th Congresses. In the 85th Congress (1957–1958) there were 49 Democrats and 47 Republicans, with 22 of the Democrats being Southerners. In the 94th Congress (1975–1976), there were 62 Democrats and 38 Republicans, with only 16 Southern Democrats. Along with this shift in partisan control of the Senate and in the regional control of the Democratic party came a shift in ideological composition of the Democratic party and the Senate. In the 85th Congress, liberals made up 41 percent of all Democrats and 22 percent of all Senators; by the 94th Congress they made up 63 percent of all Democrats and 45 percent of the

Senate. These changes came to be reflected in the pressure to redistribute power resources away from Southern and conservative Democrats and toward liberal and Northern Democrats.[11]

In the late 1940s and early 1950s, conservatives maintained their hold on the Senate by their predominance on the major "prestige" committees such as Foreign Relations, Appropriations, Finance, and Armed Services, and by chairing these committees. They also maintained dominance by controlling greater staff resources, manipulating committee activity in closed door sessions, and controlling committee appointments. In the middle 1950s, then-majority leader Lyndon Johnson, perhaps sensing the direction in which the Senate was moving and as well an opportunity to increase the debts owed him, initiated the "Johnson Rule." This rule guaranteed that every Democrat, no matter how junior, would have a major committee assignment. This rule is often seen as the first break in the dominance of the Senate Club.

As liberal and Northern senators, aided in committee assignments by the Johnson rule, gained numerical advantage and seniority throughout the 1960s and into the early 1970s, subtle shifts in power distribution began to occur. A first shift, and perhaps the most important, was that Northern senators used their greater visibility to use the Senate as a steppingstone for presidential campaigns. The quest for the presidency shattered the insulation of the Senate that the inner club had fostered in the 1940s and 1950s and increased the potential equality of senators by establishing the possibility that a lowly junior senator (such as John Kennedy in 1960) might become president.[12]

With the Senate increasingly a forum for prospective presidential candidates and with liberal activists coming to the Senate

---

[11]See Norman J. Ornstein, Robert L. Peabody, and David W. Rohde, "The Changing Senate: From the 1950s to the 1970s," in *Congress Reconsidered,* pp. 4–6.

[12]See Norman J. Ornstein, Robert L. Peabody, and David W. Rohde, "The United States Senate as a Presidential Incubator: Many Are Called But Few Are Chosen," *Political Science Quarterly,* Summer, 1976.

in increasing numbers, one of the key underpinnings of the inner club—the norm of apprenticeship—began to crumble. When the junior Senators of the early 1960s became senior members, expectations regarding the norm began to disappear altogether. "Today, not only do junior members not want or feel the need to serve an apprenticeship, but also the senior members do not expect them to do so."[13] With the disappearance of the apprenticeship norm, the Senate has become a more egalitarian institution.

This change in an informal norm has resulted in formal rules changes that have made the Senate more responsive to all senators and more open. Earlier, power in the Senate had been in the hands of a relatively few senators. This limited the ability of junior senators to make the Senate accountable and responsive to their policy views—views that increasingly seemed to reflect a Senate and national majority. During the 1970s, buoyed by the effects of the Johnson rule and the decline of apprenticeship, younger senators moved to limit the ability of senior senators to retain concentrated resources. One such move came in 1970 when a rule was adopted limiting members to service on only one of the Senate's top four committees (Appropriations, Armed Services, Finance, and Foreign Relations). Between 1973 and 1975, both the Republican and Democratic caucuses established rules altering the procedure for selecting their ranking committee members. In the case of the Democratic party (the majority party responsible for selecting committee chairs), the new procedure allows secret votes by the Democratic caucus on any chair nominee if one-fifth of the Democratic senators so request. And in 1975, the junior members decided that staff assignments were biased in favor of senior senators. Under their calls for reform, the Senate adopted a plan allowing junior members to have additional legislative staff.

Reform efforts to spread senatorial power gathered momentum in 1976 and 1977. In 1976, a temporary committee headed by Senator Adlai Stevenson investigated the Senate committee

---

[13]Ornstein, Peabody, and Rohde, "The Changing Senate," p. 8.

system and suggested numerous proposals for change. These proposals, discussed in the next chapter, had wide reaching implications for Senate power distribution, both among committees and individual senators. Among other accomplishments, the Stevenson committee succeeded in establishing the rule that each senator could chair only one committee and only two subcommittees, thus forcing a spread of existing committee and subcommittee chairs.

In line with efforts to increase the accountability and responsiveness of the Senate to all its members by devolving power, Senate reformers in the early 1970s moved to liberalize the Senate's cloture rule. For decades, many analysts had argued that the cloture rule, which required an extraordinary majority of two-thirds of those present and voting to close debate, allowed a minority of one-third of the membership plus one to obstruct the Senate and hinder its responsiveness to national policy sentiments by undertaking filibusters. In 1975, liberal senators led by then-Senator Walter Mondale succeeded in overcoming a filibuster against changing the cloture rule and instituted a new and less stringent rule. Under the new rule. sixty senators are required to support a cloture vote on legislative matters in order to close debate and allow a vote on the legislation. Under the 1975 rule, the old cloture rule of two-thirds present and voting still applies to votes on rules changes, including future changes in the cloture rule.

These moves to a more egalitarian Senate have carried with them the appearance of making the Senate a more accountable and responsive institution. As part of the same reform process, reformers moved to make the Senate less insulated. As noted in Chapter 3, congressional insulation results from at least three factors: closed meetings, a multiplicity of committees, and overlapping jurisdictions. In 1975, almost three years after the House acted to open its committee meetings, the Senate adopted rules requiring that markup sessions be open to the press and public. The Senate also voted to open conference committee meetings. In addition to these changes, the Senate moved to make itself less insulated by passing a set of committee reforms—the Stevenson reforms—that were directed toward reducing the multiplicity of committees and the overlap of committee jurisdictions.

Power Dispersion and Subsystem Politics

By the mid-1970s, Congress had institutionalized *subcommittee government*. In the three decades following the 1946 reforms, Congress had moved to proliferate subcommittees for legislative work, to guarantee a relatively equal spread of committee and subcommittee chair positions among members, to establish rules and procedures that allowed a greater disciplining of committee chairs through a slightly modified system of committee seniority, to establish clearer jurisdictional responsibilities for subcommittees, and to give the chairs of subcommittees greater autonomy and authority. As part of the same reform spirit, Congress had voted to open its committee and subcommittee sessions to public purview. Most of the reformers defended these moves as a democratization of the Congress—as effort to make Congress more accountable to its "real" majority and less insulated from the public. It was the second attempt by Congress in the sixty years since the progressive era to resolve the problems of *accountability* and *insulation* that had been magnified by the rise of committee government.

These post-war moves to disperse power within Congress were closely intertwined with congressional relations to the bureaucracy and had a number of consequences for congressional control of the administrative state. First and most obvious, the drive toward decentralization gave the average member of Congress the possibility of a greater role in subsystem politics. Instead of having a subsystem in which one committee chair would exercise influence over authorization legislation affecting numerous bureaus of a department, power dispersion created a situation in which a number of subcommittee chairs could claim jurisdiction over these bureaus and their programs. The administrative pie was cut into smaller pieces.

From the 1950s to the 1970s, the number of legislators directly involved in subsystem politics increased significantly. This increase had two significant characteristics. First, the subcommittee chairs of the 1950s had less authority and autonomy than those of the 1970s. Second, as power shifted from one committee chair to numerous subcommittee chairs, it was not the case that the new subcommittees cleanly and easily divided up responsibility for different agencies and programs that fell under a committee's jurisdiction.

Even with overt attempts to specify subcommittee jurisdictions, overlaps and ambiguities existed. Several subcommittees could claim responsibility for particular bureaus, agencies, and programs. In addition, as the number and significance of subcommittees increased, it became increasingly difficult to follow the actions of the hundreds of committees and subcommittees; and thus it often became difficult to enforce jurisdictional boundaries. The rise of subcommittee government, in short, meant a vast proliferation in the number of congressional actors who could claim some authority with regard to agencies and programs of the bureaucracy. As the number of congressional actors increased, the number of subsystem relationships increased. Instead of four or six committee chairs being the key actors in the programs and agencies of a particular department, the number of legislators who might claim authority doubled, tripled, quadrupled.

From the standpoint of individual members, this increased access to the subsystem arena carried personal advantage. It gave many more of them an opportunity to develop close ties to key interest groups and to key bureaucratic agencies, thereby increasing their claims for financial support from interest groups and favorable bureaucratic decisions from the agencies. It goes almost without saying that these close ties bring electoral benefits. In the years during which this power dispersion occurred, as work by Al Cover and David Mayhew has shown, incumbent members of Congress have dramatically increased the margin by which they win general elections. This increase in incumbent "safeness" has occurred particularly with respect to the northern congressional seats that in the late 1940s and early 1950s were considered marginal. It is not by accident that the group of individuals leading the drive for democratization of

Congress and for subcommittee government came from these districts.[14]

Political scientist Morris Fiorina argues persuasively that this increased security of incumbents results at least in part from the rise of subcommittee government, the increased perquisites that members of Congress have given themselves, and the ability of more and more members to use interest group money and bureaucratic help in casework and pork barrel projects to build unassailable electoral bases in their home districts.[15] Subcommittee government has also given members more chair positions that they could use to gain publicity and advertise themselves, to take visible positions on salient political issues, and to claim credit for the investigation of key problems and the passage of key legislation.[16] In other words, by creating subcommittee government as one means of democratizing Congress, its members have created a system of congressional prerogatives, opportunities, and relationships within Washington that gives them financial and political advantages that challengers cannot match.

In addition to the attempt to ensure electoral security, the move toward power dispersion within Congress occurred for two additional reasons. First, the reform efforts resulted from the increasing numbers of moderate to liberal Democrats elected to the Congress, from the fact that these members had genuine policy commitments that they wanted fulfilled, and from their conviction that the post-war system of committee government was unresponsive to them and to the majority sentiments of the

---

[14]Albert D. Cover and David R. Mayhew, "Congressional Dynamics and the Decline of Competitive Congressional Elections" in *Congress Reconsidered;* for the initial study demonstrating the decline of competitive elections for the House, see David R. Mayhew, "Congressional Elections: The Case of the Vanishing Marginals," *Polity* 6 (1974): 298–302; for a necessary qualification to these findings and arguments see Thomas E. Mann, *Unsafe At Any Margin* (Washington, D.C.: American Enterprise Institute, 1978).

[15]Morris Fiorina, *Congress: Keystone to the Washington Establishment* (New Haven, Conn.: Yale University Press, 1977); see also Morris Fiorina, "Congress and the Washington Establishment" in *Congress Reconsidered,* second ed., Lawrence C. Dodd and Bruce I. Oppenheimer, eds. (New York: Holt, 1980).

[16]David Mayhew, *Congress: The Electoral Connection* (New Haven, Conn.: Yale University Press, 1974).

nation. These liberals saw dispersion of power through sub-committee government and greater openness as a way of making Congress more responsive to their policy concerns.

Finally, the move toward dispersion was a matter of power: members of Congress wanted to have the ability personally and directly to influence policy formulation and implementation. It was not enough to be electorally secure or to be a member of the winning policy team. Individual members wanted to call the shots and gain the psychological and power rewards derived therefrom. Those who had power positions and prerogatives wanted to keep them. Those who lacked them wanted to possess them. To a degree this factor cut across the reelection concerns and ideological complexion of members. Quite often the most distinguishing characteristic was not whether the member was from a marginal seat or liberal or conservative, but whether the member was a junior or senior member of Congress. Those dispossessed of power, whether liberal or conservative, sought to democratize Congress as a way of gaining power. In light of these goals, the rise of subcommittee government has had a paradoxical impact on Congress.

A first paradox of congressional reform is that subcommittee government, though it may serve the short-term reelection interests of members, simultaneously threatens the ability of the Congress as an institution to be responsive to changing policy concerns of the nation. This paradox arose for three reasons. First, incumbent members of Congress are generally tied to the existing subsystems, to the Washington establishment, and to the policy perspectives that dominate subsystem politics. The spread of committee and subcommittee chair positions widely among members ties so many of them so closely to the *status quo* that they are often insensitive to new political forces that would chal-lenge it. They are often not free to change because they are hooked on a "subsystem fix": if they defend the status quo by using their subsystem positions, they will be rewarded with elec-toral support from interest groups and political support from the agencies. A second reason is that so many members accept the benefits of subsystem politics that incumbents often cannot be challenged successfully at the polls. Thus it is difficult for new political forces to "throw the rascals out" and elect new members. Third, the rise of subcommittee government undermines congressional responsiveness for the same reasons that caused committee government to undermine responsiveness and accountability in the 1920s and 1930s. If Congress relies on subcommittees as its basic unit for legislative action, then the confusion and chaos discussed in Chapter 3 regarding committee government are increased manyfold.

This leads to the second paradox of modern reform. Insofar as Congress relies on a system of *subcommittee* government as its basic means of legislative initiative and oversight, Congress undermines its own institutional power even more greatly than under committee government. This is not to suggest that subcommittees are lacking in value or that moves to create subcommittees were totally wrongheaded. Obviously, subcommittees may help make Congress more innovative by bringing a wider group of people into the action and thereby render it more creative. But if subcommittees and power dispersion are the predominant mode of legislative action, if subcommittee government is not balanced by party leadership, by central planning committees, by incentives and mechanisms for independent bureaucratic oversight, then the problems of leadership, coordination, and policy surveillance that arose from committee government will be exacerbated in subcommittee government. As Congress moved to disperse power, this is precisely what happened.

As power was spread out in the post-war years, the executive branch came to gain a stronger hand in policy formulation as well as policy implementation. With the dispersion of power within Congress, only the president had a truly national view and only the president could respond rapidly to domestic and international crises. The spread of power positions within Congress among numerous individual members meant that there was no central figure within Congress who owed allegiance to numerous factions and who had the ability to act rapidly and authoritatively for Congress. Rather, the many committee and subcommittee chairs each had a regional and committee constituency, with no strong incentive to be national in focus. And since many committees and subcommittee chairs had jurisdictional influence in overlapping policy areas, rapid agreement in response to crises was difficult to produce. Leadership in handling such issues as civil rights, urban violence, or an international crisis came to be expected primarily from the president, the Executive Office, or from the bureaucracy.

This pattern emerged in foreign and much of domestic policy and had a devastating effect on the role of the Congress in national politics. In foreign policy, "by the 1960s and 1970s, Presidents began to claim the power to send troops at will around the world as a sacred and exclusive presidential right," a right derived from the greater capacity of the executive branch to respond rapidly to international events and to create a coherent and rational foreign policy.[17] Domestically, Kennedy and Johnson asserted in Rooseveltian tradition the primacy of the president as chief legislator and chief budgetary officer, a role reinforced by the desire of the country for a planned and prosperous economy. By the 1970s the presidency was again ascendant in American politics and undertaking political actions far in excess of its legitimate constitutional role. In Schlesinger's term, "constitutional comity" between Congress and the President had broken down. Vietnam, Cambodia, and Watergate were obvious symptoms. But the most serious and direct assault on Congress came with the attempts by Richard Nixon to impound appropriated funds. That crisis stimulated Congress to undertake a series of reforms, designed to strengthen internal fiscal coordination and policy leadership, that represent a countervailing force to subsystem politics.

Fiscal Coordination: The New Budgetary Process

The budgetary process is a central dimension of policymaking in the federal government. The decisions made in budgets set the priorities of the nation, establish the fiscal parameters with

[17]Arthur M. Schlesinger, Jr., *The Imperial Presidency* (New York: Popular Library, 1973), p. 298.

which specific policies must be conducted, and determine the context within which both public and private economic choice will occur. The power to shape the nation's budget carries with it the power to shape the major contours of American public policy. Struggles over the budget thus are critical struggles over the direction of public policy and the nation's social, economic, and political life.

If Congress is to control national policymaking and exert influence on executive implementation of policy, it must have a dominant influence on budgetary decisionmaking. As we noted in Chapter 3, committee government necessarily suffers from an inability to coordinate authorization, appropriation, and revenue legislation, weakening the ability of Congress to control the budget. Subcommittee government, relying on many more decision units than committee government, suffers an even greater problem of fiscal coordination. The lack of fiscal coordination within subcommittee government meant that in an age of liberal activist legislators committed to maintaining and expanding the agencies within the various subsystems, Congress found it difficult if not impossible to limit the growth of the national budget.

THE POST-WAR CONGRESSIONAL BUDGET PROCESS
Budgetary politics within Congress involves a complex journey through a seemingly unending maze of contravening ambitions, motives, jurisdictions, and reforms. Before the 1974 reform act, as Ellwood and Thurber have written, "the history of budgeting in Congress was that of war between the parts and the whole."[18] At the beginning of every congressional session, the president sent a budget proposal for the coming fiscal year. Within Congress, the president's annual budget was chopped up every year into many small pieces, parcelled out among committee and subcommittees. Each of these would make their individual policy

---

[18]John W. Ellwood and James A. Thurber, "The New Congressional Budget Process: The Hows and Whys of House-Senate Differences" in *Congress Reconsidered*, pp. 164–165.

judgments in isolation from other committees and subcommittees, and without any serious central coordination. The internal budgetary process of Congress carried the seeds of fiscal irresponsibility and budgetary crisis.

Ideally, the level and nature of expenditures of the national government in a particular year, and the level and type of revenue collected, allow the government to stimulate or restrain the economy in a rational, planned, foresightful fashion. But because Congress lacked a central budget process to coordinate authorizations, appropriations, and revenue decisions, no internal mechanism existed whereby Congress or some component of it could plan for a specific mix of spending and taxing.

This problem was exacerbated because, over the years, Congress had removed much federal spending from annual congressional control. By the mid 1970s, as much as 75 percent of the national budget was considered relatively "uncontrollable." The two major components of this "backdoor" spending were "beneficiary programs, such as social security, where Congress determines how much each eligible person shall receive, and multiyear authorizations, such as revenue sharing, where Congress approves funds to be spent over a period of several years."[19] The incentive to use such approaches was clear to members of the various authorization and revenue committees. Under annual appropriations, the congressional power of the purse was in the appropriations committees that historically attracted the attention and favors of interest groups and agencies. By moves to expand backdoor spending, the authorization and revenue committees decreased the central power of appropriations committees and increased their own significance, since they were the committees controlling decisions with regard to multiyear authorizations and beneficiary programs.

The relative shift in budgetary power toward authorization and revenue committees served to improve their personal standing with agencies and interest groups, giving them stronger ties into subsystem politics. This meant that when agencies and programs did come up for fiscal review, the review would increas-

---

[19]Ellwood and Thurber, 1976 Southwest Convention Paper.

ingly be with the committees that had created them. However, this trend also meant an overall decrease in congressional control of the budget and the disparateness of the existing budget process made it difficult for Congress to use the national budget to set priorities.

This inability to design economic policy and to control fiscal policy led to a second problem—an unplanned rise in federal spending and in federal deficits. Committee government made consultation between the spending and taxing committees difficult. And because of committee autonomy there was no way to force spending committees to spend less or taxing committees to tax more. As Congress began to decentralize in the late 1950s, its problems of fiscal coordination mounted. The various authorization, appropriations, and revenue committees lacked a system of consultation. As the authorization and appropriations subcommittees increased in number and importance, it became even more difficult to estimate from year to year the amount of money that would be promised and spent through congressional legislation.

Spending increased dramatically and deficits mounted. In constant, comparable dollar terms, federal spending more than doubled from 1956 to 1976. During this time the federal debt itself increased from $272.8 billion to $622.0. Granted, federal debt as a percentage of the Gross National Product actually declined, since GNP was growing so rapidly. Nevertheless, the constant addition to the federal debt, its massive size, and the fact that it seemed to be generated by uncoordinated decisions rather than by carefully planned economic purpose created widespread pressure for fiscal "responsibility."

The situation was primed for confrontation between the president and Congress. So long as the president and Congress were of relatively similar ideological orientation, Congress relied on the president's budget as a guide for its decisions. And to the extent that congressional decisions went beyond the president's proposals, liberal presidents normally found it politically infeasible to challenge congressional spending. But a conservative president and a liberal Congress were another matter. They had different priorities, with neither willing to follow the other's lead.

The conflict broke into the open with the presidency of Richard Nixon, particularly in his second term when he did not face reelection and thus did not have to worry about raising campaign funds from large, established lobby groups. Nixon was at loggerheads with Congress, determined to use the existing situation as a justification for imposing his policy priorities on the nation at large. His strategy was to impound funds (that is, refuse to spend money) duly appropriated by Congress to run the government and implement its laws.

As the Nixon Administration's impoundments mounted, particularly in late 1972 and 1973, a series of court cases began to test the validity of his actions. These cases were largely decided against Nixon, primarily because his impoundments resulted from conflict with Congress over policy rather than efforts to execute faithfully the law in an economical manner.[20] But congressional victories in the courts did not stem the tide of the impoundments nor secure a redress of the damage done to many programs. Litigation took several years to complete, during which time the affected agencies and programs were undermined or stalled. The administration, though losing in court, had achieved much of its purpose, and Congress could not directly discipline the president. His impoundments, while unconstitutional, were politically defensible to taxpayers who saw Congress as a fiscally irresponsible body. To many it appeared that Nixon was on the verge of consummating a major shift in the balance of power between Congress and the presidency.

CONGRESSIONAL BUDGET REFORM

In response to these pressures and in an effort to gain control over fiscal matters, Congress moved in 1973 and 1974 to reform its budgetary politics. This reform took two directions.[21] First, Congress established a procedure for revising and controlling executive impoundment. In the past, there had existed no

[20]Louis Fisher, *Presidential Spending Power* (Princeton, N.J.: Princeton University Press, 1975), pp. 148–176.

[21]For discussion of the new congressional budget process, see Ellwood and Thurber; James P. Pfiffner, "Congressional Budget Reform, 1974: Initiation and Reaction," 1975 ASPA Convention Paper.

specific procedures presidents had to follow in order to gain congressional approval of impoundments. It had simply been assumed that presidents would act within the spirit of congressional intent. Faced with a president unwilling to honor congressional intent, Congress had no procedural mechanism to use in constraining or disciplining him. The first need, therefore, was to establish a viable procedure for congressional review and approval of impoundments. To provide this, Congress included in its budget reform package an impoundment section outlining procedures the president had to follow if he wished to impound funds.

Under the new procedures, impoundments are classified into two categories: deferrals and rescissions. Deferrals are requests by the president to delay spending of an appropriated item for a relatively short period of time (no longer than the fiscal year within which the request is made). To defer spending, the president submits a deferral request to Congress specifying the precise appropriations to be deferred and arguing that deferral of spending will not undermine congressional intent as specified in the initial legislation and hearings. A deferral request by the president is *automatically approved* unless either house, by a majority vote, passes a resolution disapproving the deferral. Because a deferral goes into effect *unless* Congress acts, and because Congress is often slow to move, the procedure that governs deferral requests is biased in the president's favor, the presumption being that he should have considerable leeway in short-term control of money.

The procedures surrounding the second category of impoundment—rescissions—are much more stringent. A rescission is a permanent cut in or elimination of appropriations. If a president wishes to rescind spending authority, he must send Congress a rescission request specifying the funds to be cut and stating the rationale for the elimination of funds. A rescission request by the president is *automatically rejected* by Congress *unless* majorities in both houses pass a rescission bill supporting the president's request. Rescission requests, obviously, are biased against the president, and he must gain explicit congressional approval for the cuts within 45 days. Given the slow and deliberate nature of Congress, rescission requests face difficult going. The rescission procedure is clearly directed toward enforcing initial congressional legislation except in extraordinary circumstances where a president can make an argument to the contrary sufficiently compelling to make Congress act rapidly.

These impoundment procedures provided for a process Congress could follow in reviewing presidential impoundment requests. They did nothing, however, to remove from the president the major weapon he had used against Congress to justify impoundment—the fiscal irresponsibility of Congress. To regain control of policy priorities, Congress had to do more than pass impoundment legislation. It had to put its own house in order and create a more responsible procedure for making budgetary decisions. In doing this, Congress left the committee system intact and created a new budgetary process to overlay it. At the heart of the congressional budgetary process, Congress created two new committees: a House Budget Committee and a Senate Budget Committee. The responsibilities of these two committees are to plan a congressional budget and guide the Congress in serving its passage.

As an aid in planning and implementing the budget, Congress outlined a timetable to be followed each year, specifying the dates by which key budgetary decisions must be made. The Congress and the budget committees are assisted in meeting this timetable and making budget decisions by a newly created Congressional Budget Office. This office, somewhat analogous to the Office of Management and Budget in the executive branch, provides full time staff to the budget committees and Congress, a staff capable of undertaking sophisticated analyses of economic trends, agency spending patterns, and so forth. In order to help make the new process work, Congress changed the beginning of the federal government's fiscal year from July to October. This change was important because Congress, which goes into session in January, cannot be expected to design and enact a budget in five months. Nine months is a much more reasonable length of time in which to create a budget and pass supporting legislation. Table 4-1 outlines the timetable of the new process.

Table 4-1.
Congressional Budget Timetable

Deadline	Action To Be Completed
November 10	Current services budget received
January 18[a]	President's budget received
March 15	Advice and data from all congressional committees to budget committees
April 1	CBO reports to budget committees
April 15	Budget committees report out first budget resolution
May 15	Congressional committees report new authorizing legislation
May 15	Congress completes action on first budget resolution
Labor Day +7[b]	Congress completes action on all spending bills
September 15	Congress completes action on second budget resolution
September 25	Congress completes action on reconciliation bill
October 1	Fiscal year begins

[a] Or fifteen days after Congress convenes.

[b] Seven days after Labor Day.

Source: U.S. Congress, Senate, Committee on the Budget, *Congressional Budget Reform,* 93d Cong., 2nd sess., March 4, 1975, p. 70.

From a conceptual point of view, the new budgetary process is quite simple. When Congress convenes in January and starts planning for a budget that will be implemented in October it first devotes about three months (January to March) gathering and assessing information necessary to assist it in planning the budget. In this first stage, the Congressional Budget Office (CBO) and the Budget Committees collect information and advice from the President and from the various congressional committees. The information will include projections of the rate of inflation, economic growth, and employment in the country, summaries of the current national budget, and details about the programs that various authorization committees expect to debate and submit to Congress in specific policy areas. This advice will include assertions as to the nation's needs in specific policy areas, projections about federal spending and incentives the nation's economy needs to provide employment and prosperity, and advice on policy priorities. This data and advice is collected and sorted into a set of alternative budgets.

By the end of the first stage, the CBO and the Budget Committees will have some general idea of the competing sets of budget alternatives that Congress could consider. These alternatives include the president's proposed budget and those drawn up by various members of the budget committees and party leadership. The competing budgets will differ to some extent in the level of spending and taxing that they propose and in the deficit or surpluses that they project. These alternatives will include differences in policy priorities (military versus domestic spending, for example), and differences in the nature of the revenue mix. The alternate budgets arise from contrasting philosophies about federal spending, varying estimates about the nature and direction of the economy, and different beliefs as to the priority items facing the country.

In the second stage, from the middle of March to the middle of May, Congress decides what its spending priorities are and which of the alternatives it would most like to follow. This decision is first made in the separate budget committees of each house. Each committee reports its decision to the appropriate house in the form of a budget resolution. By May 15, the two houses are expected to have agreed on budgetary "guidelines"—a set of statements specifying how much money the Congress is willing to spend; how the money should be distributed among different broad policy areas like defense, education, agriculture, and so forth; how the government will pay for the expenditures (income taxes, corporate taxes, tariffs, etc.); and what the projected surplus or deficit of the federal budget would be if the planned budget were followed exactly. This May 15 statement is called the First Concurrent Budget Resolution. It must be passed in identical form by both houses. This first resolution is a *target* resolution, a plan presented to the authorization, appropriations, and revenue committees as guidelines they are supposed to follow.

In the third stage of the new budget process, from May 15 to early September, the various legislative committees of Congress report legislation and Congress passes or rejects it. The committees have considerable leeway in the type of legislation they pass. The budget resolution sets broad goals rather than narrow program specifications. Thus the committees are guided by a general target of spending in the area of, say, education, but within the target they can construct the type of education program that they want. Analogously, the revenue committee has broad revenue goals given to it, but a wide range of choices concerning the type of tax structure it will employ in meeting revenue targets.

In addition, there is nothing at this stage that automatically forces authorization, appropriations, or revenue committees to stay within the budget guidelines. Either by oversight, design, or by lack of discipline, the Congress may pass legislation during the third stage that violates the goals specified in stage two. Those goals exist as broad guidelines, not mandatory prescriptions. By the end of stage three, in early September, Congress should have passed all spending legislation. The spending patterns that emerge by the end of stage three may deviate somewhat from the goals of the first budget resolution.

The "binding" part of the budget process comes during stage four in middle and late September. At this stage Congress reassesses the legislation it has passed. The Congressional Budget Office provides detailed information on the extent to which summer legislative activity has violated the first budget resolution. It provides updated information on the state of the nation's economy—information that will be needed to reassess the adequacy of the initial budget resolution for a national economic program. At this stage, the budget committees will review all of the foregoing information and report to each house a second budget resolution. This resolution will detail the final, mandatory budget figures that the budget committees believe the Congress should implement. These figures may deviate from the spending or revenue legislation already passed by Congress. If Congress votes to accept the Second Concurrent Budget Resolution, it commits itself to the figures entailed in that resolution.

Since these are mandatory figures, Congress may direct some committees to redraw previously passed legislation in a manner that will bring spending or revenue items into line with the requisites of the Second Budget Resolution. Once the second resolution is passed, and all spending legislation is reconciled with the resolution, Congress has completed its budget for the fiscal year that begins in October. This process has a certain elegant simplicity to it, and a common sense order that makes it difficult to understand why Congress has found it so difficult in the past to create a congressional budget process.

The new process, however, has left a number of problems unsolved. The passage of the Budget and Impoundment Control Act in 1974 involved numerous compromises. A first and major one was the decision to leave the existing committee structure alone and simply enact the new budgetary process on top of that structure. This meant that from the outset the new budget committees would be in a struggle with the other committees, particularly appropriations and revenue.

A second problem facing the new process is its dichotomization between the House and the Senate, with separate committees operating in the two houses. By separating the process in this way, the two houses may generate highly dissimilar budget resolutions that are difficult to reconcile. The likelihood of conflict between the houses is increased by the differences between the two committees. Because of differences in the way members are appointed to the House and Senate budget committees "the Senate Budget Committee is populated with junior members who can build their career in the Senate around their budget committee membership"[22] whereas this potential is less real for House members. As a result, the Senate committee may be more likely to take a tough position in budget resolutions—to try to set serious guidelines for other committees and use the budget process as a serious policymaking process. Since the House committee is less likely to follow this approach, it is probable that the Senate will emerge as the defender of the new budget

[22]Ellwood and Thurber, *op. cit.,* p. 184.

process while the House may well become the defender of the committees.

A final problem that the new budget process faces is the inherent difficulty of finding a majority in favor of any one budget. Even if there were no structural problems associated with the new process, it might be difficult to make it work well. Members of Congress come from vastly different constituencies and have widely differing ideologies. Given these differences, it is quite probable that the 535 members of Congress have 535 different views of the nation's priorities and 535 different views of what spending and taxing levels are desirable. These differences may be very genuine: they may reflect the geographical origin of representation in Congress with every member wanting to represent the interests of his or her district or state to the fullest extent possible. The ultimate success of the new budget process in the Congress thus may depend on the existence of mechanisms that can encourage compromise among legislators and assist the budget committees in building majority support for their budget resolutions.

Congressional Leadership: The Move to Party Government

Political parties are the primary mechanism in modern democratic governments devoted to the aggregation of interests and the nurturing of political compromises among conflicting factions.[23] The problems that the Congress has faced in adjusting to the demands of twentieth century government demonstrate quite clearly the difficulty entailed in creating and sustaining party government in the modern era of big government, particularly in a country based on a separation of powers constitution. By dividing the election of the president from that of members of Congress, by dividing the House elections from the

[23]On the nature of political parties, see Frank J. Sorauf, *Party Politics in America* (Boston: Little, Brown, 1968).

Senate, and placing no limit on congressional tenure in office, our constitution eliminates many of the incentives that other countries use to encourage legislators to band together in political parties. Unlike virtually all other western democracies, the election of our legislature is not a direct referendum on the executive, is not tied directly to the success or popularity of the executive or the Congress, and is not subject to constant revocation by dissolution of parliament. Our legislators can develop electoral careers independent of the president and independent of their congressional colleagues. Thus there seems little short-term electoral incentive for members of Congress to coalesce into strong parties that can maintain a strong organization and cohesion within Congress.

Once legislators get into Congress, their preoccupation with policy and personal power reinforces the tendency away from strong political parties. Each legislator wants to represent his or her policy perspectives. And each legislator wants to exercise personally some levers of power. If legislators can personally influence policy and exercise power, they can gain support from key interest groups and agencies, thus reinforcing their electoral security. In addition, success in policy and power arenas fulfills numerous psychological needs that legislators have and provides them a reason for entering and staying in the political struggle. With the electoral, policy, and power goals, and with psychological rewards as underpinnings, legislators are easily led to believe that power decentralization and dispersion are necessary requisites of American representative government. Power dispersion, after all, seems more democratic. And power dispersion serves the immediate electoral, policy, and power goals of legislators. Thus the turn to committee government.

Unfortunately, as we have argued, the move to power dispersion through committee and subcommittee government spreads internal congressional authority so widely that the resulting institutional impotence cripples the ability of Congress to perform its constitutional roles. The move toward a new budgetary process is an attempt by members of Congress to protect the institution's power prerogatives. Its success is critical to the maintenance of the power of Congress in our separation-of-powers

system and thus to the maintenance of representative government in America.

The success of the budgetary process depends on the ability of
members of Congress to aggregate interests and to compromise,
and on the efficacy of political parties. Unfortunately, the impetus of congressional change, starting with the Progressive era,
has been away from reliance on parties. Strong political parties
have been seen as an unnecessary threat to the power of individual legislators and to their ability to exercise personal policy
judgments. In addition, strong parties have been viewed as a
threat to electoral security: a party might well force a member to
support a controversial issue that was unpopular at home and
could cost one reelection.

Today the drama has come full circle. The power of members
of Congress ultimately depends on the power of Congress as an
institution. Congress as an institution cannot be powerful if it
relies solely on a system of dispersed power. Some means must
exist to provide for internal leadership and coordination, for
interest aggregation and compromise. Political parties currently
appear to be the only congressional mechanism that can pull
together factions and groups into workable compromises, that
can generate support for norms and rules of behavior that place
limits on political conflict. Political parties seem to be the only
mechanisms that can lead members of Congress to identify their
common interests, provide central leadership necessary to help
members see the need for institutional integrity and power, and
blend together a majority coalition based on policy compromise.
But if political parties in Congress are to play the role of coordination and leadership, reform of the party system is in order.
Reform efforts in Congress, particularly in the House starting in
1973, give some signs of a growing concern for and commitment
to party government as another counterbalance to the power of
subcommittee government.

PARTY GOVERNMENT IN THE HOUSE

The first move toward party government in the House of Representatives came with the use of the Democratic party caucus to

attack the power of committee chairs and disperse committee power to subcommittees.[24] The success of liberal reformers in using the caucus to this end underscored the potential utility of a strong central party. When the threats of the Nixon administration became clear, congressional activists moved back into the caucus and used it to strengthen party leadership so that the leadership could be used as a weapon against the Nixon administration. In the context of twentieth century congressional politics, as discussed in Chapter 3, this move was a remarkable one.

The related move toward a strong speakership came in two waves. The initial effort, which came with the Hansen reforms of 1973, placed the Speaker, as well as the majority leader and caucus chair, on the Committee on Committees. This was a curtailment of the power of Ways and Means and the power of its chairman, Wilbur Mills, who had chaired the Committee on Committees. Simultaneously it was a strengthening of the Speaker, giving him a role in the selection of committee members and committee chairs. The 1973 reforms also created a new Steering and Policy Committee to replace the dormant Steering Committee. This new committee consisted of 24 members: the Speaker, the majority leader, the Committee on Committees, the majority whip, the chief deputy whip, the three deputy whips; 4 members appointed by the Speaker; and 12 members elected by regional caucuses within the House Democratic Party. The role of the new committee was to help devise and direct party strategy in the House. The Speaker was made the chairperson of the committee. In addition, the Speaker had a dominant role in selecting the members of the committee, since not only the four members appointed by him would owe their service on the committee to him but also the five whips would be indebted since they are appointed to their whip positions by the Speaker in conjunction with the majority leader.

The second wave in strengthening the Speaker came at the

---

[24]For an excellent discussion of the role of parties in the House of Representatives and the Senate, see Robert L. Peabody, *Leadership in Congress* (Boston: Little, Brown, 1976), Chapter 2.

end of 1974 and early 1975. During this period the House strengthened the Speaker by giving him considerable control over the referral of bills. Under the new rule, the Speaker can send a bill to more than one committee, either simultaneously or sequentially; can split up a bill; or can send portions of it to different committees. In addition to these changes the early organization caucuses of the 94th Congress strengthened the Speaker by giving him the power within the Party to nominate the Democratic members and the chairperson of the House Rules Committee, thus bringing that committee more clearly into control of the Speaker and the party.[25] The early caucus also took the role of Committee on Committees away from Ways and Means Democrats and placed it in the Steering and Policy Committee. This considerably increased the role of the party leadership, particularly the Speaker, in selecting committee members and committee chairs.

While these two stages of party reforms were occurring, an additional set of changes occurred that served to strengthen the Speaker. First, throughout the 1970s, the financial and staff resources of the party whip office were increased and the number of whips appointed by the party leadership was increased.[26] The end product was a stronger and more active whip system at the disposal of the party leadership in efforts to pass legislation. Second, as Oppenheimer has shown, the Speaker was gaining control of the Rules Committee.[27] Third, the creation of the new budgetary process provided mechanisms through which a skillful party leadership could control budgetary matters and

---

[25]On the House Rules Committee in earlier eras, see James A. Robinson, *The House Rules Committee* (Indianapolis: Bobbs-Merrill, 1963). For more extensive discussions of the new Rules Committee, see Bruce I. Oppenheimer, "The Changing Role of the House Rules Committee," paper presented at the Annual Meeting of the Southwest Political Science Convention, Dallas, April 7–10, 1976.

[26]See Lawrence C. Dodd, "The Expanded Roles of the House Democratic Whip System," *Capitol Studies,* in press.

[27]Bruce I. Oppenheimer, "The Rules Committee: New Arm of Leadership in a Decentralized House" in *Congress Reconsidered.*

coordinate decisionmaking by house committees. The Speaker's potential control of the House budgetary process resulted from his appointment (in conjunction with the Senate's President pro tem) of the Director of the Congressional Budget Officer, the leadership's appointment of one of its lieutenants to the House Budget Committee, and the ability of the Speaker, as chair of the Steering and Policy Committee, to oversee appointments of Democrats to the Budget Committee.

The test of the durability and efficacy of the renewed power of the speakership revolves around the ability of Speakers to retain and institutionalize the new authority, to build on it through formal and informal accumulations of additional authority, and to provide leadership and coordination through the skillful, subtle, yet vigorous use of their authority. In January 1977, the House replaced retiring Speaker Carl Albert (D-Okla.) with a new Speaker, Rep. Thomas P. "Tip" O'Neill (D-Mass.), who was reelected in January 1979. O'Neill has prior experience as a Speaker, having served in that post in the Massachusetts House of Representatives. In that post he was seen as a strong, assertive leader. It is generally conceded that he is more activist, more partisan, and more forceful than Albert. Yet O'Neill faces serious problems in sustaining the speakership. The crisis environment of Vietnam, Watergate, and impoundment is now gone. The fading of the crisis mentality removes a major stimulus that was necessary to the strengthening and sustenance of the speakership.

Speaker O'Neill and those who follow him will now face a highly dispersed system of subcommittee government in which there are numerous independent actors with independent resources, yet little external pressure for these actors to work together with the Speaker. O'Neill cannot exercise power by working through a small inner club. He will have to build and sustain a broad supporting coalition in a highly diverse and fragmented House. As an aid in this process, O'Neill cannot rely on the presidency as strongly as Speakers such as McCormick; to do so would allow executive cooptation and further weakening of Congress. Finally, O'Neill faces serious legislative problems that are politically explosive, problems such as energy, ethics legislation, and government reorganization. All these factors mean that the sustenance of a strong speakership is both quite necessary yet problematic.[28]

SENATE PARTY LEADERSHIP

In many ways the greatest organizational difference between the House and the Senate lies in the area of party leadership. In the House, the leader of the majority party has the constitutionally prescribed and prestigous position of Speaker. This position gives the party leader a central visible status that raises him above the other members of the House, particularly when his symbolic status is supplemented by formal authority within the party caucus. Under the Speaker comes an elaborate hierarchical organization composed of the majority floor leader, the whip and an increasingly elaborate whip organization. A fairly similar structure—sans the speakership—exists for the House minority party. By contrast, as Robert Peabody notes, "Top party leadership in the Senate is, almost without exception, collegial in nature."[29]

The leader of the majority party in the Senate is the majority floor leader, and this position is not a constitutionally prescribed one. The primary aid to the majority leader is an elected majority whip with whom he can work in scheduling legislation and rounding up votes. Because of the smaller size of the Senate and its more collegial nature, there does not exist as an elaborate a whip system as in the House. In the Senate, party leaders are much less distinct from regular party members, more one among equals. They derive little formal authority and few organizational resources from their position. Their power and influence depend not so much on formal rules and party reforms as on their personality and legislative skill.

[28]On O'Neill and the problems he faces, see *Congressional Quarterly Weekly Report,* Vol. 34, #52, pp. 5–6.
[29]Peabody, *Leadership in Congress,* p. 325. Chapter Eleven of this book provides an excellent overview of Senate party leadership.

In the House, the power of party leaders, particularly the Speaker, is regulated to a large extent through the rules and norms of the House and the party. In the Senate, the power and authority of the party leaders depends much more on the personality and leadership style of the individual party leader and his legislative competence. The power of the Senate party leaders will also be strongly influenced by environmental constraints—factors such as the size and ideological diversity of the party, the party's control of the executive branch, and the personal characteristics of committee leaders.

Because of the more informal nature of the Senate party leadership, changes in their strength and authority come less with alterations in formal rules and more through variations in the style of party leaders themselves and in their environmental constraints. The classic illustration of this phenomenon is the contrast between Lyndon Johnson, Democratic floor leader during most of the 1950s, and Mike Mansfield, Democratic floor leader from 1960 to 1976. During the period in which Johnson and Mansfield served as party floor leaders, the formal authority of that position was largely constant and the power deriving from it rested mostly on the persuasive abilities and skill of its occupants. Yet by all accounts the actions of these two party leaders differed drastically. Lyndon Johnson had an extensive staff, dominated an active and aggressive Policy Committee, had rather considerable influence over committee nominations, and took a strong role in developing legislative programs and strategy. Among other accomplishments, he is often credited with passing the first civil rights bill of the twentieth century, and is often acknowledged as the most effective majority leader in Senate history.[30]

Mansfield followed Johnson and, instead of building on the authority of Johnson, let it wither. He worked with a small, "tight" staff, democratized the Policy Committee and allowed it to glide along without great direction or impact, failed to exert

[30]On Lyndon Johnson, see Rowland Evans and Robert Novak, *Lyndon B. Johnson: The Exercise of Power* (New York: New American Library, 1966): Harry McPherson, *A Political Education* (Boston: Little, Brown, 1972).

personal control over the committee selection process, remained neutral in party whip contests, and did not take a strong role in legislation. Whereas Johnson developed the reputation of being the most powerful majority leader, Mansfield became known as the most beloved majority leader. He was perceived as a gentleman and was continuously elected to his post for 16 years—twice as long as any other individual. His legacy is less one of legislation personally guided through the Senate and more one of harmony.[31]

How does one explain the contrast between Johnson and Mansfield? To a degree, differences in their style and actions must be attributed to different environments in which they operated. Throughout most of Johnson's tenure, Democrats composed a slim majority of the Senate. In addition, its majority relied on a large segment of conservative southerners who were quite likely on many issues to bolt the party and vote with Republicans. And Johnson faced a Republican president. All these factors meant that Democratic success within the Senate required aggressive leadership. By contrast, Mansfield's tenure was blessed with a large Democratic majority, a declining reliance on southern Democrats, and an increase in northern Democratic loyalists. And through the first eight years of Mansfield's tenure—the formative years—Democrats controlled the presidency. Thus it can be argued that Mansfield did not have to exert strong leadership because legislative success would flow rather naturally from the surrounding circumstances.

The difference between the two men's power also seems to lie at least in part in their personality differences. As Peabody has noted, "By all contemporary observations and accounts the two men appeared to be nearly polar opposites in terms of such personal qualities as aggressiveness, dominance, and power-seeking."[32] LBJ actively sought the job of party leader and intensely cultivated the inner club of southern oligarchs who could give it to him. By contrast, Mansfield did not want to be either

---

[31]On Mansfield. see Andrew J. Glass, "Mike Mansfield, Majority Leader" in *Congress in Change*, Norman J. Ornstein, ed. (New York: Praeger, 1975).
[32]Peabody, *Leadership in Congress*, p. 240.

whip or majority leader, at least by all appearances, and had to be drafted to both positions. Johnson as an individual thrived on the exercise of power whereas Mansfield always seemed to disdain the exercise of power. Because the majority leadership position in the Senate is largely what its occupant makes it through collegial involvement and persuasive abilities, a majority leader who wants power and is skillful at legislative strategies is probably far more likely to make the party leadership a powerful force than one who assiduously avoids power.

Because the power of party leadership in the Senate is such a complex interplay of environmental constraints and the personal goals of the party leaders (with the latter having perhaps a stronger influence on the power of party leaders than personality does in the House) it is difficult to identify systematic directional change in the power of party leadership in the Senate. One cannot look easily to Senate or party rules to indicate the direction of party leadership; one must instead analyze the political environment of a given Congress and the personality of the party leader. As those change, the power of party leaders in the Senate will shift, a shift far more rapid yet far less formal and overt than in the House.

With the advent of the 95th Congress, both the environmental constraints and the occupants of the party leadership positions in the Senate changed dramatically. For the first time in eight years, the majority party in the Senate also controls the presidency. If the Carter/Mondale administration succeeds in shoring up its popularity and surviving in office, Senate Democrats may turn a bit inward, with senators of the majority party focusing more on institutional and policy roles. With such a shift, power and prerogatives within the Senate could be expected to increase in value and visibility. Junior senators would be forced to take a slightly more deferential attitude toward their seniors. Insofar as the presidential politics of the Senate served in the past two decades to break down its insulated inner club of the 1950s, the dampening of presidential opportunities among Democrats by the potential 16 year hegemony of the Carter/Mondale administration could serve to increase the viability of a new inner club within the Democratic party.

The possibility of a reemergence of more centralized power in the Senate Democratic party was increased by the selection of Robert Byrd as Majority Leader in early 1977 and his reelection in 1979. Byrd was majority whip during the last several years of Mansfield's tenure as majority leader. Byrd's background is that of a poor West Virginia orphan who rose to political prominence out of poverty by hard work and diligence. His dedication to work and success characterizes his Senate career and is evident in his approach to party leadership. As one appraisal of Byrd has noted:

> He rose to majority leader . . . from the assistant leader post by being a superb legislative tactician. He mastered the rules. He was willing to work tirelessly on boring routine floor details. He did favors for Senators ranging from giving them little gifts like tickets to ball games, playing his fiddle at their campaign rallies, giving them campaign funds, scheduling their legislation or blocking votes on matters of special concern to them if they were absent.[33]

Overall, Byrd's style evokes reminiscences of LBJ.

> The flattery and persuasion, the reminder of a past favor and the hint of a new one, suggest a style that is more like Lyndon B. Johnson than Mike Mansfield, his two immediate predecessors. It is a style more forceful than that of Mansfield, who disdained the use of power to persuade his colleagues, and less punitive than Johnson, who relished the stick as well as the carrot. It is an approach that seems, even at this early stage, to be having an impact on the Senate.[34]

From all appearances, Byrd is concerned about protecting the prerogatives of the Senate as an institution, prerogatives that have been severely battered by Vietnam, impoundment crises, and so forth. Early in the Carter administration Byrd admonished Carter for not consulting more closely with congressional leaders in legislative matters, an admonishment that has served to make Carter more respectful of the Senate leadership.

---

[33]Spencer Rich, "Disparate Byrd-Cranston Senate Team Pulls Together," *Washington Post,* Sunday, April 17, 1977, p. G1.
[34]Martin Tolchin, "Byrd Persuasive as Senate Chief," *The New York Times,* March 27, 1977, p. 1.

Byrd has been a strong supporter of ethics legislation and Senate reorganization, both moves designed to increase public support for the Senate. Byrd sees strong party leadership in the Senate as a key element of a strong Senate and sees an increase in organizational capacity as a key element of a strong party leadership. During his first months as the majority leader, for example, he moved to reactivate the Democratic Policy Committee and increased its staff from three to seven professional aides. He reportedly has put his own close staff aides in the key positions as head of the Democratic Policy Committee, secretary for the majority party, and assistant for floor business. Byrd himself, as majority leader, is the chairman of the Steering Committee, which makes appointments to committees. Byrd has retained control over floor scheduling, and he spends a great deal of time on the floor directly managing the business.[35] From all signs, Byrd is moving the Senate democratic party back toward a stronger party leadership.

The New Congressional Policy Process

One cannot study Congress for very long, or study congressional history very extensively, without realizing that Congress is a changing, dynamic institution. Certainly that has been the case in the twentieth century. When the century dawned, Congress was in the midst of the flourishing of party government in both the House and the Senate. Twenty years later the structure of party government lay in shambles and Congress was rushing pellmell into an era of committee government. The transition from party government to committee government had a dramatic impact on the congressional process, on the ways in which Congress makes laws. It made the policy process in Congress more insulated and less accountable to national policy sentiments. It undermined the ability of Congress to coordinate policy initiatives or provide policy leadership to the nation. It placed responsibility for policymaking on a disparate set of committees

[35]Rich, "Disparate Byrd-Cranston Senate Team Pulls Together," pp. G1, G6.

and subcommittees that eventually came to rely on executive dominance of much of the policy formulation process. The end result was a decline in congressional authority and moves to reform Congress through the 1946 LRA. That Act tried to salvage congressional authority by strengthening and streamlining the committee system in Congress.

As the post-war years began, Congress was experiencing the great age of committee government. Twenty-five years later the golden era of committee chairmen had given way to a proliferation of subcommittees and subcommittee chairs. The Congress, particularly the House, was a "liberated" institution, both with respect to the formal structure of power and the informal norms of interpersonal relationships. Virtually all members of Congress could hope to "be somebody" irrespective of region, limited seniority, or sex. Yet side by side with the growth of subcommittee government and the dispersion of power there also developed new mechanisms of centralization—a new budget process and stronger party leaders. This seemingly incongruous combination of power dispersion along with power centralization was a congressional response to the problems of insulation, accountability, coordination, and leadership that continued to plague Congress even after the 1946 reform. The power dispersion that led to the subcommittee government and sunshine laws was rather clearly an effort by reformers, particularly liberals, to make Congress more accountable and less insulated. In the process, they sought to gain personal power for themselves. The move to a coordinated budget process and stronger party leadership was a response to problems of coordination and leadership, problems that power dispersion had actually exacerbated.

Today the policy process in Congress is far more elaborate and complex than it has ever been. Significant power rests in many different positions of authority. When a bill is introduced it must first go to subcommittee, where it will receive extensive consideration, including open hearings, open debate, and open markup. Then it goes to full committees, where it may face a similar process. Then it proceeds to the floor, via an open Rules Committee meeting in the House. At the floor level it will again be subject to serious debate and deliberation, all open to the public. Under the new rules, it is quite possible that a bill will be amended significantly on the House floor as well as on the Senate floor. At the floor stage, the party leaders and whips may be extensively involved. After passing both houses, the bill may well go to a conference committee that is held in open view of the press and interested public. If the conference committee concludes successfully, the bill will return to each house for a final vote.

As a bill proceeds along this path, the environment in which it exists is more complex than in the past.[36] In both the House and the Senate, major bills may have been initiated by or at least nurtured by the Policy Committee of the majority party. In addition, legislation will be monitored by the Congressional Budget Office and guided and constrained by the congressional budget resolution and the watchful eye of the congressional Budget Committees. For a bill to succeed, it must survive each of the steps in the new congressional process—from subcommittee through conference committee to final passage and through review during the second budget resolution. Although no single actor along the way has the extensive arbitrary power over a bill that a standing committee chair had in the early post-war years, more actors have some authority over a bill. A bill has more hurdles, though the hurdles are less imposing.

The new policy process is characterized by a proliferation of overlapping and competing policy subsystems, with legislative proposals spewing forth from hundreds of subsystems in an often conflicting and contradictory fashion. The role of the central budgetary process and central party leaders is to guide the numerous proposals into a fairly consistent, coherent set of programs, and to articulate the justification for major policies emerging from Congress. Because so many congressional actors

---

[36]For example, see Norman J. Ornstein and David W. Rohde, "Shifting Forces, Changing Rules and Political Outcomes: The Impact of Congressional Change on Four House Committees" in *New Perspectives on The House of Representatives,* Robert L. Peabody and Nelson W. Polsby, eds. (Chicago: Rand McNally, 1977), pp. 186–269; David E. Price, "Policy Making in Congressional Committees: The Impact of Environmental Factors," *APSR* (June, 1978), Vol. 72, #2, pp. 548–574.

have some degree of significant authority, the role of the central leaders is extremely difficult. The power dispersion of the post-war years enmeshed far more members of Congress in subsystem politics than ever before, linking their loyalty to particular interest groups and agencies, not to an overall congressional or national program.

Thus the new congressional policy process is a delicate balancing act, a balance between dispersed and centralized power centers, between particularized and general policy interests. And, as the history of the past century should indicate, there is nothing inherently permanent about a new congressional order or the policy process that results from it. Much depends on how well the new process works to both solve the problems of accountability, insulation, coordination, and leadership while maintaining a significant role for the average member of Congress. In addition, much depends on the relationship that grows up in the new era between Congress and the executive. If Congress is able to develop and maintain a strong policy formulation role vis-à-vis the executive under the new congressional structure, it may endure.

But the power of Congress depends not only on its ability to solve its post-war problems with policy formulation. Congressional power also depends on its ability to influence the *implementation* of public policy. Thus the success or failure of the new congressional process also turns on its capacity to conduct effective oversight of administration. An examination of that capacity is the task of the next two chapters.

5
Congressional Oversight: Structure and Paradox

Political analysts have long argued that a key to successful representative government lies in the ability of the legislature to oversee and control the administration of public policy.[1] The power to legislate is largely meaningless if the legislature lacks the ability to ensure proper administration of public policy. The controversy over impoundment during the Nixon years dramatized this issue and emphasized that legislative control of administration is closely linked to the legislative process itself. A legislature that cannot control itself ultimately cannot effectively control administration because it will lack popular support and legitimacy.

If the public is to support congressional efforts to control the executive, the public must be convinced that Congress is capable of acting in a rational, foresightful, forthright, and responsible manner. The best way for Congress to demonstrate this capacity is through responsible behavior within that area of legislative process that is most visible to the public: lawmaking. The moves toward a new budgetary process, greater openness, greater accountability, and central leadership are efforts by Congress to put its own house in order and justify public faith in its legislative capacity and thus its ability to oversee policy implementation. Unfortunately, the increased ability of Congress to follow a

[1]See, for example, John S. Mill, *Representative Government* (London: Longmans, Green, 1878); Woodrow Wilson, *Congressional Government* (Gloucester, Mass.: Peter Smith, 1885, 1965).

rational course in lawmaking does not actually guarantee that Congress will successfully control *administration* of public policy.

Oversight of the executive entails more than ensuring the rational expenditure of money or publicizing congressional positions on key policy conflicts with the executive—areas of administrative control to which budgetary and party leadership reform are most closely geared. *Oversight* also involves attempts by Congress to review and control policy implementation by the agencies and officials of the executive branch.[2] As an all-pervasive process, it can lead Congress into every facet of administration; precisely for this reason, oversight is often a slippery and ephemeral process that is difficult to identify, measure, or study in a precise manner.

A recent study by the Senate Committee on Government Operations indicates that there are numerous goals associated with congressional oversight.[3] Five goals appear to be primary:

1. Ensuring that the administrative branch implements the laws in accordance with Congressional intent.
2. Determining policy effectiveness by gauging the appropriateness of a policy and determining whether its impact is in line with congressional standards.
3. Preventing waste and dishonesty by ensuring that agencies operate honestly and efficiently.
4. Preventing abuse in the administrative process by keeping tabs on agency use of discretionary authority.
5. Representing the public interest by monitoring and constraining agency-clientele group relations.

---

[2]For various uses and definitions of the term oversight see Joseph Harris, *Congressional Control of Administration* (Washington, D.C.: The Brookings Institution, 1964), p. 9; Morris S. Ogul, *Congress Oversees the Bureaucracy* (Pittsburgh: University of Pittsburgh Press, 1976); John D. Lees, "Legislatures and Oversight: A Review Article on a Neglected Area of Research" *Legislative Studies Quarterly*, Vol. II, No. 2, May 1977; and Joel D. Aberbach, "The Development of Oversight in the United States Congress: Concepts and Analysis" discussion paper prepared for the Commission on the Operation of the Senate, University of Michigan Institute of Public Policy Studies, October, 1976, p. 2.

[3]*Congressional Oversight of Regulatory Agencies*, Committee on Government Operations, United States Senate, Vol. II, February, 1977, pp. 4–5; see also Joseph Harris, *Congressional Control of Administration*, pp. 1–2.

These five goals all involve attempts to make agencies and executive officials accountable to Congress. This need for accountability stems from the wide-ranging and multifaceted nature of modern government. The constitutional responsibility of Congress is to decide those issues that involve a clash of competing interests and determine the allocation of national resources. Yet today there exist so many issues that Congress cannot "legislate" all the decisions that face it; it has to delegate some decisionmaking authority to executive officials and agencies. Nevertheless, delegated authority derives from Congress, which has a responsibility to ensure that this authority is used in a responsible and responsive manner.

The Committee Structure and Oversight

In conducting oversight, the primary structural mechanism that Congress uses is the committee system. Within the committee system the responsibility for oversight falls largely to the appropriations committees, the authorization committees, and the government operations committees. Each of these three types of committees has a different fundamental role—roles specified in the 1946 Legislative Reorganization Act. The *appropriations committees* have responsibility for "fiscal" oversight: the duty to ensure that agencies spend funds in efficient and appropriate ways. The *authorization committees* have responsibility for "legislative" oversight of agencies within their jurisdiction. Their task is to determine whether particular programs work and to propose remedies to problems they uncover. The *government operations* committees have a responsibility for "investigative" oversight: a mandate for wide-ranging inquiry into government economy, efficiency, and effectiveness that may follow policies and programs across many agency lines. These committees also have jurisdiction over government reorganization.

THE APPROPRIATIONS COMMITTEES AND OVERSIGHT
Congress historically has relied heavily on the Appropriations Committees for oversight, particularly oversight focused on in-

dividual departments and agencies.[4] The dominance of the appropriations committees in departmental oversight derives from
these committees' control over the "power of the purse."[5] Within
the committee structure of Congress, the appropriations committees have the responsibility to review and "mark up" all appropriations bills. Whenever an agency desires a new appropriation, even if the agency activities have been authorized on an
open-ended basis by the authorization committees, the agency
must seek appropriations through the Appropriations Committees.

Appropriations for departments and agencies are not automatically granted to fulfill authorization authority. When an
agency seeks new funds, the Appropriations Committees have
the right to review agency organization, activity, programs and
personnel performance. Since most agencies must seek appropriations annually, the review of agency behavior gives the Appropriations Committees each year an opening that they can use
to keep tabs on agencies, bring agency personnel before them
for questioning, and "suggest" improvements or redirections in
agency activity.

Each house of Congress has a separate Appropriations Committee. Because of the different institutional imperatives and
environments of the two houses, these two Appropriations
Committees do not always act in a similar fashion. A major difference between the two derives from the fact that the Constitution requires the House to originate all bills for raising revenue.
The House historically has expanded this constitutional mandate to claim the exclusive right to originate all general appropriations bills, arguing that the revenue mandate was a general
endorsement for House predominance in all fiscal matters.
Based on this claim, the House Appropriations Committee has
developed a predominance over the Senate Committee, one
reinforced by the different characteristics of the House and
Senate as institutions.[6]

[4]Arthur Macmahon, "Congressional Oversight of Administration: The Power of
the Purse," *Political Science Quarterly,* 58 (1943), p. 380.
[5]Harris, *Congressional Control of Administration,* p. 292.
[6]On the different environments of House and Senate Committees see Richard
Fenno, *Congressmen in Committees* (Boston: Little, Brown, 1973), p. 145.

Virtually all oversight in the appropriations committees of both houses occurs within their subcommittees. These subcommittees are autonomous actors with full control over the review of agencies and programs in their jurisdiction: each standing appropriations committee largely honors the decisions of its subcommittees. While recent analysis suggests that Senate Appropriations subcommittees may be moving increasingly toward earlier and more thorough hearings,[7] Senate subcommittees do act primarily to review House decisions, and Senate subcommittee hearings are considerably shorter and less extensive than in the House.

The differences between the roles of House and Senate appropriations committees and subcommittees affect their relations to the executive agencies. The House Committee, through its subcommittees, performs the role of reviewing the appropriations requests of the agencies; during this review process the subcommittees will often make numerous cuts. The Senate Committee, divided into subcommittees whose jurisdictions parallel those of the House Committee, normally reviews the House Committee decisions and, as noted, acts as an appeals court for those agencies and groups that believe themselves unfairly treated in the House. In their budget reviews, the subcommittees in each chamber inquire into the performance of the agencies and programs and will make known their pleasure or unhappiness with agency performance.

Actually, however, the most intensive appropriations review is directed toward agency requests for funds above and beyond its current budget. In the appropriation's review process, past funding levels normally are taken as a baseline, and subcommittees focus on the increment above that baseline that agencies request. This *incremental* form of appropriations review, taken primarily to maximize the use of the relatively small staff and resources the subcommittees have, usually focuses on those agencies requesting the largest appropriations increases. A primary way that subcommittees discipline agencies is through cuts in this increment, thereby signaling to agencies that success in future appropriations requests depends on: (1) following the

[7]*Congressional Oversight of Regulatory Agencies,* pp. 22–23.

"guidelines" specified by committee members in agency hearings or (2) being responsive to informal guidance from committee members throughout the year. When an agency fails to justify itself in both the House and Senate subcommittees and suffers significant cuts in its requested incremental increase, the message from Congress to the agency is a clear one. From this viewpoint, the existence of two separate appropriations committees with different decision processes can be an effective way of communicating to agencies—if both committees are in agreement as to their desires for agency behavior.[8]

In addition to the discipline exercised through cuts in agency funds, the Appropriations Committees have three broad, interrelated ways of overseeing the executive. First, they can involve themselves in surveillance after appropriations bills are passed. This process is the same as the day-to-day techniques of the authorization committees and does not constitute a process unique to the appropriations committees. The other two forms of oversight, statutory and nonstatutory appropriations controls, have characteristics and problems distinct to the appropriations process.[9]

Statutory appropriations controls are the constraints the appropriations committees place on agencies by specifications they write in appropriation legislation. There are three types of statutory controls:

1. Statements that specify the purpose for which funds must be used.
2. Specifications of the funding level for an agency as a whole as well as for programs and divisions within the agency.
3. Provisions that specify that no part or only a fraction of an appropriation may be used for certain purposes.

Statutory appropriations controls are generally viewed as effec-

---

[8]On incrementalism in the budgetary process, see Aaron Wildavsky, *The Politics of the Budgetary Process* (Boston: Little, Brown, 1975).

[9]For discussions of statutory and nonstatutory controls, see *Congressional Oversight of Regulatory Agencies,* pp. 30–33; Michael W. Kirst, *Government Without Passing Laws* (Chapal Hill: University of North Carolina Press, 1969).

tive oversight techniques because they are so direct, unambiguous, and virtually self-enforcing. As a recent committee report concluded, "while agencies are able to bend the more ambiguous language of authorizing legislation to their own purposes, the dollar figures in appropriations bills represent commands which cannot be bent or ignored except at extreme peril to agency officials."[10] The primary limitation on statutory controls is that the Appropriations Committees must use statutory language in a negative rather than a positive manner; they cannot direct executive agencies to initiate a program that is not based on authorizing legislation, but they *can* refuse funds for certain programs. The distinction between negative and positive statutory controls is often ambiguous, however, leading appropriations committees to stretch the outer limits of their power, thereby angering agencies, interest groups, and authorization committees.

When an appropriations subcommittee wishes to avoid the entanglements of statutory controls, it often can employ nonstatutory restrictions. The category of nonstatutory controls includes the use of appropriation hearings, reports, and debates to control and guide the administration. The importance of nonstatutory controls arises from the fact that while they are not legally binding, administrators may feel "morally bound" to obey them. This sense of moral commitment is reinforced because administrators know that they will appear annually before the appropriations committees for funds, having to answer for failure to follow nonstatutory guidance.

The basic power of the appropriations committees in agency oversight is their ability to grant or withhold budget requests. Partially as a result of conflicts between authorization and appropriation committees, and partially because of the nature of the modern welfare state, several developments have occurred in the past few decades that limit the portion of the annual budget subject to control by the appropriations committees.

First, authorization committees have evaded the appropriations process by allowing agencies to expend funds without ad-

[10]*Congressional Oversight of Regulatory Agencies,* p. 31.

vance appropriations. This procedure, known as *backdoor spending*, has increased significantly in recent years. The second development, *permanent appropriations*, bypasses both the appropriations committees and Congress itself. These appropriations "are those which become available without any current action by Congress. These include multiyear appropriations as well as obligations such as interest on the public debt and civil service retirement funds."[11] As a result of these changes in appropriations procedures, together with a series of reforms and changes in authorization committee activity, the overarching predominance of appropriations committees in departmental oversight may be lessening, with the authorization committees playing an increasingly active role in oversight.

AUTHORIZATION COMMITTEES AND OVERSIGHT

Most committees within Congress are authorization committees, and the bulk of activity within Congress each year involves these committees. Their authority stems from their control over the initial establishment of agencies and programs and over all subsequent congressional action that involves changes in statutory authority or reauthorization of agencies and programs. The House and Senate each have separate authorization committees whose jurisdictions largely parallel one another. The authorization committees of each house are autonomous standing committees insofar as oversight is concerned—independent within their own house.

Each authorization committee has an internal life and decision process of its own that are determined largely by the goals of its members and the environmental context within which the committee operates. Because of the large number of authorization committees and subcommittees, their autonomy, and the existence of very different decision-processes within them, the authorization process lacks any visible appearance of regularity, order, or coherence. Different authorization committees or subcommittees conduct oversight in a variety of ways, using dif-

[11]Kirst, *Government Without Passing Laws,* p. 6.

ferent mechanisms for different reasons and in vastly different degrees.

The major way in which authorization committees exercise control of administration is through the *authorization* or *reauthorization* act itself. Each agency and program must have legal authorization for its activities, and many agencies and programs must receive periodic reauthorization. When committees write authorization or reauthorization legislation, they are specifying the actions that they expect to be taken. The more clearly and precisely they specify these actions, the greater guidance the agencies have in implementing programs. The reauthorization act, in particular, can be quite important. Often committees will be unable to write highly specific legislation the first time, or even later. But they can require an agency or program to return periodically for renewal of its authorization. This process is somewhat analogous to agencies returning annually to receive appropriations. During the renewal process, committees may be able to write far more specific and limiting legislation.

For agencies and programs that operate under permanent authorization, the major statutory form of oversight after the initial authorization is the *amending process.* In situations where agency or program mandates are too broad, where agencies implement programs in ways that Congress did not intend, or where evidence arises that initial statutory language is producing undesired consequences, the authorization committees can propose that Congress change statutory language by amendments to the original act. The amending process may change the statutory basis on which agencies exist; the use of (or threat of) amendments can serve to keep agency officials responsive to Congress in program areas where they have open-ended authorization. Despite its potential significance, the amending process has real limits as an oversight technique. It is time consuming, and necessitates considerable agreement within Congress on specific matters of agency behavior. Without general congressional consensus, it may be difficult to pass amendments because a small faction can filibuster them in the Senate or often delay committee or subcommittee action. For these reasons, members of Congress seeking to exert control or influence on administration in particular areas often prefer less time-consuming and more informal methods. Only when these other nonstatutory techniques fail will members normally attempt to amend a statute.

Nonstatutory authorization controls include hearings, investigations, committee reports, meetings, letters, and other informal arrangements. These mechanisms can be used to develop certain "understandings" in situations not covered by statute. They can also be used in situations where committee members prefer informal arrangements with bureaucrats rather than fixed legal relationships.

As the foregoing should indicate, authorization committees have numerous techniques that they can use in oversight. And these do not exhaust the list. Additional oversight occurs in the *confirmation process* when the Senate committees hold hearings to confirm presidential appointments to head departments and agencies. In the confirmation process, committee members may extract pledges regarding agency implementation of policy or information about agency organization and personnel. Oversight also occurs through *casework*—efforts by members to obtain satisfactory treatment of constituents by bureaucratic agencies. Casework can uncover examples of agency unresponsiveness that committees then can use as a basis for investigating an agency and forcing changes in agency behavior or personnel—as with inquiries in the mid-1970s that resulted from inadequate processing of veterans benefits by the Veterans Administration. Finally, oversight can occur through a technique that crosses the line between statutory and nonstatutory action: the *legislative veto*.

Conduct of oversight can be both manifest and latent: it can involve explicit and overt use of oversight techniques, or it can occur through informal contacts.[12] There is a general view among many scholars and political actors that latent oversight, while difficult to measure and study, may be as effective as man-

---

[12]This differentiation is stressed by George W. Shipley *Patterns of Committee Surveillance in the House of Representatives* (Doctoral Dissertation, The University of Texas, Austin, 1976); and Ogul, *Congress Oversees the Bureaucracy.*

ifest oversight. The informal contacts that members of Congress have with executive officials, and their subtle, sensitive use of these contacts, can often produce a positive response from the agencies far more quickly and more productively than would occur as a result of overt committee actions. The reason for this is fairly obvious: bureaucrats are as sensitive as anyone else to public embarrassment. If attacked publicly, they may fight back openly; if approached privately, they may seek a compromise both because of genuine agreement with members of Congress and because of a desire to avoid public humiliation. Latent oversight must not be overemphasized, however. Its effectiveness is geared to the existence of manifest oversight techniques: "Evidence of a general desire to oversee, and the existence of formal structures capable of performing such function, can trigger administrative responses in anticipation of possible inquiries."[13]

THE GOVERNMENT OPERATIONS COMMITTEES AND OVERSIGHT

Political analysts have long recognized the need for an oversight committee that would be independent of both the appropriations and authorization process. The reasons for creating such a committee stem from the inadequacy of both appropriations and authorization committees as oversight mechanisms. The appropriations committees are inadequate both because many agencies and programs increasingly do not fall under annual appropriations review and because so many agencies and programs *do* require annual review that the appropriations committees tend to be overwhelmed. And they often lack the opportunity and time to focus only on a few "deserving" agencies or programs and investigate them thoroughly.

With regard to the authorization committees, oversight is severely limited by the very nature of the authorization process and the structure of the committee system. First, authorizing responsibility can involve committee members so deeply with

[13]John D. Lees, "Legislatures and Oversight: A Review Article on a Neglected Area of Research," p. 197.

agencies and interest groups that they may find it extremely difficult to achieve a detached perspective from which to evaluate agency and program performance. Second, the autonomous yet overlapping nature of the authorizing committees inhibits coordination and cooperation in agency surveillance while exacerbating the possibility of intercommittee conflict.

As a means to avoid the problems inherent in appropriations and authorization oversight, Congress has created a Committee on Government Operations in each house. These committees are descendents of several committees first created in the early 1800s to control federal expenditures in the various executive departments.[14] As a result of the 1946 LRA, the Government Operations Committees have been charged with "studying the operation of government activities at all levels with a view to determining its economy and efficiency."[15] The Government Operations Committees differ from other standing committees in that their primary responsibility is to investigate and oversee, not to legislate. This is not to suggest that these committees have no legislative jurisdiction; they are given legislative responsibility for such items as "presidential reorganization proposals, housekeeping bills which tidy up minor problems in administrative procedures, budget and accounting measures, and amendments to the Federal Property and Administrative Services act of 1946."[16] Nevertheless, these are relatively minor matters.

The foundation of the committees' activity is their oversight responsibility. As *the* congressional oversight committees, they are charged with investigating the operation of government activities at all levels, and are not bound by departmental or programmatic jurisdictions that constrain the authorization committees. Following the 1946 LRA, there were three basic formal restrictions on the committees' potential as oversight agents: (1)

[14]Walter J. Oleszek, "Committee on Government Operations," Monographs on the Committees of the House of Representatives, Prepared by the Select Committee on Committees, 93rd Congress, p. 61.

[15]Thomas A. Henderson, *Congressional Oversight of Executive Agencies; A Study of the House Committee on Government Operations* (Gainesville, Fla.: University of Florida Press, 1970).

[16]*Ibid.*, p. 8.

their investigations had to focus on administrative agencies; (2) their review was restricted to policy execution, not policy itself; and (3) the committees were to investigate problems, not legislate their solution. To conduct oversight within these parameters, the committees have been given several powers: (1) they can require the submission of documents and the appearance of witnesses through the use of subpoena power, an authority not granted most committees; (2) they can conduct their investigations both inside and outside of the United States; and (3) the committees can sit while Congress is not in session, thus allowing them to continue investigation after adjournment.[17]

Because of their broad investigative jurisdiction and special powers, the Government Operations Committees would appear well suited to fill the oversight vacuum left by the appropriations and authorization committees. Historically, this potential has not been fulfilled. Several reasons account for this failure. First, just as the effectiveness of legislative power depends on the ability to investigate and oversee, so the ability to investigate policy administration and enforce proper policy implementation effectively requires the authority to write legislation that can alter statutes, specify executive responsibility more clearly, and follow through on the implementation of statutory directives. The Government Operations Committees have lacked these powers. Second, and closely related to the first problem, the Government Operations Committees are constrained by the jealousies and animosities that other committees show them. Their investigative jurisdiction is so broad that they can move into the substantive jurisdiction of any committee. Because of this, and because the authorization committees are so often closely associated with agencies and interest groups, the authorization committees view the Government Operations Committees with a jaundiced eye.[18]

Hostility of the other committees creates a real problem for the Government Operations Committees. As Henderson writes

---

[17]*Ibid.,* pp. 11–12.
[18]U.S. Congress, House, Select Committee on Committees, *Hearings* on Committee Organization in the House, 93rd Congress, Ist Session. Vol. I, Part I, p. 173.

of the House Committee, "the danger . . . is not that it might be abolished. The rigidity of the congressional committee system makes that possibility remote. Rather, the threat lies in its being rendered totally ineffective through a shortage of funds, an in- difference to its recommendations, or the assignment of un- wanted people to its ranks." For this reason, the GOC in each house has "had to be especially sensitive to the expectations and demands of the larger body."[19] In an effort to demonstrate such sensitivity, members of the committee who investigate agencies tend to consult closely with the appropriate authorization com- mittees, be restrained in their use of publicity, constrict investi- gations to avoid direct conflict with other committees, and rarely conclude investigations by proposing specific legislative solu- tions to problems they may uncover. While these norms may be effective in sustaining support for the GOCs' existence and funding, they clearly can inhibit broad-ranging, well-publicized oversight that not only uncovers problems but identifies solu- tions to them. Thus the GOCs simply have not proved to be aggressive oversight agents of Congress.

PATTERNS OF COMMITTEE SURVEILLANCE

As one would expect, the oversight activism of standing commit- tees, and their use of the different oversight mechanisms varies greatly among committees. This variation is rather difficult to specify because the oversight process itself is changing and fluid. One measure of oversight activity does exist, however, that is reasonably objective and applicable to all committees: committee hearings. An examination of hearings allows some insight into the variation in oversight activism among committees.

One study of hearings is the work by Dodd, Shipley, and Diehl,[20] which examines the approximately 14,600 published

[19]Henderson, *op cit.*, pp. 21–22.
[20]See Lawrence C. Dodd, George Shipley, and Philip Diehl, "Patterns of Con- gressional Committee Surveillance," a paper presented at the 1978 Midwest Political Science Convention, Chicago, April, 1978; See also Shipley, *Patterns of Committee Surveillance in the House of Representatives, op. cit.;* Philip Diehl, *Patterns of Committee Surveillance in the Senate* (Masters Report, The University of Texas, Austin, 1976).

committee hearings held by Congress from 1947 to 1970. Of these hearings, the House of Representatives held 7771 and the Senate held 6840. The study indicates that the number of committee hearings has increased rather dramatically during the post-war years from 1947 to 1970 (Figure 5–1), with the growth in hearings particularly pronounced in the Senate. Within the two houses, the number of hearings varies dramatically by committee, with some committees holding more than a thousand hearings over the 24 year period while others held less than 100

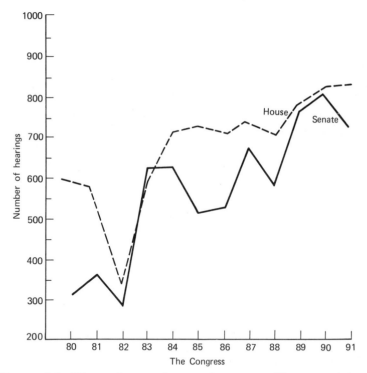

Figure 5-1. The volume of committee surveillance activity, 1947–1970. *Source:* Lawrence C. Dodd, George Shipley, and Philip Diehl, "Patterns of Congressional Committee Surveillance," a paper presented at the 1978 Midwest Political Science Convention, Chicago, April, 1978, p. 3a.

(Table 5–1). However, committees in the two houses that have similar jurisdictional responsibilities are rather similar in the relative number of hearings they hold.

Regarding the focus of hearings, committees in both houses tend to give more attention to investigations of broad policy questions than to inquiries into agency implementation of programs. This conclusion is reached by classifying each committee hearing according to whether its predominant focus was on agency behavior or policy concerns. Both the House and Senate have devoted between 70 and 80 percent of all hearings to policy rather than agency questions, though the Senate increasingly has focused more on agency behavior than the House.

The greater aggregate focus of the Senate on agency behavior is a general characteristic of most Senate Committees. Table 5–2 divides all committees into five categories based on the percentage of committee hearings devoted to agency investigations. Clearly, most committees in each house devote most of their hearings to policy questions. In both houses, the most agency-oriented committees are the appropriations committees. Among the authorization committees, committees devoted to national security and military questions are more apt to devote their hearings to agency inquiries than are the committees responsible for domestic policy and public works activity. Although the Government Operations Committees have the clearest mandate to oversee executive agencies, both the House and Senate Government Operations Committees devote a majority of their hearing activity to policy rather than agency questions.

Decentralization and the Oversight Paradox

The responsibility of Congress to oversee the performance of the executive agencies is scattered among many committees that possess a diverse set of oversight tools. Judging from analysis of committee hearings, congressional committees and the two houses vary greatly in their attentiveness to agency behavior. Overall, congressional attention to bureaucratic agencies is haphazard. Even the committees most responsible for oversight—the Government Operations Committees—fail to devote the bulk of their hearings to investigations of agencies.

Table 5-1.

The Volume of Surveillance Activity by Committee by House, 1947–1970

Committee House/Senate	Number of Hearings House/Senate	Percentage of Total House/Senate
Agriculture/Agriculture	556 / 298	7.2 / 4.4
Appropriations/ Appropriations	653 / 554	8.5 / 8.1
Armed Services/ Armed Services	1137 / 638	14.6 / 9.3
Banking/Banking	309 / 511	4.0 / 7.5
Commerce/Commerce	712 / 784	9.2 /11.5
District of Columbia/ District of Columbia	153 / 117	2.0 / 1.7
Education and Labor/ Labor and Public Welfare	460 / 605	5.9 / 8.8
Foreign Affairs/ Foreign Relations	374 / 412	4.8 / 6.0
Government Operations/ Government Operations	725 / 464	9.3 / 6.8
House Administration/ Rules	57 / 99	0.7 / 1.4
Interior/Interior	437 / 534	5.6 / 7.9
Internal Security (HUAC)/	203 /	2.6 /
Judiciary/Judiciary	325 /1005	4.2 /14.7
Merchant Marine/	342 /	4.4 /
Post Office/Post Office	284 / 179	3.7 / 2.6
Public Works/Public Works	321 / 312	4.1 / 4.6
Science/Aeronautical and Space Sciences	88 / 65	2.4 / 1.0
Veterans/	264 /	3.4 /
Ways and Means/Finance	266 / 245	3.4 / 3.7
TOTAL	7771 /6840	100/100

Source: Lawrence C. Dodd, George Shipley and Philip Diehl, "Patterns of Congressional Committee Surveillance," paper presented at the 1978 Midwest Political Science Convention, Chicago, April, 1978, p. 4a.

Table 5-2.

The Surveillance Focus of Congressional Committees, 1947–1970

Surveillance Focus	House of Representatives	Senate
Group A: Exclusively agency oriented (90% or more agency hearings)	None	None
Group B: Predominantly agency oriented (60 to 90% agency hearings)	Appropriations Armed Services	Appropriations Rules Aeronautical and Space Sciences
Group C: Balanced focus (40 to 60% agency/policy hearings)	None	Armed Services Government Operations
Group D: Predominantly policy oriented (60 to 90% policy hearings)	Banking and Currency Government Operations Post Office and Civil Service Space and Astronautics	Agriculture Banking and Currency District of Columbia Education and Labor Foreign Affairs Interior Commerce Judiciary Post Office Public Works
Group C: Exclusively policy oriented (90% or more policy hearings)	Agriculture District of Columbia Education and Labor Foreign Affairs House Administration Interior Unamerican Activities Interstate Commerce Judiciary Merchant Marine	Finance

Source: Lawrence C. Dodd, George Shipley, and Philip Diehl, "Patterns of Congressional Committee Surveillance," paper presented at the 1978 Midwest Political Science Convention, Chicago, April, 1978, p. 35.

The dispersed and haphazard nature of oversight is even greater than this summary indicates. A fair amount of oversight occurs *ad hoc* through casework in members' offices. Some oversight responsibility falls on the new budget committees, on the revenue committees, and on select nonlegislative committees such as the House and Senate Select Committees on Intelligence that investigated the CIA in the mid 1970s. Finally, as we see later, Congress has also relied for oversight assistance on such staff agencies as the Congressional Research Service and the General Accounting Office.

The highly dispersed nature of oversight responsibility, the lack of strong central oversight committees, and the natural conflict among committees all undermine severely the ability of Congress to conduct serious, rational control of administration. As one might expect, the decentralization trends of the post-war years have made the conduct of oversight even more problematic. In fact, the decentralization of congressional committees has led to an oversight paradox.

As we noted earlier, power within Washington depends largely on one's ability to influence subsystem politics. The foregoing sections indicate that the ability to influence specific bureaucratic agencies or executive officials falls largely to the committees whose legislative jurisdiction provides them responsibility for authorizing or funding specific agencies and programs. With the power dispersion within committees that has taken place during the post-war years, this oversight responsibility increasingly has flowed to subcommittees.

The move to disperse power within committees by instituting subcommittee government derived in large part from the desire by members of Congress to increase the number of positions within Congress that could provide access to subsystem arenas. Members of Congress attempted to increase the number of power positions so that more members could possess reasonably direct access to a subsystem. Paradoxically, while power dispersion has increased the number of members active within subsystem politics, as well the number of hearings held by Congress into agencies and programs, it has at the same time weakened the ability of Congress to conduct serious oversight and administrative control. The reasons for this are threefold.

THE DECLINE IN CONGRESSIONAL BARGAINING
POWER VIS-À-VIS AGENCIES

The power of Congress within a particular subsystem is very much a function of the authority of the individual members who head the congressional side of a subsystem triangle. The power of individual congressional actors is itself a product of numerous subsidiary resources that they possess: such committee resources as staff and informational capacity; external resources and support they derive from congressional agencies; the consensus of their members behind them; the legal-constitutional constraints that they possess over agencies or program; and their unfettered access to agency data and information. Within a system of decentralized oversight responsibility (granted that some reasonable level of the foregoing resources exists), the most important resource congressional actors can possess lies in their strategic bargaining position vis-à-vis agencies and interest groups. This position depends on the number of agencies and programs falling within their general purview and the dependence of agencies on them for support.

Within the administrative branch of government, agencies are often functionally interdependent. Many bureaus fall within a general departmental jurisdiction that links them organizationally. Additional interdependence derives from joint or overlapping responsibilities for a program or policy area. The personnel in these agencies often have a common loyalty to a general goal (such as an equitable social welfare system in HEW or a strong defense capacity in DOD). And they are connected by a loyalty to the federal bureaucracy itself and by the realization that congressional raids on the power or funding of one agency may ultimately lead to attacks on others.

This interdependence of administrative agencies provides Congress an opportunity for influencing agency behavior. To the extent that Congress can keep responsibility for a large set of related agencies within the hands of one central person or group—a committee chair, for example—that central entity can have considerable leverage over all those agencies. A committee with jurisdiction over numerous related agencies can threaten to discipline one agency or bureau because the administrators know that the committee can carry out its threat; after all, a committee with many agencies under its jurisdiction is not likely to be excessively dependent on one particular agency. Because the agencies are intertwined, the committee has a number of different hostages it can hold to force compliance from one particular agency. If the committee in question is the one committee with clear authority over the agency, the agency knows it will have to adhere to the committee's requests or suffer the consequences.

The coming of subcommittee government has undermined the strategic bargaining position of Congress in regard to the agencies. By its very nature, subcommittee government involves carving up committee jurisdictions into a larger set of smaller jurisdictions. In such an arrangement, individuals who chair subcommittees have considerably fewer agencies or policy areas to oversee than had the committee chairperson prior to power dispersion. While such an arrangement allows these individuals to become more expert, more informed, and thus more attentive to agency oversight than were committee chairs, the increase in surveillance activity and interest generally means a decrease in the effectiveness of their oversight efforts. This ineffectiveness of the subcommittees occurs in part because it is difficult for a member of Congress to threaten, discipline, or control an agency when the agency personnel know that the agency's function is central to the continued existence, jurisdictional integrity, and funding of the member's subcommittee.

Subcommittee chairs do try to improve their effectiveness by increasing the number of agencies that they investigate—and thereby decrease their dependence on one or two agencies. And because of the imprecise division of a committee's jurisdiction among subcommittees, some expansionist activity occurs as subcommittees within a committee move into each others jurisdictional turf. However, this form of empirebuilding can be dangerous because authorization committee caucuses increasingly control the selection and resources of subcommittee chairs and can discipline a subcommittee chair who encroaches on the jurisdiction of another subcommittee.

Similar discipline is less likely, however, if a subcommittee moves into a jurisdictional area of another *committee*. As congressional decentralization has occurred, there has been a considerable breakdown in respect for the jurisdictional boundaries among committees. As noted in Chapter 3, a goal of the 1946 LRA was to reduce the number of committees so as to streamline legislative decisionmaking and oversight. Crossing of jurisdictional lines had occurred as committee or subcommittee chairs delved into popular and politically profitable topics. With several committees concentrating on the same agencies or programs, many others went unexamined—a poor use of congressional time and resources. In addition, the agencies and bureaus were often able to play committees off one against another.

The 1946 Act tried to address this problem of multicommittee surveillance by reducing the number of committees and subcommittees and by clarifying committee jurisdictions. In particular, the Act tried to structure jurisdictional lines so that committees paralleled departmental lines in the executive branch. The assumption was that a smaller number of committees and subcommittees together with clearer jurisdictional lines would reduce the opportunity for jurisdictional crisscrossing and lead committees to focus more critically and extensively on all agencies and programs within their own jurisdiction. While systematic studies of the pre-war era are lacking, the 1946 Act apparently did reduce committee overlap, since the level of multicommittee surveillance in the immediate post-war years was quite low.

Unfortunately, from the standpoint of those seeking to hold the line on multicommittee surveillance, the 1946 Act did not constrain either the growth of subcommittees or their increased autonomy. As more subcommittees were created and became the locus of committee power, subcommittees of one parent committee began to examine agencies or programs falling in the general domain of another committee. This occurred partly because new legislation passed during the post-war years confused jurisdictional lines by putting programs that fell under the substantive jurisdiction of one committee in departments or agencies whose activity was the substantive responsibility of a different authorization committee. This situation allowed a wider range of committees to investigate a particular department than had been the intent of the 1946 Act, but at the same time destroyed the simplicity and coherence of committee jurisdictions.

Such crisscrossing was fueled by the nature of subcommittee government. The congressional rules under subcommittee government spread subcommittees more widely among members of Congress than did rules prior to the 1946 Act. As a result, more legislators had a vested interest in holding hearings. Individuals who chaired subcommittees had a number of incentives to cross into other committees' jurisdictions: (a) crossing into other committees' jurisdiction avoided intracommittee conflict; (b) it expanded the number of agencies or programs that one could investigate, making a subcommittee less reliant on the small number of agencies or programs falling into its initial jurisdiction; (c) it allowed members of Congress to help their reelection chances by following popular issues, thereby gaining publicity back home and by undertaking action beneficial to key groups within their constituency, even if such action was not clearly warranted by their subcommittees' jurisdiction; and (d) in cases where the policy areas covered by their subcommittee were less geared to their own interests than related areas, they could follow personal interest by delving outside the subcommittee's jurisdiction. In the face of these incentives for jurisdictional crisscrossing, there were few clear disincentives. As subcommittee chairs went outside of their own committees, little means existed to discipline them for poaching.

In the post-war years, as Figure 5-2 indicates, jurisdictional crisscrossing increased dramatically. Based on the recent study by Dodd, Shipley, and Diehl, the graph indicates the average number of committees holding hearings into departments (counting only those departments existing both in the early post-war years and the late 1960s). In the figure's calculations, hearings held by a subcommittee were attributed to their parent committee so that hearings by fifteen subcommittees of a committee are treated as the hearings of one committee, *if* all hearings covered the same department.

Figure 5-2 indicates that increase in multicommittee surveillance of departments occurred in both the House and Senate,

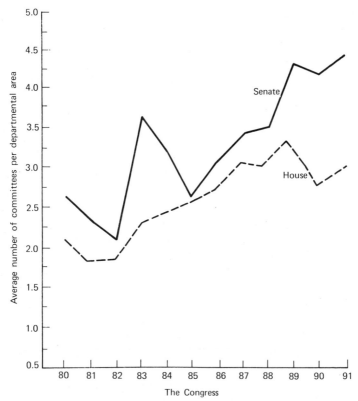

Figure 5-2. Multicommittee surveillance of departments by House by Congress, 1947–1970. *Source:* Lawrence C. Dodd, George Shipley, and Philip Diehl, "Patterns of Congressional Committee Surveillance," a paper presented at the 1978 Midwest Political Science Convention, Chicago, April, 1978, p. 19a.

though far more dramatically in the Senate. In both houses, the late 1940s witnessed an average of around two committees holding hearings into each separate department (with the Senate scores slightly higher than the House scores). This average would approximate the figure expected in a situation where an authorization and appropriation committee investigated each department. By the late 1960s, by contrast, the average number of committees holding hearings per departmental area had increased significantly. In the House the average ranged between 2.50 and 3.0. In the Senate, the average was approximately 4.0. The dramatic increase in Senate multicommittee surveillance underscores the greater preoccupation of the Senate with executive agencies.

The pattern of increase in multicommittee surveillance of departments does vary by department. With respect to the House of Representatives, 7 of the 12 departments or functional areas examined experienced a proportional increase in multicommittee surveillance: the Congress, the Executive Office, the State Department, the Treasury, the Interior Department, Labor Department, and the Independent Agencies. Only two areas evidence clear decreases in multicommittee surveillance by House committees: the Supreme Court and the Commerce Department. In the Senate, virtually all departmental areas show increases in multicommittee surveillance.

The rise in multicommittee surveillance has further weakened the bargaining power of Congress vis-à-vis the agencies. Not only does an individual subcommittee have just a few agencies that are clearly under its jurisdiction, and thus faces a challenge if it should try to discipline an agency by reducing the agency's authority; a subcommittee that attempts to discipline an agency will learn that the agency quite likely can find some other subcommittee to defend and fight for it. The overall result is a rise in the independence of executive agencies. In the midst of chaos, agencies can go their own way. This tendency is reinforced by the second problem caused by power dispersion: the *difficulty* of Congress in gaining access to information.

ACCESS TO INFORMATION

It goes without saying that information is the lifeblood of the congressional process. Congress has a constitutional responsibility to determine what the nation's policy problems are, to make a reasonable judgment about solving those problems, and to ensure that the executive branch is adequately implementing policy. If Congress is to fulfill this responsibility in a reasoned, deliberative fashion, it must possess information that is reliable and sufficiently detailed to allow a balanced, independent analysis.

Much of the information that Congress needs to make such judgments must come from executive agencies. In fact, it is often their role, specified in legislation, to possess the expertise, the advanced technology, and the financial resources necessary to gather data and interpret it. However, the information gathered by bureaucratic agencies is often very sensitive data—sensitive not only regarding foreign policy but also concerning personal lives and economic fortunes. The indiscriminant leaking of such information could do damage to the national security, to civil liberties, and to the domestic economy.

As Congress moved to a system of dispersed power and as multicommittee surveillance increased, the executive branch became faced with a growing number of committees and subcommittees all demanding information. As their numbers grew, so did the probability that the information would be leaked. This possibility stemmed from the nature of Congress. As a representative assembly, Congress is an open institution, at least relative to the rest of government. Its members gain admittance by election, not by passing a security clearance. Its staff is often chosen with attention to constituency connections, rarely if ever with regard to whether they are security "risks." In addition, members of Congress, as politicians, will often have political reasons to make information public that executive officials would prefer be kept secret.

Although executive agencies might have developed a system to protect information so long as they worked with a few members of Congress, it became extremely difficult to do so with the dramatic growth in the numbers of members seeking information. The executive response to this situation was to expand a secrecy and clearance system in which information was classified and placed off limits not only to members of the public but also to members of Congress.[21] By the late 1960s and early 1970s, this system pervaded not only the area of foreign policy but some areas of domestic policy as well. Thus, while Congress held more hearings, its hearings often seemed to elicit less substantive information.

The agencies were able to enforce this situation for two simple reasons: (a) it was often true that, in a dispersed system of subcommittee government, leaks of sensitive information might occasionally occur; (b) even if the information was not as sensitive as agencies liked to suggest, subcommittees were so dependent on agencies for the reasons discussed earlier that the agencies could often simply bluff or ignore subcommittees. As a result, Congress was placed in an increasingly vulnerable position insofar as information from the executive branch was concerned. The natural inclination was to turn to interest groups for help and information. Yet here too Congress found itself in a weakened position.

THE GROWING POWER OF LOBBYISTS

Just as a committee or subcommittee's authority over an agency depends on its strategic bargaining position vis-à-vis the bureaucracy, so does a committee or subcommittee's relations with an interest group depend on its strategic bargaining position in relation to interest groups in general. If numerous interest groups fall within a committee's policy domain, the committee and its leaders often have the upper hand; each interest group knows that it needs the committee more than the committee needs it. (This is particularly true where committees do not overlap in their policy jurisdictions.) By contrast, if a committee or subcommittee deals with legislation affecting only a small range

---

[21]On the existence and nature of this secrecy system, see Arthur M. Schlesinger, *The Imperial Presidency* (New York: Popular Library, 1973); Leon V. Sigal, "Official Secrecy and Informal Communication in Congressional-Bureaucratic Relations," *Political Science Quarterly*, Vol. 90, #1, Spring, 1975; and Morton H. Halperin and Daniel N. Hoffman, *National Security and the Right to Know* (Washington, D.C.: New Republic Books, 1977).

of interest groups, the members of the committees are limited in the number of groups they can help and from whom they can receive electoral support.

If, simultaneously, the interest groups have numerous other subcommittees or committees to whom they can turn, any one subcommittee tends to become more dependent on one interest group than that group is on the committee or subcommittee. Instead of key committee members being in a position to encourage support for the committee from interest groups, the interest groups are in a position to demand support from the committees and subcommittee members. If such support is not forthcoming, the interest group can withdraw electoral assistance from the key members of the committees. The result is a situation analogous to congressional committee dependence on bureaucratic agencies.

As Congress moved to a system of dispersed power, this third and final problem, congressional dependence on interest groups, exploded like a time bomb. With power dispersion, the work units that increasingly had the real responsibility and authority for policy formulation and surveillance were subcommittees, not the standing committees. The subcommittees had policy jurisdiction over matters of concern to only a small number of interest groups. As a result, members of Congress who had sought access to subsystem politics as a means of gaining financial support and shoring up their electoral base were faced with the fact that the price of electoral support from these interest groups often was dependence on them. Power dispersion did not give to subcommittee chairs the same broad-ranging authority, power, and electoral benefits that standing committee chairs had previously inherited from their more extensive involvement in subsystems.

The consequences for Congress and oversight of the executive were severe. First, it increased the difficulty that Congress had in achieving cooperation and information from interest groups. In many ways, this development went largely unnoticed because power dispersion did increase the number of hearings on Capital Hill and thus the more frequent presence of interest groups. It was also hidden to a degree because the 1960s and

1970s witnessed the growth of such "public interest" groups as Common Cause or Nader's Raiders that thrived on information gathering and dispersal along with the popularization of issues. Nevertheless, with regard to groups such as large financial corporations, power dispersion put Congress at a disadvantage. Since it is often the case that major corporations are the only reliable and direct source of much information needed for policy formulation or surveillance (i.e., oil companies with respect to petroleum production or reserve figures, auto manufacturers with respect to the ability to implement safety measures, and so forth), this problem of access to information was a serious one.

Second, greater dependence on interest groups often creates a reluctance for members of Congress to undertake serious oversight. As we have noted earlier, a key problem that often undermines legislative intent in policy implementation is that interest groups develop sweetheart relations with the agencies that are supposed to regulate them or which implement policy that affects them. This is particularly true in connection with the larger, well-heeled, and influential interest groups. These groups are the same ones likely to penetrate Congress most easily and to have the greatest potential electoral leverage over members. As members become more dependent on such groups, they are less likely to challenge the existing relationships between agencies and interest groups; they may be less likely to investigate agencies' implementation of policy unless that implementation flies in the face of these major interest groups.

As a growing number of sweetheart relationships between interest groups and members of Congress developed, a third problem emerged: widespread suspicion about congressional ethics and evidence of congressional corruption. By its very nature, power dispersion involves more members more directly and extensively with interest groups. More members of Congress must be wined and dined. More must be given electoral help. This highlights the existence of close relationships between lobbies and Congressmembers, arousing suspicions. In addition, the possibility for serious scandals and the difficulty of hiding improprieties are both enhanced. As a consequence, Congress and its members have been put in an increasingly unfavorable light, thereby delegitimizing the authority brought to the investigation of the executive, sidetracking Congress from investigating the executive to investigating and defending itself, and giving the executive more leverage over Congress. Such leverage is expressed, for example, through employment of the Justice Department to investigate congressional scandals and use of the resultant information to the advantage of the executive.

In sum, power dispersion in Congress during the post-war years served to generate problems that seriously undermined the ability of Congress to effectively oversee the executive. Power dispersion served the short-run interests of individual members, giving many more of them access to subsystem politics via important and autonomous subcommittee positions. As they dispersed power and thus developed closer ties with the bureaucratic agencies and interest groups, members were able to increase their electoral security remarkably, as well as their personal treatment within Washington. Simultaneously, members of Congress became more dependent on agencies and interest groups, more enmeshed in both intra- and intercommittee conflict, and more isolated from the information needed for policy formulation and surveillance.

Congressional Reform and the Oversight Process

For decades, members of Congress and political scientists alike have lamented the inadequacy of congressional oversight of the bureaucracy.[22] But the decentralization of Congress during the post World War II period did not improve the situation. Rather, because of widespread congressional involvement in subsystem politics, power dispersion in Congress brought about a general

---

[22]For example, see Samuel P. Huntington, "Congressional Responses to the Twentieth Century," in *The Congress and America's Future,* David B. Truman, ed. (Englewood Cliffs, N.J.: Prentice-Hall, 1965–1973); Richard E. Neustadt, "Politicians and Bureaucrats," in *The Congress and America's Future;* John F. Bibby, "Oversight and the Need for Congressional Reform," in *Republican Papers,* edited by Melvin Laird (Garden City, N.Y.: Anchor Press, 1968), pp. 477–488.

decline in the aggregate policy influence and governmental power possessed by the members as a group, particularly a loss of ability to use the committee system to challenge and control administrative implementation of policy. While this decline occurred steadily throughout the post-war years, it came to a head most visibly in the late 1960s and early 1970s, just as did the negative consequences of power dispersion for fiscal coordination and leadership. The most salient symbols of the congressional dilemma were those linked to foreign affairs: the inability to gain information about Vietnam, Cambodia, or the CIA, and the embarrassment of the Korean scandal.

These incidents sent members of Congress a clear message. If their positions within subsystem politics were to do more than provide a means of electoral security, if the system of subcommittee government was to provide a basis for policymaking and the exercise of governmental power, Congress had to find some way of handling the three problems power dispersion caused for oversight. Ironically, these problems were ultimately rooted in the committee structure itself, in the reliance on appropriation and authorization committees to conduct surveillance of the executive. The resolution of these problems would seem ultimately to lie—or at least begin—with a reform of the system itself, centralizing responsibility for oversight in a committee outside the authorization and appropriations process and thus independent of subsystem politics.

By and large members of Congress chose not to reform the oversight process by centralizing responsibility. They moved neither to significantly restructure the oversight process nor give greater power to the government operations committees. The solution was instead to retain decentralization of oversight but to make up the ground lost by dispersion, and perhaps gain new ground, by strengthening the general resources possessed by committee and subcommittee chairs, and by attempting to correct the most obvious problems within the committee structure.

Specifically, members of Congress moved to resolve the three problems of oversight by employing three separate but interrelated strategies. (1) They tried to increase their strategic bargaining power vis-à-vis the agencies by reducing problems of conflict within and among committees; this strategy entailed committee reforms to clarify jurisdictional responsibilities and provide mechanisms to better coordinate oversight activity. (2) As a way of increasing congressional information, Congress sought to use statutory reform to force more open information processes on the executive; expanded its own staff system within committees; initiated the use of computer facilities; and enlarged and improved its system of support agencies. (3) Finally, to decrease dependence on interest groups and thereby remove the major political disincentives to oversight, Congress moved to reform the campaign finance laws, to improve lobby laws, and to impose significant ethics legislation on itself.

REFORMING THE COMMITTEE STRUCTURE

As we noted earlier, the post-war committee system has suffered increasingly from a breakdown in committee jurisdictional lines, and consequently, in a rise in multicommittee surveillance and intercommittee conflict. One result, as we have seen, has been a weakening of congressional potential to conduct vigorous oversight. Adding to this problem is a fundamental flaw in the congressional committee structure: Congress lacks powerful and independent Government Operations Committees to conduct vigorous investigations and coordinate the oversight activities of other committees. During the early and mid 1970s, both the House and the Senate moved to resolve some of the jurisdictional problems by reforming their committee systems. In this process, some attention was given to strengthening the House Government Operations Committee, as well as other devices to enhance committee and subcommittee oversight of administration.

Jurisdictional Reform.   The House of Representatives was the first house to move to clarify its jurisdictional boundaries. In 1973 it created a Select Committee on Committees, popularly known as the Bolling committee because Representative Richard Bolling (D-Mo.) was its chair and its chief instigator. This committee held hearings for over a year into the nature and inadequacies of the committee system in the House and, in 1974, reported a proposal to restructure the House committee system. Under its plan, two standing committees (Internal Security, and Post Office and Civil Service) were to be eliminated while 14 others were to be affected significantly.[23] In addition, the Bolling Committee felt that a key problem with the existing committee system was the excessive workload many representatives had because of service on two standing committees. The committee thus proposed to make most committees exclusive committees, with legislators who served on those committees ineligible for service on others.

When the plan reached the Democratic Caucus in 1974, a great deal of uncertainty existed among the committee and subcommittee chairs over the extent of jurisdictional revision and the effect of revision on existing subcommittees; there also was uncertainty about which members would compose the new committees or subcommittees and/or chair new committees and subcommittees. The Subcommittee Bill of Rights that had passed in the previous Congress had given a number of members new power or the hope for new power. The Bolling plan threw this new power into doubt, thus the most potent opposition to it came from the committee and subcommittee chairmen. In the 93rd Congress—as a result of the earlier decentralizing reforms—these individuals composed a majority of the members of the Democratic caucus in the House. Their response was predictable, as then-Majority Leader Thomas P. O'Neill (D-Mass.) argued: "The name of the game is power and the boys don't want to give it up."[24]

After reviewing the Bolling plan for about two months, the House Democratic Caucus moved by a 16 vote margin to refer the plan to the Hansen Committee. The committee, which included some of the most vocal opponents of the plan, produced a counterplan. Both programs were introduced on the floor of the House of Representatives in September 1974, with the Han-

[23]Roger H. Davidson and Walter J. Oleszek, "Adaptation and Consolidation: Structural Innovation in the U.S. House of Representatives," *Legislative Studies Quarterly,* Vol. 1, # 1 (Feb., 1976), p. 51.

[24]*Ibid.,* p. 49; originally in Richard L. Strout, "Democrats House Reforms," *Christian Science Monitor* (June 28, 1974).

sen plan winning over the Bolling plan by a vote of 203 to 165. According to Davidson and Oleszek, "the Hansen plan was simply the Bolling report with the controversial features excised."[25] With respect to the major policy areas in which jurisdictional centralization had been proposed:

a.   A major improvement came in the field of transportation, where all major categories except railroads—a plaything of Commerce Chairman Harley O. Staggers (D-W.Va.)—were gathered into Public Works and Transportation.
b.   An invigorated Science and Technology Committee assumed overall responsibility for governmental research and development programs, including such fields as energy and the environment.
c.   The Foreign Affairs Committee, now styled the Committee on International Relations, gained only a portion of the duties proposed by the select committee, but operated under broadly worded new language.
d.   There was some concentration of health responsibilities in Commerce, although Ways and Means retained most of its crucial leverage on medical financing through payroll taxes.
e.   Energy and environmental issues remained as scattered and uncoordinated as ever.

In retrospect, the defeat of the Bolling plan is a testament to the tenacity of political subsystems and the preoccupation of legislators with personal careers and personal political alliances. The decentralization of the House over the preceding 25 years had created a set of vested interests that were exceedingly hard to break. Individual members, having only recently gained control of subcommittees, were loathe to give up newly won authority. Thus, of the 118 subcommittee chairs in the 93rd Congress, only 25 voted against the Hansen program, with the vast majority either not voting (16) or voting for Hansen (77).

Committee and subcommittee chairs, of course, were not sufficiently numerous to defeat the Bolling proposal by themselves. But, as members of the subsystem elite that had proliferated

[25]*Ibid.*, p. 53.

over the previous 25 years, they did have resources to draw on in protecting themselves—their subsystem allies outside Congress. Since many members of Congress who did not benefit immediately from the decentralized system of subcommittee government were nevertheless indebted to numerous outside interest groups for campaign funds and assistance, the activation of outside groups provided a way of affecting these members.[26] Through such efforts and through their own large numbers, committee and subcommittee chairs in the House were able to defeat many of the most significant elements of the committee reorganization plan. The Bolling Committee, however, had succeeded in focusing attention on the problems of the committee system, perhaps implanting seeds that will yet germinate in the coming decades. And it created a concern for committee reform that stimulated the Senate to look at itself.

Meanwhile, in the 94th Congress, a series of senators led by Adlai Stevenson moved to create a Bolling-type committee for the Senate. On March 31, 1976, they succeeded and the Senate approved a resolution creating a 12-member bipartisan Temporary Select Committee to Study the Senate Committee System. Under the direction of Adlai Stevenson as its chair and Bill Brock as co-chairman, the committee held hearings in July-September 1976. On October 15, 1976, Senators Stevenson and Brock introduced the committee proposals to the full Senate. These proposals affected three distinct aspects of the committee system.

The first impetus of the Stevenson plan was to reduce the number of Senate and joint committees from 31 to 16. By the time the resolution had passed the Senate Rules Committee and the full Senate, the number of committees was reduced only from 31 to 25 for the first session of the 95th Congress, with the prospect that four more committees would be phased out by the end of the 95th Congress. Among its major accomplishments, however, the reform resolution did succeed in its attempts to

---

[26]*Ibid.,* p. 55; for an excellent analysis of the Bolling Committee see Roger H. Davidson and Walter J. Oleszek, *Congress Against Itself* (Bloomington: Indiana University Press, 1977).

abolish (a) the Aeronautical and Space Sciences Committee, transferring its jurisdiction to the expanded committee on Commerce, Science and Transportation; and (b) the District of Columbia and Post Office and Civil Service Committees, transferring their jurisdictions to the Government Operations Committee (now renamed the Government Affairs Committee).

A second major aim of the Stevenson committee plan was to realign committee jurisdictions to place responsibility over broad policy areas in committees whose jurisdictions would have included all major aspects of that policy. Members of the various committees affected by jurisdictional changes fought them furiously. In the resolution that passed the full Senate, the only fundamental jurisdictional change came in the area of energy. The Senate renamed the old Interior Committee as the Committee on Energy and Natural Resources, and expanded its jurisdiction to cover numerous energy-related areas, including control over naval petroleum reserves and oil shale reserves in Alaska, water power, nonmilitary development of atomic energy, solar energy, energy regulation and research, and coal production and distribution. (In creating an energy committee, the Senate succeeded where the House had failed. On the other hand, the House created a central transportation committee but the Senate did not.)

The third area of change proposed by the Stevenson Committee, perhaps the most far-reaching, had to do with the number of committees and subcommittees on which a Senator could serve and chair. In previous years, the average Senator had served on approximately 18 committees and subcommittees, with some serving on as many as 31. The first Stevenson plan that passed allowed each senator to serve on three subcommittees in her or his major committee assignments and on two subcommittees in her or his minor committees. A member thus can serve on 11 committees and subcommittees altogether.

Of even more importance than limitations on committee service was action taken to limit the number of committees and subcommittees a member could chair. Under the original Stevenson plan, each senator could serve as chair of only one standing committee; in addition, each senator could chair one subcommittee on *each* of his or her standing committee assignments. Senator Dick Clark (D-Iowa) went to the floor of the Senate in opposition to this portion of the resolution, arguing that it was too generous and that it would give senior members too much leeway to stack up chair assignments. Clark proposed to reduce the maximum number of subcommittees a senator could chair from three (as allowed by the Stevenson plan) to two, thus reducing the overall number of chair positions possible per member from four to three. The Clark proposal passed the full Senate and was seen as a victory for younger members. All sitting committee chairs opposed the passage of the Clark amendment.[27]

In the end, the Stevenson plan suffered much the same fate as the Bolling plan, although the process was not so brutal nor the defeat so obvious (perhaps because the Stevenson plan did not attempt such wide-ranging reforms). The reduction of the number of committees was only partially accomplished and the realignment of committee jurisdictions no more successful than in the House. The reduction of the number of committees on which members could serve and the number of committee chairs they could have merely served to bring Senate practice in line somewhat with the House.

Strengthening Intercommittee Coordination and Oversight Capacity. Aside from the attention given jurisdictional reform, the primary focus in the Bolling Committee (though not the Senate Stevenson Committee) was on strengthening the oversight authority and capacity of the standing committees. The hearings and debates touching this portion of the Bolling plan centered on the need for oversight coordination and the need for more vigorous investigations.[28] In an attempt to improve oversight capac-

[27]*Congressional Quarterly Weekly Report,* February 13, 1977; for an analysis of the Stevenson Committee and a comparison with the Bolling Committee see Roger H. Davidson, "Two Roads of Change: House and Senate Committee Reorganization" in *Congress Reconsidered,* second ed., Lawrence C. Dodd and Bruce I. Oppenheimer, eds. (New York: Holt, 1980).

[28]Select Committee on Committees, *Hearings* on Committee Reorganization in the House, Vol. 1, Part I, p. 243. The material on the Government Operations Committee relies in part on Melissa Pratka, "Oversight: The Congressional Pipe Dream?" Honors Thesis, University of Texas, Austin, 1977.

ity, therefore, the Bolling Committee proposed to strengthen the Government Operations Committee and to strengthen the oversight capacity of other committees.

Regarding the Government Operations Committee the Bolling Committee took a three-pronged attack. First, it sought to increase the investigative role of the Committee by permitting it to conduct investigations in areas where other committees were also holding investigations; to offer privileged floor amendments to legislation based on its oversight findings; and to insert its oversight findings in reports of authorization and appropriations committees. Second, the Bolling Committee proposed that the Government Operations Committee be used as a vehicle to assist coordination and communication among other committees attempting to undertake oversight activity by directing it to prepare an oversight report for the House at the beginning of each year. This report

> would be developed after discussion by the HCGO with appropriate representatives from the standing committees. . . . After consultation with the Speaker and minority leader, the oversight report would include, among other matters, (1) a discussion of what the review plans of each standing committee are expected to be, (2) recommendations involving the coordination of oversight activities among the authorizing, appropriations committees and HCGO, and (3) suggestions regarding which programs and agencies ought to receive priority consideration as oversight is concerned.[29]

Third, to increase the status of the Government Operations committee, the Bolling plan proposed that the committee be designated a "major" committee and given an expanded work load, including jurisdiction over such items as internal security, census and the collection of statistics generally, and general revenue sharing.

As a means to improve the oversight capacity of the other standing committees, the Bolling plan recommended two approaches. First, it proposed that all standing committees (except Appropriations) be directed to establish oversight subcommit-

---

[29]U.S. House of Representatives, Select Committee on Committees, *A Report on the Committee Reform Amendments of 1974.* 93rd Congress, 2nd session, 1974, p. 69.

tees; to conduct future research and forecasting in their areas of responsibility; and to review tax expenditures affecting programs and policies within their jurisdiction. Second, the Bolling Committee proposed that six committees be granted "special oversight" responsibilities, permitting them to exercise comprehensive scrutiny over matters of direct concern to their jurisdictions even if those matters were also the legislative responsibility of some other committee. This grant, however, was not to carry with it any new legislative authority.[30]

As was the case with the jurisdictional reforms, these reform proposals generated much debate and opposition. First, there was fear of the added clout given the Committee on Government Operations, particularly the priviledged floor status to offer amendments to other committees' bills. This was seen as inviting direct encroachment by it on the legislative affairs of the other committees.[31] Similarly, opposition arose, within the GOC as well as outside of it, to the proposed upgrading of its status and the expansion of its legislative jurisdiction. Outside members resented giving the GOC jurisdiction that their committees had previously possessed. Members of the GOC feared that new legislative responsibilities would overwhelm the committee with work, straining its resources. Finally, there was some opposition to the requirement that other committees establish oversight subcommittees. The opposition was based particularly on the fear that such subcommittees might be too active and usurp authority of other subcommittees within a committee.

As the Bolling plan made its way through the party caucus, the Hansen committee revisions, and the House floor fights, the opposition took its toll. The privileged floor status was defeated soundly, the upgrading of the Government Operations Committee was considerably weakened, and the proposal for oversight subcommittees was made a recommendation rather than a requirement. Despite the Bolling Committee defeat on these three proposals, the first and third of which were really the heart of a revitalized approach to committee oversight, some advances

---

[30]Davidson and Oleszek, "Adaptation and Consolidation," p. 26.
[31]*Ibid.*

were made. The Government Operations Committee was given authority to prepare the oversight report, authority to investigate subject areas despite the existence of similar investigations by other committees, and the authority to have its oversight findings presented in the relevant reports of other committees.

In addition to the passage of these proposals, the House passed others affecting a wide range of other committees. As summarized by Davidson and Oleszek, these are as follows:

(1) all committees now have the authority to review the impact of tax expenditures on matters that fall within their jurisdiction;

(2) each committee (except Appropriations and Budget) has a future research and forecasting responsibility;

(3) seven committees have a "special oversight" function, i.e., the right to conduct comprehensive review of programs and agencies that fall partly within the jurisdiction of another committee;

(4) committees are authorized to create oversight subcommittees or to require their subcommittees to conduct oversight in their jurisdictional areas;

(5) committee reports on measures shall include their oversight findings separately set out and clearly identified;

(6) the costs of stenographic services and transcripts for oversight hearings will be paid from the House contingent fund rather than from committee budgets.[32]

IMPROVING INFORMATION RESOURCES

If Congress is to make adequate use of the oversight techniques at its disposal, it must possess information about national problems and agency activity. Its ability to gain information rests on a variety of factors: statutory rules governing information availability; the technology Congress provides itself for information processing; the external support agencies Congress can utilize in gathering and assessing information; and congressional staff. During the 1970s, Congress moved on all four fronts.

Sunshine and Freedom of Information.   The 1970s saw numer-

[32]*Ibid.,* p. 30.

ous laws requiring greater public and congressional access to information possessed by the executive branch. The two landmark laws were the Freedom of Information Act Amendments and the so-called "Government in Sunshine" Act. In 1966 the Congress passed the Freedom of Information Act, requiring the federal government to make documents, opinions, records, policy statements, and staff manuals available to citizens who requested them, unless the material fell into at least one of nine exempted categories. Citizens were given the right to bring suit under the act, with the burden of proof falling on the agency that refused to release the materials. In September 1972, the House Government Operations Subcommittee on Foreign Operations and Government Information released an oversight progress report on the act. That report concluded that the act had been "hindered by five years of footdragging" by the federal bureaucracy. In particular, the committee felt that the bureaucracy had undermined the intent of the Freedom of Information Act by a series of bureaucratic hurdles thrown in the way of those seeking access to information—hurdles as seemingly trivial but quite significant as excessive charges levied by agencies for finding and providing the requested material.[33]

As a result of the oversight hearings and a Supreme Court ruling that limited the applicability of the 1966 Act, a set of amendments to the act was debated and ultimately passed Congress in October 1974. In November 1974, Congress overrode President Ford's veto of the bill and enacted it as law. The new amendments basically reduced the possibility for bureaucratic footdragging. Among other provisions, they set out in some detail the ways in which agencies were to publish information to make it easily available; required each agency to publish a uniform set of reasonable fees for providing documents; and set out time limits for agency responses to requests. It required agencies to release unlisted documents to someone requesting them if the person had a reasonable description of the document. (Previously, some agencies had refused to provide material simply

---

[33]On the Freedom of Information Act, see the *Congressional Quarterly Weekly Report,* Vol. 32, #12, 41, and 47, 1974, pp. 775, 2882, and 3151.

because the applicant could not give a precise title.) And it clarified some of the exemptions written into the previous act to make clear their limited use.

The Government in Sunshine Act followed the Freedom of Information Act Amendments by two years. Its enactment capped a four-year lobbying effort by reform groups such as Common Cause. The Act required for the first time that all multiheaded federal entities—some fifty of them—conduct their business regularly in public session. The requirement covered regulatory agencies, advisory committees, independent offices, and the Postal Service. The Act specified only ten kinds of matters over which a meeting could be closed—items such as court proceedings, personnel problems, trade secrets, or sensititive national defense issues. Perhaps most importantly, the Act provided for district court enforcement and review of the open-meetings requirement and placed the burden of proof in disputes on the agency involved.

The Sunshine Act represented a significant victory for those individuals seeking greater access to executive information. The Act was particularly tough in defining very broadly the meaning of an agency meeting to include almost any sizable formal or informal gathering of agency members, including conference telephone calls. In addition, the Act represented an advance over the Freedom of Information Act in specifications of certain information that should be open to the public; in these cases the Act stated that its provisions would take precedence over the Freedom of Information Act in cases of information requests. Although the Act was not enthusiastically embraced by President Ford at the time, he nevertheless signed it in September 1976—in the midst of a heated presidential campaign against a strong advocate of sunshine laws, Jimmy Carter.[34]

The Development of Computer Facilities.   Gaining access *to* information, of course, is only part of the battle *over* information. Congress must have some means to process information, store it efficiently, analyze it. Modern technology, particularly the computer, has made all these processes much easier than they were

[34]See the *Congressional Quarterly Almanac,* 1976, p. 473.

just a few decades ago. Yet Congress has been slow to utilize the new technology. Computers require technical expertise on the part of those who use them. Members of Congress are not elected to office because of their technical ability, and have historically been loathe to hire staff with technical expertise, partly out of fear that they would become tools of the experts they hire. In addition, Congress has feared the impact that computers would have on the internal balance of congressional power. In the early years, when computers were coming of age, their implementation in Congress would have required a centralized system since there were too few computer technicians to provide specialized staffs for each member and subcommittee and there did not exist the technology to distribute terminals throughout the Congress.

As our discussion suggests, the "reforms" and "improvements" that are easiest to pass in Congress are those that can be easily spread among all members and that virtually all members can envision using. The implementation of a congressional computer system in the 1950s and 1960s would not have been such a reform. In fact, the move toward decentralized congressional government then taking place threw roadblocks in the way of such developments, since those seeking to disperse powers were not about to support a reform that would give committee chairs a significant power resource. Rather than struggle over computers, therefore, Congress chose to let the executive branch experiment—leading to a highly sophisticated bureaucracy confronting a Congress that, as late as 1967, had no significant computer capacity.

Quietly, but with accelerating speed, computers emerged in Congress during the 1970s and began to change the nature of information processing.[35] Their first major use came in 1967 when the Clerk of the House computerized the payroll system. Since that time, Congress has computerized a variety of support

[35]*Congressional Quarterly Weekly Report,* May 28, 1977, pp. 1045–1051; see also Stephen E. Frantzich, "Improving the Knowledge of Congress through Computerized Information Technology," a paper presented at the 1978 Southwestern Political Science Convention, Houston, Texas, April 12–15, 1978.

functions. In 1967 the House moved to a computerized assembly of committee calendars, followed by the Senate in 1972. In 1972 the Clerk of the House and the Secretary of the Senate began a computerized compilation of those campaign documents filed with them. And in 1973 the House installed computerized electronic voting machines. In addition, some members of Congress have began to use mini-computers to facilitate the performance of office functions, including the handling of constituent mail and the processing of constituent casework.

These moves to use computers to process very basic congressional functions have "legitimized" them on Capitol Hill to the point that they are now being incorporated increasingly in ways that influence fundamentally committee oversight activity. In 1976, Congress spent $25 million dollars on congressional computer services. A member of Congress with the appropriate terminal can gain access to hundreds of different data bases and services offered by the federal government and private companies. Among these services are access to the files of the Library of Congress; information about the status, legislative history of, and pending amendments to bills; and Justice Department files providing updated versions of the U.S. Code, Supreme Court briefs, and other legal items. In April 1977, the House began an experiment with computerized printing of Congressional hearings.

Congress now appears to be on the verge of launching new programs that would extend the computer into virtually every aspect of congressional operations. The leading missionary for this expansion on the Hill is Rep. Charles Rose (D-N.C.), chair of the computer policy group of the House Administration Committee; prior to election to the House, Rose helped introduce computerization to state government in North Carolina. Rose foresees a day when congressional computers will be linked with those in the executive branch to provide Congress with an electronic system to help monitor the activities of federal agencies. Under the proposed system, every time an executive agency issued a regulation, spent or collected money, or took other action it would be noted in the congressional computers. Members of Congress or staff interested in a specific program could dial into the computer and receive up-to-date accounting of agency actions. According to Rose, "This kind of a system would restore Congress as a check and balance to the power of the executive branch. It would make Congress a co-equal branch of government."[36]

Congressional Resource and Support Agencies.   While Congress experiments with computers and envisions a day when it can tap the vast informational resources of the executive branch, still it is the case that members of Congress and congressional committee staff need access to staff agencies that have the expertise and resources to provide independent analysis to Congress. So long as Congress lacks direct access to executive files, such independent support agencies will be critical in gathering information through more circuitious means. And even if Congress adopts computer technology, it will need support agencies with the personnel skills and resources to analyze the data received from executive departments, and to gather independent data. In fact, should Congress develop direct computer connection to the vast executive branch information system, it would be so overwhelmed with data that it would have no way of clearing a path without support agencies to cull and analyze it.

Today, Congress has access to four resource or support agencies: the Congressional Research Service; the Office of Technology Assessment; the Congressional Budget Office; and the General Accounting Office. The CRS and the GAO, both of which have a long congressional history, have enjoyed an expansion and upgrading in the 1970s; the OTA and the CBO are recent congressional creations. Since Congress historically has had an aversion to reliance on technical experts, particularly those who would possess some measure of independence from individual members of Congress or specific congressional committees, the move to expand the resources and number of support agencies demonstrates the seriousness of congressional concern with development of independent information capacity. These agencies and their impact on the bureaucracy are discussed more extensively in Chapter 6.

[36]*Ibid.,* p. 1049.

The Growth of Congressional Staff. No matter how extensive the congressional support agencies are, of course, Congress ultimately must assess information internally, and much of this assessment is done by the personal and committee staffs of Congress. One of the major trends in Congress in the post-war years has been an increase in the number of staff. Prior to 1946, personal and committee staffs were small, and neither committee staffs nor personal staffs had increased significantly from the time of World War I. Congress found itself increasingly overburdened with casework, legislation, and oversight activity, and by the late 1930s and early 1940s the need for more staff was apparent. The request by members for more staff was one of the reasons behind the appointment of the Joint Committee on the Organization of Congress in 1945, and a major concern of the 1946 Legislative Reorganization Act. That Act expanded congressional staff, legitimizing staff growth as a major element of congressional reform.[37]

After the passage of the 1946 LRA, congressional staff grew incrementally throughout the 1950s and 1960s. In the mid-1960s, however, attention turned again to staff and, as noted earlier, another Joint Committee on the Organization of Congress was created. As with the 1945 Committee, "the 1965–66 investigation was spurred by the feeling both in and out of Congress that the legislature had lost its initiative to the executive branch."[38] A major issue of the new committee was the perceived inadequacy of congressional staff capabilities vis-à-vis executive staff capabilities.

The final report of the Joint Committee recommended that the number of permanent professional committee staff members be increased and that, on their request, minority committee members be authorized to appoint professional and clerical staff

---

[37]On the growth of staff, see particularly Harrison W. Fox, Jr., and Susan Webb Hammond, *Congressional Staffs: The Invisible Force in American Lawmaking* (New York: The Free Press, 1977), p. 171; and Martin Machowsky, "On the Growth of Committee Staff," a paper presented at the 1978 Annual Meeting of the Midwest Political Science Association, Chicago, April, 1978. U.S. Congress, Joint Committee on the Organization of Congress *Organization of Congress,* Report, March 4, 1946., p. 9.

[38]Congressional Quarterly. *Congressional Quarterly Almanac,* 1966, p. 542.

members. In 1970 Congress passed these provisions as part of the 1970 Legislative Reorganization Act. The Act also provided explicit recognition of professional staff as personal aides in congressional offices. During the 1970s both the House and the Senate have continued to focus on staff as a major area for reform, with both houses expanding the authorization for committee and personal staff.

A broad overview of the historical increases in congressional staffs is contained in Table 5–3. This table, the result of a study by Fox and Hammond, indicates the dramatic growth in staff that has occurred since World War II both with respect to personal and to committee staff. The table also demonstrates that a sizable proportion of that growth occurred in the 1970s. In addition, it should be noted that the growth in committee staff is a pervasive phenomenon, as Machowsky indicates, characterizing practically all congressional committees. In both the House and Senate, finally, the growth in staff has come in "investigative" staff more than in "professional" staff. This pattern is particularly true for the Senate.[39]

Today the Congress has a professionalized staff system that probably surpasses that of any legislature in the world. The two major types of staff—committee and personal—undertake a wide range of tasks. As Fox and Hammond conclude from their extensive study:

> *Major personal staff tasks are handling constituent problems: casework and projects, requests for information, correspondence, visits with constituents and special interest groups. Press and legislative work are also important activities. Senate offices with larger staffs tend to be more specialized than House offices. In both House and Senate personal offices, six major activity clusters are found: administration, legislation, research, press, correspondence, and oversight. Committee aides' activities include bill drafting, investigating and dealing with lobbyists. Administrative, research, correspondence, oversight, and some press functions are also performed.*[40]

Overall, the congressional staff are a key element of the congressional relationship with the executive.

[39] These conclusions summarize the findings of Fox and Hammond, *op. cit.*, and Machowsky, *op. cit.*

[40] Fox and Hammond, *op. cit.*, p. 88.

Table 5-3.
Personal and Committee Staff Employees of Congress (selected years)

Year	Committee		Personal	
	Senate	**House**	**Senate**	**House**
1891	41	62	39	not appropriate
1914	198	105	72	"
1930	163	112	280	870
1935	172	122	424	870
1947	290	193	590	1440
1957	558	375	1115	2441
1967	621	589	1749	4055
1972	918	783	2426	5280
1976	1534	1548	3251	6939

Source: Harrison W. Fox, Jr., and Susan Webb Hammond, *Congressional Staff: The Invisible Force in American Lawmaking* (New York: The Free Press, 1977), p. 171.

CONTROLLING CONGRESSIONAL-LOBBYIST RELATIONS

Ultimately, reforms in organizational and committee structure and increases in congressional information capacity will have little impact on oversight if members of Congress are unwilling to take oversight seriously. And members of Congress may often be hesitant to undertake rigorous oversight because of their close involvement with and commitment to interest groups that benefit from favorable relationships with existing bureaucratic agencies. Today, "Lobbyists approach their jobs with more intelligence, hard work and persuasive argument than ever before. While fewer than 2,000 lobbyists are registered with Congress under a largely ignored 1946 law, their actual number has soared from about 8,000 to 15,000 over the past five years. . . . It is estimated that lobbyists now spend $1 billion a year to influence Washington opinion, plus another $1 billion to orchestrate public opinion across the country."[41]

[41]"The Swarming Lobbyists," *Time*, August 7, 1978, p. 15.

The close association between members of Congress and the lobbies has become particularly evident in the 1970s as a result of a series of scandals. In 1977, for example, Former Representative Edward A. Garmatz (D-Md., 1947–1973) was indicted by a federal grand jury on charges of conspiracy to take $25,000 bribes from two shipping firms in exchange for his sponsorship of legislation favorable to the companies; during the time covered by the indictments, Garmatz chaired the House Merchant Marine and Fisheries Committee that handled such legislation.[42] The Justice Department filed a suit alleging that representatives of South African sugar interests had illegally provided campaign contributions and gifts of travel and other favors to two members of the house Agriculture Committee. During the time period covered by the suits, 1970–1974, the two members involved in the suit had served as chair and ranking minority member of the committee that had jurisdiction over sugar import quotas.[43] Finally, and most explosively, there were the accusations surrounding the Korean scandal.

The Korean scandal has been called one of "the most sweeping allegations of congressional corruption ever investigated by the federal government."[44] While the truth surrounding the scandal may be years from complete revelation (if in fact it is ever fully uncovered), the prevalent view of the scandal is that the South Korean government, fearing a reduction in congressional support for the maintenance of American troops in Korea, drew up a list of 90 or more members of Congress who were deemed critical to Korean interests. Starting in 1970, agents of the Korean government are alleged to have distributed "between $500,000 and $1-million per year . . . for bribes, gifts and congressional travel."

One major Korean figure in the probe was Tongsun Park; his alleged role in the scheme "was to pass out money, host lavish parties and acquaint himself with as many members of Congress as possible, with the hope that having friends in Congress would

[42]*Congressional Quarterly Weekly Report,* Vol. 35, #32.
[43]*Congressional Quarterly Weekly Report,* Vol. 35, #30, p. 14927.
[44]*Congressional Quarterly Almanac,* 1976, p. 32.

pay off in favorable legislative action." Aside from this activity, a member of Speaker Albert's staff was accused of being a Korean Central Intelligence Agency agent who used her position to gain critical information for Korean lobbyists and to influence key members of Congress. In addition, "a former South Korean embassy employee was quoted as saying that he had seen the South Korean ambassador 'stuffing hundred dollar bills' into envelopes and charging off to deliver them to Capitol Hill." In response to such allegations, both the Justice Department and the Congress began extensive investigations. In the Congress, after initial confusion and conflict between its own investigative committee and its staff, it turned to former Watergate prosecutor Leon Jaworski, who later resigned, to head the probe.[45]

In the wake of such allegations and ongoing investigation, one assertion stands out to illustrate the potential damage that intimate congressional-lobbyist association can have on congressional-executive relations. In March 1977, newspaper columnist William Safire "alleged that in essence: (1) the National Security Council had in 1974 and 1975 accumulated significant information regarding congressional complicity in an influence-buying scheme by the South Koreans, and (2) that the House leadership in late 1975 had been blackmailed by the White House, by threats of releasing that information, into relenting its support of the Pike committee investigation into the C.I.A."[46] Because Safire had been a member of the Nixon White House staff and had good connections into the top echelons of the Republican party, the story seemed to have some potential credence as a description of behind-the-scenes manuevering in the Republican years.

Immediately following the release of this story, Representative Otis G. Pike (D-N.Y.), former chair of the House Select Committee on Intelligence, along with 10 other former members of that committee, requested a Justice Department inquiry into the allegations. In the months following that request, Attorney General Bell and the Carter Justice Department themselves

[45]*Congressional Quarterly Weekly Report,* Vol. 34, # 51, p. 3337.
[46]*Congressional Quarterly Weekly Report,* Vol. 35, # 13.

became the focus of allegations. Safire and others argued, for example, that Bell might be moving to quash the Korean investigation rather than indict fellow Democrats in Congress. If true, such a move would obviously give the executive branch a considerable degree of leverage over certain members of Congress.

The Korean scandal is symbolic of the type of congressional involvement with lobbies that can arise. And it is just one more case, though admittedly a dramatic one, in a long string of miniscandals such as allegations of congressional involvement with and favoritism to certain airline companies, to defense contractors, to oil companies, and so forth. These scandals have involved allegations that include explicit bribery, excessive and/or illegal campaign funding, backdoor financial support of members of Congress through the payment of retainers, excessive lecture fees, and numerous other activities. Many of these activities are, in moderation, elements of the democratic process: supporting candidates through campaign funds or inviting members of Congress to speak are both necessary to free elections and free speech. Yet in excess and in secret, and in the context of bribery, they clearly compromise these members and can be used by the executive branch to compromise the aggressiveness of oversight by the entire Congress. In realization of this fact, in response to the public outcry to clear up the congressional "mess," and out of fear that inaction would lead to electoral defeat for large numbers of them, members of Congress have moved on three fronts to reform the structure that underlies congressional-lobbyist relations: campaign financing; lobbyist laws; and rules governing congressional ethics.

Campaign Finance Laws. Congress has labored over campaign finance laws for years. In 1971, it passed the Federal Elections Campaign Act that set up the financial procedures that were a major factor in breaking open the Watergate scandal. In 1974 it passed the Federal Elections Campaign Act Amendments that introduced the first spending limits ever for congressional primary campaigns and set new expenditure limits for general election campaigns for Congress. The Act also introduced the first use of public money to pay for political campaign costs by providing for public financing procedures to cover presidential primary and general election campaigns. The final bill did not contain Senate-passed funding of primary and general election congressional campaigns. It did include some rigorous limitations on the contributions that individuals could give candidates, including an individual aggregate limit of $25,000 for all federal candidates annually. The Act set up explicit procedures for candidate disclosure of financial support. It also established a bipartisan, fulltime supervisory board controlled by six voting public members; two of these members were to be appointed by the Speaker of the House, two by the president of the Senate, and two by the president, all of whom would be confirmed by the Congress. The purpose of this board was to implement the act and to enforce the provisions of the Act through both civil and criminal means.

The 1974 Act was challenged in court, and in 1976 the Supreme Court ruled that the process whereby members of the Federal Elections Commission were appointed was an unconstitutional abridgment of the president's power of appointment. This ruling undermined the major provisions of the 1974 Act, since they relied on the existence of the Federal Elections Commission. In 1976, in an effort to resolve this problem, Congress passed yet another campaign finance law. Aside from reconstituting the FEC with all members appointed by the president, the Act also changed a number of aspects of the finance law, but added nothing fundamentally new. The passage of the Act, however, did not defuse demands for additional campaign financing reforms. Early in 1977, members of the 95th Congress moved the reform of congressional campaign financing to a new topic—public financing of congressional races. In both the House and Senate, members introduced relatively similar bills that proposed a mix of public and private funding of congressional races. In August 1977, a bill with such a plan in it was killed by a Senate filibuster.

Lobby Laws.   The second major element of the attempt to reduce members' dependence on lobbies is stricter regulation of the lobbies themselves. The 94th Congress attempted to reform lobbying practices by replacing the existing lobby law, the 1946 Federal Regulation of Lobbying Act (Title III of the Legislative

Reorganization Act of 1946), with a more rigorous law. The lobby revision bill of the 94th Congress attacked the existing structure of lobbyists' activities in a number of ways. First, it tried to clarify the meaning of "lobbyists." The definition of the 1946 Act, as limited by a 1954 Supreme Court decision, was considered too vague to be enforceable. This revision proposed a much more explicit definition that provided clear financial measures to determine what constituted a lobbyist. Second, the bill required lobby organizations to register annually with the General Accounting Office and to file with the GAO quarterly reports on their activities. The bill provided detailed descriptions of information required in these reports. Finally, the GAO was to be given responsibility for enforcing the Act, including authorization to refer suspected violators to the Justice Department for civil or criminal action.

The 1976 lobby revision bill was "opposed by virtually every major lobby group in Washington other than Common Cause."[47] In the end, while the House and Senate passed separate versions of the bill, the congressional session ended before a final version could be passed. Supporters of the bill blamed this inaction on the House Democratic leadership. New lobby disclosure legislation was introduced in the 95th Congress. On April 4, 1977, the House Judiciary Subcommittee on Administrative Law and Governmental Relations began the first hearing into these new proposals. While the bills under consideration in the 95th Congress varied over a wide range of specific details, there was fundamental agreement on the central goal: replacing the 1946 Federal Regulation of Lobbying Act with a tighter system requiring public disclosure of the organized efforts to influence governmental decisions. In addition to consideration of this legislation, the Korean scandal has forced Congress to focus more extensively on foreign lobbies.[48] In that area, as well, no law has been forthcoming.

Ethics Legislation. The final way in which Congress has moved to regulate the impact of lobbies in Congress is through

[47]*Congressional Quarterly Almanac,* 1976, p. 477.
[48]*Congressional Quarterly Weekly Report,* Vol. 35, # 16, pp. 701–704.

the approval of new codes of ethics for its members. These moves were fueled by the widespread scandals of the mid-1970s, and by the perception that the existing ethics codes for members of Congress contributed little to the avoidance of such scandals.[49]

The responsibility for drafting a new code of ethics for the House of Representatives went to a bipartisan, 15 member Commission on Administrative Review, chaired by David Obey (D-Wis.). The Commission included five Democrats, three Republicans, and seven public members. It was created July 1, 1976, in the wake of a sex-payroll scandal involving allegations that Wayne Hays (D-Ohio), Chairman of the House Administration Committee, had kept a mistress on the public payroll who had little if any job competence or responsibility.

The reform efforts of the Obey Commission came in two waves—first, a set of proposals to strengthen the ethics codes of the House and, second, a set of proposals to change administrative procedures in the House to enforce and reinforce the provisions of the ethics code. The first set of proposals emerged in February 1977. These proposals called for virtually total financial disclosure by members of the House, a ban on private unofficial office accounts, and limits on income members could make outside of the House. The ethics proposals of the Obey Commission went before the House in March 1977 when they were adopted by a vote of 402–22, virtually in the form proposed by the Commission. The only negative votes came from a few Republicans and southern Democrats.

The provisions of the House ethics code were fairly stringent. They required all House members and major staff members to disclose all income in excess of $100 or gifts in excess of $100 from a single source, reimbursements in excess of $250 from a single source, liabilities that exceeded $2500, as well as regulations on stock and real estate transactions. The code also

---

[49]For a more extensive discussion of the ethics legislation in the House and Senate, see the 1977 *Congressional Quarterly Almanac*, pp. 763–797; Joseph Cooper, "Reforming Congressional Ethics," in *Congress Reconsidered,* second edition.

provided for disclosure of spouses' finances under certain conditions; public inspection of the reports; and closer regulation of office accounts, franked mail, and foreign travel. Perhaps most importantly, the code prohibited any member from earning income outside Congress in excess of 15 percent of his or her official salary, except for income from stocks or bonds or income from a family-controlled business or rade.

The second set of proposals from the Obey Commission came in the fall of 1977. This set of proposals included the creation of a House Administrator in whom would be centralized the control of most administrative aspects of the House, including financial and payroll responsibility. The administrator, appointed by the Speaker subject to House approval, was seen as an example of additional effort to strengthen the power of the majority party leadership. The Commission also proposed a new Select Committee on Committees (like the earlier Bolling Committee) to recommend new changes in the House committee system, expansion of computer facilities in Congress, regulation of racial discrimination in employee hiring practices in the House, and the publicizing of member trips. These various proposals seemed to open the House to a series of greater reform efforts in the future and to a further diminishing of the autonomy of the individual members. But the move to bring the proposal before the floor of the House in October 1977 was defeated, ending the momentum of the Obey Commission.

The Senate moved more slowly on ethics legislation than the House, waiting until January 1977 to establish the 15 member Senate Special Committee on Official Conduct. The Senate Committee, headed by Gaylord Nelson (D-Wis.), drew on the work of the Obey Commission to prepare a new code. The Senate passed its ethics code in April 1977. The code included financial disclosure for Senators and for employees making over $25,000; these disclosure rules closely followed the House rules. The Senate also limited outside income to 15 percent of official salary, and strengthened the Senate Ethics Committee.

Overall, the House and Senate ethics codes have altered the life of the members of Congress. The financial disclosure requirement makes service in Congress even closer to life in a goldfish bowl. And it ended the Senate career of one member, Edward Brooke (R-Mass.), after discrepancies were found between his congressional income statement and his financial disclosures in divorce proceedings. Likewise, the curtailment of outside income increased the hardship of serving in Congress, discouraging service by less affluent politicians and encouraging retirement of those members who cannot live on a congressional salary (a very real possibility given high Washington prices, the cost of political life, and the need to maintain a residence in the home district).

The impact of the ethics legislation on the influence of powerful financial lobbies is less clear, especially those supporting conservative causes. Because of its stringency, the ethics legislation may make service in Congress attractive primarily to those who are already wealthy—who come from careers or family backgrounds that predispose them to look favorably on the legislative proposals of groups that serve wealthy interests. In addition, by regulating income and gifts according to whether they come from a single source, the ethics legislation encourages large umbrella lobbies to break up into smaller and more specialized lobby groups, actually encouraging the proliferation of single-issue lobbies on the Hill. This increases their number and reinforces the move to subcommittee government in which single interest lobbies can attach themselves to a subcommittee that serves their specific interest. Finally, the ethics legislation does nothing to regulate or control the amount of lobbying the groups can undertake on the Hill or in reelection campaigns. For these reasons, one must question the extent to which the ethics legislation actually decreases the significance of lobby influence in Congress or serves to increase congressional propensity to oversee the bureaucracy.

CONCLUSION

As we have seen in this chapter, Congress has moved during the 1970s to improve its capacity to monitor the bureaucracy and oversee the executive branch. The reforms it has undertaken are numerous and affect a wide range of activities. On the surface, they may appear to represent a reshaping of the orientation of Congress toward the executive—a major move in redefining that relationship. However, the reform efforts described above are primarily a continuation of the previous oversight "system" (if that is an appropriate term) on a broader scale. They do not, in our judgment, really address the fundamental problems of aggressive, centralized, sustained, and coordinated oversight. Because these changes are wide ranging, one may be tempted to expect much of them; and because they fail to restructure oversight procedures, one may be overly pessimistic regarding their influence on bureaucracy and administration.

What of their impact on the administrative state? It is probably too early to determine *precisely* what their influence will be or the extent to which they counter the pressures of subsystem politics and subcommittee government, but there are enough straws in the wind to enable us to speculate about their impact. Thus we turn now to a preliminary assessment of recent changes in Congress as they affect the bureaucracy, to initial judgments as to the impact of recent oversight reforms, and to a consideration of what these developments may imply for the policy role of the administrative state. This assessment is the task of the following two chapters.

6
Congressional Oversight and the Federal Bureaucracy: Patterns of Impact

The development of subcommittee government and subsequent reforms, traced in the preceding pages, have not gone unnoticed in the corridors of our national bureaucracy. The increased time and effort that Congress has come to devote to its dealings with departments and agencies in the "modern" era of subcommittee government has brought new challenges and opportunities for the administrative state. In this chapter, we explore the changing context of congressional-administrative relations in the modern period, with particular attention to the impact of the expanded use of key oversight devices and the ways in which the national bureaucracy has responded to or avoided the oversight efforts of Congress.

The strong presence of Congress in the day-to-day life of administrative agencies is a relatively recent phenomenon—certainly much stronger and persistent than in the period around the turn of the century that we earlier characterized as the formative period of the modern administrative state. Agency interaction with Congress in this early period was generally limited to presentation of budget requests by individual agencies and to ad hoc investigations, usually of the economy-and-efficiency variety. The rise of Congress as a professional, or at least "institutional" body in the decades between the overthrow of Speaker Cannon and World War II roughly paralleled the growth of the administrative state in its most rapid phase of development. In this same period, however, neither institution seemed to bulk particularly large in the consciousness of the other; a kind of psychic distance characterized their relations.

The "distance" between Congress and national administration began to narrow rather markedly during and immediately after World War II, when, as we have seen, Congress began to deal with oversight of administration in a more systematic fashion. This new impetus, coupled with the development of new oversight techniques, forced federal agencies to take greater cognizance of the role of Congress in surveillance of their activities. Perhaps more importantly, the proliferation of powerful subcommittees and the spread of subsystem politics helped pull bureaus and agencies more deeply into the vortex of congressional activity.

That the distance between agencies and Congress was beginning to narrow is suggested in the emergence in this period of the first scholarly treatments of administrative-congressional relations, including seminal studies (beginning in the early 1940s) of congressional attempts to control administration through the appropriations process, confirmation of appointments, statutes governing the public service, and such newer devices as the legislative veto.[1] These early contributions to the literature of oversight were soon followed by the first analyses of agency-committee relations and of subsystem politics.[2]

[1]See, among others, Elias Huzar, "Legislative Control Over Administration: Congress and the WPA," *American Political Science Review,* Vol. 36 (February, 1942), pp. 51–67; Arthur MacMahon, "Congressional Oversight of Administration: The Power of the Purse," *Political Science Quarterly,* Volume 58 (June and September, 1943), pp. 161–190 and 380–414; Harvey C. Mansfield, Sr., "The Legislative Veto and the Deportation of Aliens," *Public Administration Review,* Vol. 1 (Spring, 1941), pp. 281–286; and Leonard D. White, "Congressional Control of the Public Service," *American Political Science Review,* Vol. 39 (February, 1945), pp. 1–11.

[2]Among them were Arthur Maas, *Muddy Rivers: The Army Engineers and the Na-*

One problem for the modern student of Congress and administration is that the literature in this area, though growing, has more often been the concern of observers of Congress than those who study administration. Treatments of oversight and case studies of committee and subcommittee-agency relations often focus on internal committee dynamics and congressional politics rather than the impact of increased efforts at oversight on the agencies themselves. The implications for the bureaucracy of the developments in Congress traced in the preceding chapters, in short, remain to be studied by scholars.

Because little research on the impact of Congress and congressional oversight on the bureaucracy exists, our assessment must be somewhat impressionistic. We hope, however, to spur other scholars to recognize that study of oversight ultimately must address not just the quantity of oversight activities but their *impact* on the agencies. We hope to give students of national government a perspective from which to evaluate congressional-bureaucratic relations. And we hope to broaden the study of congressional-bureaucratic relations—arguing that one of the major influences that congressional organization, oversight, and reform may have on the bureaucracy is not on specific aspects of policy implementation but on the structure and role of the bureaucracy. Just as the rise of the administrative state has influenced the organization and role of Congress, so has the congressional response influenced the organization and contemporary role of the administrative state.

The Impact of Oversight on Agencies: General Considerations

Relations between agencies and their bureaus and congressional committees and their subcommittees are varied and complex. No two patterns of agency-committee interaction are the same;

---

tion's Rivers (Cambridge: Oxford University Press, 1951) and J. Lieper Freeman, *The Political Process: Executive Bureau-Legislative Committee Relations* (New York: Random House, 1955).

most are so different from each other as to make accurate generalizations quite difficult. In addition, the significance of agency-committee interaction is conditioned by the fact that an agency often faces numerous committees and subcommittees that are trying to influence it. If one attempts to understand the influence of Congress on an agency by focusing on the efforts of one committee or subcommittee, one is likely to be led astray. Thus one must consider the *range* of conditions that help determine the effectiveness of congressional oversight efforts, as well as the extent to which recent reforms in Congress nurture or undermine conditions that are conducive to meaningful congressional oversight.

INTERNAL COMMITTEE FACTORS

As we stressed previously, most intentional oversight activity within Congress occurs at the committee and subcommittee level. Committees are, of course, congeries of individual members, and the disposition of individual members toward agency surveillence is a key to understanding committee behavior. Most studies of congressional oversight are quick to point out that among the various functions of the members of Congress—including legislation, representation, and policy surveillance—oversight ranks low. Engaging in oversight does not, as a rule, pay off for a member of Congress in additional votes garnered for reelection; it is an activity with low visibility. Few congressional careers (though there are exceptions) are built on oversight; policy initiation through legislation rather than policy surveillance tends to be the primary role orientation of members.[3] On the other hand, the increasing realization among members that oversight may contribute to legislative initiatives as well as serve constituency interests provides some counterpressure—as does the potential for increased agency-committee interaction provided by the flowering of subsystem politics.

---

[3]For an early discussion of the lack of incentives for individual members to pursue oversight roles, see Seymour Scher, "Conditions for Legislative Control," *Journal of Politics,* Vol. 25 (August, 1963), pp. 526–551.

Opportunity for close committee supervision of the bureaucracy appears to be enhanced by a committee structure that allows a good deal of freedom and autonomy for its subcommittees. The frequency and intensity of surveillance tends to increase in committees where individual subcommittees are given a loose rein by the parent committee, especially where the subcommittees play a central role in their respective policy areas.[4] A proclivity to take oversight seriously is stimulated by a committee or subcommittee whose chair takes a positive view toward oversight. In addition, oversight activism appears to be enhanced by committees that have adequate staff and financial resources, and which are composed largely of members who are pleased with their assignment, interested in their work, and enthusiastic about their subcommittee's role in surveillance.[5]

From the perspective of the individual committee or subcommittee, congressional reforms in the 1970s have nurtured oversight activism. The move to subcommittee government has given greater independence to subcommittees. The legitimation of oversight subcommittees for authorization committees has increased the number of subcommittees and subcommittee chairs likely to evidence an interest in oversight. The expansion of congressional staff, the implementation of computer usage at the committee and subcommittee level, the strengthening of procedures whereby committees and subcommittees can gain information from the bureaucracy—these and other reforms have increased the resources that subcommittees possess in oversight efforts.

The democratization of committee and subcommittee assignment procedures and those governing selection of committee and subcommittee chairs has created a situation in which members can feel more committed to and enthusiastic about their committee and subcommittee work. In addition, the re-

---

[4]John Bibby, "Committee Characteristics and Legislative Oversight of Administration," *Midwest Journal of Political Science,* Vol. 10 (February, 1966), pp. 78–98; Morris S. Ogul, *Congress Oversees the Bureaucracy* (Pittsburgh: University of Pittsburgh Press, 1976), p. 15.

[5]*Ibid.*

forms designed to constrain the influence of lobbyists may reduce a major congressional disincentive toward oversight—the fear that oversight efforts might produce reelection problems for a member of Congress if a powerful lobby group chose to retaliate by withholding support or financing an opposing candidate. The efforts at ethics reform also reduce somewhat the possibility that oversight efforts may be inhibited by subtle or overt forms of bribery.

Many recent reform efforts may increase the capacity and motivation of individual committees and subcommittees to attempt oversight activity. Granted, many of the reforms themselves are quite limited. Nevertheless, to the extent that congressional influence on the bureaucracy is increased by active attention to bureaus and agencies by numerous subcommittees and committees, reform efforts probably have increased congressional influence.

THE INFLUENCE OF POLICY COMPLEXITY
ON AUTHORIZATION COMMITTEES

Characteristics of committees and individual members, however, are only part of the story. Factors external to a committee or subcommittee can influence greatly the extent and quality of bureaucratic supervision. A very important consideration is the jurisdiction and complexity of the policy arena within which an agency operates. It is the exception rather than the rule for one policy area to be handled by one authorization subcommittee of each house of Congress and by one administrative agency or bureau. The responsibility for various public policies is spread out and dispersed, both in Congress and the bureaucracy—often subject to the jurisdiction of three or more authorization committees and their subcommittees and as many agencies downtown. Bits and pieces of policies are broken up and parceled out to subcommittees and bureaus, each often struggling to unify policy formulation or execution under its aegis.

To complicate the matter further, there are instances in which a policy may be subject to the jurisdiction of a single set of substantive subcommittees but dispersed downtown, just as one federal agency may play the lead role in administering a policy whose jurisdiction on the Hill is fragmented. In both of these cases, the problem facing the subcommittee desiring to maintain effective supervision is that either it has only a small piece of the action or that the action is played out in a variety of agencies and bureaus.

We suggest that the rather neat, classical definition of a policy subsystem—a single bureau, a single set of subcommittees, and a cluster of interest groups surrounding them—is inaccurate or at least misleading, for it ignores the complexity of the relationships among policy areas, agencies, and congressional committees. Coherent, comprehensive surveillance is especially difficult where policy execution is fragmented. As one congressional staff member suggested:

> *A committee which passes a bill concerned with a given area may find that the programs to be administered are involved in several departments separately and that serious investigation of the work involved in carrying out the legislation would involve work with several departments. This is simply too time-consuming and too complex . . . so oversight is not performed.*[6]

The converse situation, where an agency or bureau may be responsible to a half dozen or so committees also limits effective oversight by Congress. Here the agency may be less than receptive to a legislative superior that speaks in a multitude of tongues—or at least delights in the possibility of playing one subcommittee off against another.

The attempts by the Bolling and Stevenson Committees to restructure jurisdictional lines among committees were in large part an effort to reduce this sort of jurisdictional complexity. Both committees largely failed in their attempt. In fact, because the reforms that did pass both the House and Senate ultimately realigned committee jurisdictions for different policy areas—for example, House reform of transportation and Senate reform of energy—the reforms may have added to the confusion and complexity of policy arenas when viewed from the broader perspec-

[6]Quoted in Ogul, *op. cit,* pp. 14–15.

tive of the entire Congress. Likewise, other reforms such as the creation of oversight subcommittees, while perhaps increasing the likelihood of oversight activity by a committee, have added to the complexity that a bureau or agency faces when it goes to Capitol Hill—thus probably reducing the likelihood that the agency will be given one single and clear message from Congress.

The leadership of Congress, of course, is not oblivious to the problems that jurisdictional complexity causes. Their attention, however, has been focused primarily on the problems that complexity causes for policy *formulation,* as witness the area of energy. To bridge the numerous authorization committees and subcommittees responsible for particular policy arenas, the leadership has created ad hoc committees composed of members drawn from the various committees that have jurisdiction in a policy area. These ad hoc committees have been given responsibility to create programs that tie together the *legislative* but not the *oversight* efforts of different committees and subcommittees. This system, which may aid in policy formulation, does not resolve the problem of oversight. Instead, it has taken some pressure to realign committee jurisdictions off Congress, reducing the likelihood that it will systematically address this problem.

THE NATURE OF A POLICY ARENA
What the foregoing suggests is that the way in which policy is "organized" (or unorganized) in Congress and the administrative state may well have important consequences for committee-agency relations. It is also likely that the kind or nature of a policy area may condition the relationship. A helpful analysis of the varying economic impacts of different kinds of policies has been suggested by Theodore Lowi and refined by others. Whether a policy is primarily *distributive* (a sharing of the wealth, such as in commodity subsidies, river and harbor improvements, or other pork barrel issues), primarily *regulative* (controlling one segment of society for the benefit of society at large), or primarily *redistributive* (taking from one group to give to another) may condition how and at what level the policy is handled in both Congress and the executive branch.

Classical subsystem politics appear to be closely associated with distributive kinds of policies. As the nature of policy moves toward the regulatory, the scope of conflict is broadened and the congressional focus tends to move upwards from the subcommittee to the full committee or the floor, and in the executive branch from the bureau to the agency or departmental level. Redistributive policies (progressive income tax, voting rights, etc.) tend to become the province of Congress and its leadership organs on the one hand and the president and his political appointees on the other. Of course, policies may change their nature over time, and there is a tendency for a policy, once established, to gravitate downwards toward the subsystem level (as has often been the case with the regulatory commissions).[7]

From this perspective, congressional surveillance of distributive policy poses a peculiar dilemma. Committee-agency relations are probably the most enduring and prevalent. Yet we have already noted that subsystem politics does not necessarily lead to agency surveillance for the purpose of control but more often for cooperation in mutually beneficial ventures. It is true that subgovernment dominance of a policy area may be challenged, as witness the threats to the tobacco subsystem in the 1960s over the issue of cigarette advertising,[8] or in housing in the early 1970s. Here a policy area may be broken temporarily from subsystem control and rise upwards into patterns of congressional treatment more common to the regulatory policy area, with the potential for control above the subsystem level. But as we have suggested previously, it is precisely here that the congressional mechanisms for policy surveillance are rudimentary or lacking. Further, the challenge to subsystem dominance is often short-lived, and after a time, agency-committee relations may settle back into established routines.[9]

[7]For a recent elaboration of these themes, see Randall Ripley and Grace Franklin, *Congress, the Bureaucracy and Public Policy* (Homewood, Ill: The Dorsey Press, 1976), pp. 71–171.

[8]See the excellent study by A. Lee Fritschler, *Smoking and Politics* (Englewood Cliffs, N.J.: Prentice-Hall, 1975).

[9]For a discussion of "overhead" congressional attempts to break into subsystem politics, see Ripley and Franklin, *op. cit.*, pp. 71–95.

In those policy areas that fall under the rubric of regulative rather than distributive politics, there is evidence that strong or persistent oversight is lacking. Scher's study of seven regulatory commissions over two decades found a basic reluctance of the substantive committees and subcommittees involved to monitor carefully the work of the commissions under their purview. The general pattern he discovered was "one of no review for long periods of time." And though there were occasional forays into the work of the commissions, he found committee members reluctant to alienate or provoke the powerful economic interests the commissions regulated.[10]

Such a finding underscores the fact that the stance an agency may take with its legislative committees is conditioned by its relations with the clientele and interest groups active in its political environment. As Francis Rourke, among others, has suggested, the amount of support (or lack of it) that an agency enjoys from its clientele, from interest groups, and from the public at large varies considerably from agency to agency.[11] Agencies that have traditionally been able to muster strong support from the public or from interest groups served by the agency—agencies such as the Office of Education, the National Park Service, or the Food and Drug Administration—may feel themselves in a strong position vis-à-vis their legislative committees. This may produce a situation where the committees may be reluctant to conduct forceful surveillance, especially where the clientele of an agency may rally to its support. It is not always the case that enduring public or interest group support translates into agency immunity from close scrutiny by its oversight committees. Some agencies, among them the Bureau of Land Management in Interior, have captured public support but have not always been able to turn this support to its advantage in its dealings with the Congress. But strong outside support, especially when coupled with the distributive effects of subsystem politics, can place an agency in a powerful position.

[10]Scher, *op. cit.*
[11]See the discussion in Francis Rourke, *Bureaucracy, Politics and Public Policy* (Boston: Little Brown, 1976), pp. 42–57.

Evidence as to what may happen to agencies that lack a strong clientele base is provided in a graphic study of the foreign aid program during the 1950s and 1960s. The Agency for International Development and its predecessors have never enjoyed a base of support for their activities at home. During the period studied, the legislative committees of both houses kept close rein on the aid program and were responsible for a number of statutory limitations and restrictions on the agency's authority, both in committee and on the floor. These restrictions included deep cuts by the legislative committees in certain programs and the mandating of others. "The relative lack of support for a program from a structured constituency," the author concluded, "tends to encourage legislative limitations on administrative discretion."[12]

The recent reforms have addressed the problems that powerful clientele groups cause in many policy areas by attempting to reduce the general influence that lobby groups can have on members of Congress. Thus the attempts to regulate campaign financing, lobbying activity, and congressional ethics all help restrict the ability of clientele groups to pressure members to go easy on pet agencies. Unfortunately, as the previous chapter indicates, the efforts to decrease lobby influence on the Hill have not been very successful, largely because lobby groups are now so numerous and powerful that they can often block or weaken attempts to regulate them. Thus the oversight motivation of members may still vary considerably by the nature of a policy area and the relative power of clientele groups within a given policy arena.

THE APPROPRIATIONS COMMITTEES
AND DUAL SUBSYSTEMS

Thus far, we have looked briefly at a number of factors that affect agency-committee relationships, the stance of agencies vis-à-vis their legislative committees, and some general consid-

---

[12]William L. Morrow, "Legislative Control of Administrative Discretion: The Case of Congress and Foreign Aid," *Journal of Politics,* Vol. 30 (November, 1968), pp. 985–1011. The citation is from page 1005.

erations that surround the oversight role. We have concentrated primarily on the legislative committees, for they are formally charged with maintaining "continual watchfulness" over the agencies whose legislation they write. And it is in the legislative committees where much of the recent innovation in oversight techniques has occurred. The appropriations committees, and the appropriations process, however, occupy a special place in an agency's constellation of legislative relationships—and one that is enduring and persistent. For the vast array of legislative committees and subcommittees, surveillance of agency activity is a secondary or tertiary concern that takes a back seat to creation and passage of legislation. For the appropriations subcommittees, however, legislative activity and oversight are nearly synonymous; agency review and appropriations legislation are done simultaneously and are mutually reinforcing.

Although the authorization committees have a number of incentives to expand instead of reduce the domain of agencies under their supervision, to view them more often as assets rather than problem cases, and to tread lightly in matters of oversight, the basic function of the *appropriations* committees implies that they will be skeptical, cautious, even hostile to executive branch agencies. Since budgets represent programs and dollars create policies, appropriations committees' decisions on areas and levels of funding are often as central to policymaking as the authorizing legislation produced by the legislative committees. Moreover, the appropriations committees have developed over time a range of nonstatutory controls over agencies that influence the execution of their programs.[13]

The characteristics of appropriations committees themselves give impetus to oversight. Of those characteristics of committees discussed above that are associated with a tendency toward strict surveillance—desirable committee assignments, relatively autonomous subcommittees, staff resources, and so on—the appropriations committees appear to exhibit most if not all. It is little wonder that the appropriations process, conducted on an annual basis rather than the occasional reviews of agency activity

---

[13] A survey of these techniques may be found in Michael Kirst, *Government Without Passing Laws* (Durham, N.C.: University of North Carolina Press, 1969).

typical of the authorizing committees, has long been regarded by members of Congress, scholars, and executive branch agency officials alike as the most persistent and thorough means of oversight.

This is not to suggest that many of the conditioning factors discussed earlier in relation to the authorization committees do not also play a role in an agency's relations with its appropriations committees. Richard Fenno, for example, found that agencies with strong external support have a better chance than agencies without such support for increasing their appropriations from year to year.[14] Yet as another scholar has cautioned, the awarding of generous appropriations does not necessarily indicate a lax attitude or sporadic attention to a particular agency.[15] But the argument can be made that the relationship between an agency and its legislative committees on the one hand and its appropriations subcommittees on the other has a different tenor. Indeed, the relationship is different enough that we feel a case can be made that subsystem politics really revolves about *two* different subsystems: one involving the agency and its authorization committees, the other its appropriations subcommittees.

This notion of a *dual* subsystem can be traced in part to the fact that, as we suggested earlier, the typical agency is often involved with a greater number of legislative subcommittees than appropriations subcommittees. Even an agency of moderate size such as the Environmental Protection Agency reports on a regular basis to subcommittees of three separate standing committees in the House and three in the Senate. The larger Agriculture Department operates under authorizations involving subcommittees of six legislative committees in the House and five in the Senate. Only one subcommittee on appropriations of each house, on the other hand, is regularly concerned with approving the agency or departmental budget.

The dominant pattern thus is for an agency to be simultane-

---

[14]Richard Fenno, *The Power of the Purse* (Boston: Little, Brown, 1966), p. 412.
[15]Ira Sharkansky, "An Appropriations Subcommittee and its Client Agencies," *American Political Science Review,* Vol. 59 (September, 1965), pp. 622–623.

ously a member of two subsystems—one involving a half dozen or more legislative subcommittees and the other involving one appropriations subcommittee in each house. These subsystems differ because the norms of the legislative committees often differ from those of appropriations; the former often attempt to expand an agency's jurisdiction or function and view an agency as a partner rather than an adversary, whereas in the appropriations committees, norms of restraint and scarcity usually dominate. Through the dual subsystems, the tension (often hostility) within Congress between legislative and appropriations committees is transmitted to the agencies, whose stance vis-à-vis their legislative master is thereby made more complex and difficult.

What is not generally appreciated is that within the agencies themselves, different actors figure more prominently in one subsystem as against the other. Generally, it is the *political executives* who are important in the agency's ties to the authorization committees. On the other hand, there is a tendency for the appropriations subcommittees to rely more heavily on the *budget directors* of the agency and its bureaus—individuals who are generally career civil servants in the supergrades and expert in the labyrinth of budget figures and procedures to an extent impossible for their politically appointed bosses. And both the career budget officers and appropriations subcommittee members are around longer than the agencies' political executives—which may help explain the effectiveness of oversight exercised through the appropriations subsystem. Because the lines of communications in the appropriations process run to careerists in the bureaucracy, messages passed along them have a greater chance of being internalized in the agency concerned.

The tension between these two subsystems means that oversight activity often is more a conflict over turf than a coordinated effort by Congress to produce a specific type of behavior within the bureaucracy. As the two subsystems struggle with each other (particularly as authorization subsystems attempt to constrain the power of the appropriations subcommittees), the bureaucracy may find that the resulting confusion and chaos leaves it free to follow its own course. The conflict within Congress is exacerbated because the rise of subcommittee government has produced a number of competing mini-subsystems within the authorization subsystem itself. Thus not only are authorization subcommittees struggling to take turf from the appropriations subcommittees and influence the bureaucracy, they are also struggling among themselves. Further, House subsystems are vying against those in the Senate.

The reforms of the 1970s did little to reduce this problem of tension and competition among subcommittees. The failure to strengthen the Government Operations Committees avoided the one approach that might have allowed a means of replacing oversight by dual subsystems or at least seriously coordinating it. In many ways, the reforms exacerbated the problems. The emphasis on authorization committee oversight, the creation of oversight subcommittees within authorization committees, and the flow of resources to authorization subcommittees strengthened their hand in relation to appropriations committees and subcommittees. In addition, the new congressional budget process, threatening the preeminence of the appropriations committees and subcommittees, may increase the competition between appropriations and authorization committees for influence over bureaucratic agencies—since the appropriations subcommittees may become increasingly assertive of their oversight task as their power wanes. Thus the recent reforms may have added to the problem of dual subsystem oversight instead of alleviating it.

CONGRESSIONAL-PRESIDENTIAL RELATIONS

Another set of factors that appears to condition the stance of an agency toward its legislative committees and the attitude of the latter toward oversight have to do with the overall tenor of the relationship between Congress and the president in general and between subcommittee members and agency officials in particular. It is a staple of the literature on oversight that agencies become more prone to close scrutiny when the Congress and president are of opposite parties. And one can hazard the guess that policy surveillance is enhanced where the ideological center of gravity of Congress is, say, to left of center and that of the president to the right—as during the Nixon and Ford administrations.

But probably more important are the peculiar personal relationships between a legislative subcommittee and the political executives responsible for an agency. Trust in the agency officials, in their capacity and openness, is likely to lead to confidence in the agency's work and to less rigorous surveillance. Morris Ogul's study of oversight patterns in the Post Office Department during the 1960s found that members of the Post Office and Civil Service Committee (the Post Office's legislative committee in the House) placed great emphasis on the personal capacities of the Postmaster General and his leadership abilities. One committee member suggested that "One variable for explaining oversight is the respect that legislators have for individual [agency] members. Individuals that they like, that they respect, and that they have had mutually satisfactory relationships with, will have more discretion and get much less flack from congressmen."[16]

Although the recent reforms within Congress cannot do a great deal to influence the general tenor of the relationship between Congress and the president, they may have some potential impact. In particular, the creation of the new Congressional Budget Office may reduce the reliance of Congress on the Office of Management and Budget for information about the national budget and agency expenditures. And the budget process may allow Congress to plan a budget independently of the executive, even when he is of the same party. If the new budget process does succeed in nurturing congressional independence of the president, Congress may become increasingly willing to maintain greater "distance" from the executive without fear that its policy process will collapse. In such a situation, Congress might undertake serious surveillance of the executive regardless of party affilation.

OTHER FACTORS
Naturally, other factors can also condition or influence the likelihood of oversight.

House/Senate Differences. Whether an interested committee is

---

[16]Ogul, *op. cit.,* p. 50.

in the House or Senate may be critical. Senators, having longer terms, may take extensive investigations more seriously than House members. The latter, having to rely on their committees and subcommittees as their main source of visibility and power (unlike senators, who have a more natural national visibility) may conduct more publicized oversight efforts.

Corruption, Crisis, and Publicity.   As Joel Aberbach has argued, "Evidence of corruption, the breakdown of a program, or the subversion of accepted governmental processes as revealed by Watergate may make oversight attractive because the overseer is almost sure to make a favorable public impression."[17]

The Influx of Skeptical Senators and Representatives.   The election of a "new breed of politicians . . . with a limited, often skeptical view of what government can accomplish" might also advance the notion that thorough and systematic oversight can yield some political payoff.[18]

These factors, together with the aforementioned ones, all condition oversight activity. The critical task, of course, is to determine whether the development of various oversight techniques has, in the context of these conditioning factors, actually led to improved surveillance of the administrative state by Congress.

Oversight Techniques: Their Expanded Use and Effectiveness

Of the various factors that condition agency-committee relations, some are relatively impervious to control by Congress. Others, such as the structure of the committee system, are subject to congressional reform. Because the reforms discussed in Chapters 4 and 5 have affected many of the conditions for oversight, and because a strengthening of the oversight capacity of

---

[17]Joel D. Aberbach, "The Development of Oversight in the United States Congress: Concepts and Analysis," a paper presented at the 1977 Annual Meeting of the American Political Science Association, Washington, D.C., Sept. 1–4, 1977, p. 8.

[18]*Ibid.,* p. 10.

Congress was a goal of so many of them, one would expect to find that serious efforts at oversight have increased. Because the reforms are so recent and because political scientists have largely ignored the overall influence that Congress has on agencies and bureaus, it is difficult to provide a thorough assessment of the actual impact of these reforms on the bureaucracy. One approach, however, is to analyze the impact of the creation and expanded use of certain oversight devices. Here we focus on four such devices and discuss in some detail their characteristics, their use by recent Congresses, and their probable contributions to oversight.

THE CONGRESSIONAL VETO

The congressional veto is a statutory provision within a law that requires the executive branch (1) to inform Congress or committees within Congress of the actions that the executive branch plans to take in implementing that law or portions of it; and (2) to receive from Congress explicit or implicit approval of the actions before actually carrying them out.[19] Legislative veto provisions always specify that the executive must submit its plans to Congress *before* they go into effect. The Congress is given a specified period—normally sixty days—to review the plans and reach a judgment on them. During the waiting period, Congress can act to disapprove or approve the action by a concurrent resolution, by a simple resolution of either house, or, since the mid-1940s, by the action of standing committees. The formal voting procedure followed by Congress will depend on the option or options written into the initial provisions of the act. "The most significant feature of the whole process is that the action of Congress or its committees is taken in a form that does not

---

[19]On the legislative veto, see Joseph P. Harris, *Congressional Control of Administration* (Washington, D.C.: The Brookings Institution, 1964), pp. 204–248; *Congressional Oversight of the Regulatory Agencies,* Committee on Government Operations, U.S. Senate, February, 1977, pp. 114–122; Joseph and Ann Cooper, "The Legislative Veto and the Constitution," *George Washington Law Review,* Vol. 20 (March, 1962), pp. 467–516; Larry Schechter, "The Legislative Veto," Honors Thesis, The University of Texas at Austin, 1977.

require the signature of the President and hence is not subject to his veto."[20]

The legislative veto is a twentieth century device, a response to the growing role of national government in American life and to the consequent difficulty of Congress to legislate with the specificity that it had in a less complex age. It provides a means whereby Congress can write legislation giving the executive broad discretion over its own organizational life and over the fleshing out of policy while retaining for Congress the ultimate authority to approve or disapprove administrative actions.

The use of legislative veto provisions emerged in the 1930s, initially involving proposals for reorganization of the executive branch by the President. In the 1940s and 1950s, the legislative veto matured as a tool of legislative oversight. In the early 1940s, it moved from a device largely limited to exercise by a concurrent solution of both houses of Congress to one exercised by a simple majority of either house. In the mid-1940s, the veto provision was altered to place responsibility in some cases not in one or both houses but in specific committees of one or both houses, bringing about congressional veto by committee. In addition, the range of bills to which legislative vetos applied was expanded beyond the area of executive reorganization to include a variety of acts, among them the Neutrality Act of 1939, the Lend Lease Act of 1941, and numerous others.

During the post-war years, most congressional veto provisions have actually involved *committee* vetos. This procedure meshes well with the desire of members of Congress to disperse power through a committee structure rather than leave it in a central body wherein it can be controlled by central party leaders. In addition, the use of committee vetoes is congruent with sub-committee government, since the actual responsibility for committee review of particular agency proposals generally falls to the subcommittees with jurisdiction over the subject. The subcommittees reach the initial decision and then seek formal ratification by the standing committee. And even in situations where the power of final approval or disapproval rests with one or both

---

[20]Harris, *op. cit.*, p. 204.

houses, the review procedure normally involves subcommittees and committees.

As Congress has decentralized, it has increasingly turned to the use of legislative vetoes. Table 6–1 presents data summarizing this trend. In the Kennedy-Johnson years, when power dispersion within Congress occurred slowly on a committee-by-committee basis, the number of acts passed by Congress with veto provisions was 41, up by 11 from the 30 passed during the Eisenhower years; the number of actual veto provisions con-

Table 6-1.

The Number of Acts and Provisions Containing Congressional Vetoes, 1932–1975

Year	Number of Acts	Number of Provisions
1932	1	2
1933	1	1
1934	0	0
1935	0	0
1936	1	1
1937	0	0
1938	0	0
1939	2	2
1940	1	1
1941	1	1
1942	2	2
1943	1	1
1944	3	3
1945	1	1
1946	3	4
1947	1	1
1948	2	2
1949	4	4
1950	0	0
1951	3	3
1952	3	4
1953	3	3
1954	4	4
1955	2	2

Table 6-1 *(continued).*

Year	Number of Acts	Number of Provisions
1956	6	6
1957	4	4
1958	6	7
1959	3	3
1960	2	2
1961	7	8
1962	7	8
1963	2	6
1964	7	10
1965	5	7
1966	5	7
1967	4	6
1968	4	6
1969	6	10
1970	11	17
1971	7	10
1972	11	19
1973	14	20
1974	25	39
1975	21	58
TOTALS	196	295

Source: "Congressional Review, Referral and Disapproval of Executive Actions: A Summary and an Inventory of Statutory Authority," Congressional Research Service, J.K. 10156, 76–886,

tained in those acts nearly doubled. During the first seven of the Nixon-Ford years, when power dispersion became institutionalized in a system of subcommittee government, Congress passed 95 acts with veto provisions, more than twice as many as in the preceding years. The number of veto provisions contained in these acts was 175, considerably more than twice as many as contained in the acts passed during the Kennedy-Johnson years.

Today, the legislative veto is clearly a part of governmental life, permeating numerous agency and policy domains. During the 1970s it has been employed in a wide variety of policy areas, ranging from the traditional area of executive reorganization to such diverse areas as motor vehicle safety, foreign assistance, construction of public buildings, mineral leasing legislation, emergency petroleum allocation, national education, and the review of National Science Foundation grants. The formulation of committee vetos has become more complex, as in the case of the National Traffic and Motor Vehicle Safety Act Amendments of 1970. In that Act, Congress required that specific executive proposals be approved by each house's Public Works *and* Commerce Committees, bringing four different committees into the approval process and sending shudders down the spines of executive officials.

During the 1970s, congressional veto provisions were written into the two legislative acts that most directly touched on the conflicts between Congress and the Nixon presidency: the War Powers Act of 1973 and the Budget and Impoundment Control Act of 1974. In these two acts Congress clearly saw congressional veto provisions as critical in regaining control over its two most basic constitutional powers—the power to declare war and the power to control the purse. Ironically, one of the most severe criticisms of the congressional veto derives from the argument that it itself is an unconstitutional procedure. Some political observers argue that it is a surrender of Congress' constitutional power to the president, or that it allows undue congressional involvement in decisions that are the realm of presidential responsibility alone.

Although the congressional veto, particularly the committee veto, is touted as an oversight device, we think an argument can be made that its emergence is less an expression of a desire for enhanced surveillance of administration than a device adopted by the legislative committees to help strengthen the authorization subsystem. Support for this argument may be seen in the shift in the *kinds* of activities and policies that have been drawn into the legislative veto process. Whereas the legislative veto as orginally developed was employed in executive reorganization and national security affairs, the committee veto has tended to be used primarily for *distributive* policies—military installations, military construction and real estate transactions, lease-purchase contracts, termination of federal activities of a business nature, and the like. Among the committees that exercise the committee veto, those which are involved in the pork barrel—Public Works, Armed Services, and Agriculture—are especially prominent.[21] The procedures employed by these committees in the use of the congressional veto suggest that maintenance of the committee role in subsystem politics, instead of oversight of administration, is the primary criterion.[22]

There are recent indications that the committee veto is also being employed in the struggle between the legislative and appropriations committees over levels of expenditures, or at least to influence the direction of expenditures. The Science Committee in the House and the relevant subcommittee in the Senate, for example, require that the National Science Foundation secure their approval should the Foundation plan to transfer more than ten percent of its appropriated funds from one major program category to another. And the House Science Committee has tried (unsuccessfully) to require through committee veto that the NSF receive its blessing before obligating any funds for research into solar energy. Another example of a committee veto that places conditions on appropriations appears in the organic act establishing the Consumer Product Safety Commission (CPSC). Before the CPSC may spend more than $100,000 on constructing testing laboratories, it must seek approval of its legislative committees through a committee veto process.[23]

As a device of oversight, the legislative veto (and its committee veto variant) may be more effective as a restraining device on presidential direction than a serious check on agency behavior. Its recent imposition in such areas as limiting the Chief Executive's power to commit U.S. forces abroad (the War Powers Act) and blocking his ability to defer appropriated funds (the Budget and Impoundment Control Act) suggest that Congress finds it especially useful in situations where it desires to check or limit

---

[21] John S. Saloma, *Congress and the New Politics* (Boston: Little, Brown, 1969), pp. 140–151.
[22] Harris, *op. cit.*, pp. 222, 231–232, 238.
[23] Authors' interviews.

presidential initiatives that Congress feels ignore its proper role. Some support for this assumption is offered by the observation that opposition to the committee veto appears to have come much more frequently and strongly from the president and Executive Office than from department and agency heads. Presidents Truman, Eisenhower, and especially Johnson took strong stands in opposition to committee veto provisions, refusing to sign a number of bills that included them.[24]

It is our impression that committee veto provisions are rarely regarded with fear and trembling by executive agencies—an impression reinforced by the observation that such provisions often bolster rather than retard subsystem relations. Indeed, there have been occasions where individual agencies have complied with committee veto provisions in spite of presidential instructions to disregard them.[25] It is likely that in the constitutional struggle between Congress and president over the legality of committee veto procedures, some agencies may find the pull of subsystem politics stronger than that of overhead executive direction.

PERIODIC AUTHORIZATIONS

Periodic authorization is precisely what the name implies—a requirement that the authorization of a program or agency be subject to periodic renewal.[26] As noted earlier in Chapter 5, the reauthorization process can be a major technique that authorization committees may use in controlling executive agencies and programs. Periodic authorization is particularly attractive to subcommittees because the responsibility for the hearings into agency reauthorization and the initial markup of reauthorization legislation can be handled by them. In fact, the reauthoriza-

---

[24]Saloma, *op. cit.*, pp. 139–142; Harris, *op. cit.*, pp. 219–226.

[25]Harris, *op. cit.*, p. 229.

[26]On periodic authorization and sunset legislation, see *Congressional Oversight of Regulatory Agencies*, pp. 44–48, 129–135; and David W. Landsidle, "Annual Authorization and the Process of Congressional Oversight," Masters Thesis, The University of Texas at Austin, 1975.

tion process provides subcommittees a clear weapon that they can use to force agencies to pay attention to them.

An increase in the use of periodic authorization is a very attractive way to seek a strengthening of congressional oversight capacity while maintaining subcommittee government. While most agencies historically have been endowed with permanent authorizations, there has been an increasing trend in the post-war years, particularly in the last decade, toward requirements for limited authorization. In addition, there has been a move to eliminate permanent authorizations and to substitute limited ones in agencies operating under open-ended statutory mandates.

One of the most striking aspects of the move to periodic authorization is the occasional use of annual authorizations. Prior to the post-war years, Congress had never required agencies to receive authorization renewal every year. In the immediate post-war years, at a time in which Congress was quite concerned with control of the executive, it "invented" annual authorizations and has continued to expand their use since that time. The first target of the new device was the 1948 European Recovery Program, popularly known as the Marshall Plan. Congress has utilized annual authorizations in subsequent foreign assistance programs, the Atomic Energy Commission, the National Aeronautics and Space Administration, aspects of armed services authorizations, Amtrak, the National Science Foundation, and several other major programs.

The generally accepted view of annual authorization is that it is a relatively effective oversight device, allowing for increased involvement of legislative committees in policymaking and surveillance, providing increased access to agency bases of information, improving the ability of Congress to focus attention on crucial programs, and producing an increased knowledge base from which to examine agency activity.[27] We argue, however, that the conventional wisdom surrounding the utility of annual authorization as an oversight device is open to question. This is partly because of some questions concerning the motivation (of

[27]Saloma, *op. cit.*, pp. 151–152.

at least some committees) behind the adoption of annual authorization procedures and partly due to our analysis of the impact of annual authorization on those federal agencies subject to it.

Imposition of annual authorization has resulted, on occasion, not from a pristine desire to improve policy surveillance but from the struggle for policy hegemony between the legislative and appropriations committees, and more broadly, between the opposing subsystems of which they are a part. This appears to be the case, for example, in the annual authorization requirement placed on NASA. In pushing annual authorization, the House Science and Astronautics Committee argued that the requirement would strengthen the Committee against the House Appropriations Subcommittee involved. NASA annual authorization had the unanimous backing of the members of Science and Astronautics, while it was opposed by nearly three-fourths of the members of the House Appropriations Committee.[28] The Appropriations subcommittee involved. NASA annual authorization would gradually flow to the legislative committees—a fear that over time appears to have been justified. In their study of NASA and its legislative environment, Redford and White suggest that annual authorization has contributed to the preeminence of the legislative committees, rather than appropriations, in congressional surveillance and policymaking regarding the space program.[29]

In addition to its use as a pawn in the struggle between legislative and appropriations committees, annual authorization has also made a convenient foil for Congress in its policy struggles with the president. This is particularly evident in the foreign affairs area beginning in the 1960s, when annual authorization was specified for the Alliance for Progress, and more recently in the extension of annual authorization to the State Department and U.S. Information Agency. Here, annual authorization may

[28]*Ibid.*, pp. 148–149.
[29]Emmette S. Redford and Orien White, *What Manned Space Program After Reaching the Moon?* (Syracuse: Inter-University Case Program, 1971), pp. 33–34. Also see Landsidle, *op. cit.*, pp. 42–43.

be seen as less a product of internal struggles within Congress than part of a broader congressional effort to reassert its authority against the president in matters of foreign policy.[30]

As far as the agencies are concerned, annual authorization does not always represent more intensive oversight or imply greater program restraint. Granted, the requirement is burdensome. Additional time is required to prepare each year for appearances before authorizing committees in addition to the yearly defense of budget requests before the appropriations subcommittees. High-level political appointees in agencies and programs subject to annual authorization may spend up to half their time preparing for or taking part in congressional hearings. Moreover, annual authorization tends to increase the uncertainty in an agency's legislative environment. Not only is the agency subject to the vagaries of a yearly appropriations process but also to the whims of its authorizing committees. Carefully considered long-range planning may be disrupted. And from the perspective of the overhead executive, control and coordination of the bureaucracy may be weakened. President Johnson's budget director, Charles Schulze, commented that annual authorization "creates a real difficulty for the executive branch . . . in the indecisiveness and inability to make sound plans for the year being considered . . . in the immersion of the legislative committees as well as the Appropriations Committees in the details of administration to the detriment of the longer range, broader view of missions and objectives."[31]

For some agencies, however, it appears that the burdens of annual authorization are well worth bearing. Indeed, some agencies find it of positive value to their programmatic development and their ability to defend themselves on the Hill. Agencies have often been able to turn annual authorization to their advantage by increasing the visibility of their programs in Congress and mustering support for them. Annual authorization can lead to a close rapport between an agency and its legislative committee and to a strengthening of policy subsystem ties

---

[30]*Ibid.,* pp. 67–71; Morrow, *op. cit.,* p. 1001.
[31]Quoted in Saloma, *op. cit.,* p. 150.

which both may play off against the appropriations committees. Apparently, this occurred with NASA, one of whose legislative liaison officers maintained that the agency "profits from the exposure" produced by yearly review.[32] A similar view obtains in the National Science Foundation, where a legislative liaison official volunteered that annual authorization was less a rein than a shot in the arm. This same official described the relationship of the Foundation to its legislative committees as "almost incestuous at times."[33] In other agencies, annual authorization is used to help justify the agency's budget before the appropriations committees. A strategy often adopted by agency officials is to argue that since the legislative committees have examined the program with a fine-toothed comb, the appropriations committee may rest assured that the request has received intense scrutiny and passes muster.[34]

Although the evidence is impressionistic, it appears that annual authorization may not be the rigorous tool for oversight it is often judged to be. Annual authorization may even offer advantages for the agencies; indeed, there are occasions when agencies have even sought an annual authorization requirement from their legislative committees to enable them better to bring their programs to the attention of Congress.[35] And annual authorization may be less than powerful where the motive behind its introduction, as we have seen above, has more to do with struggles between authorization and appropriations subsystems than with a desire to bring an agency or program to heel.

Our caveats concerning the utility of annual authorization extend also to periodic authorization. In fact, the major impact of annual or periodic authorizations may be to inhibit authorization committees from doing the one thing that they are best prepared to do—write legislation. Rather, they spend time reviewing the behavior of agencies and programs that they are almost surely not going to question seriously, given their com-

---

[32]Landsidle, *op. cit.*, p. 103.
[33]Authors' interviews.
[34]*Ibid.*
[35]Landsidle, *op. cit.*

mitment to them. In the very process of review, moreover, the agency gets an opportunity to defend itself and ask for expansion of its authority.

One type of periodic authorization that might benefit congressional oversight is sunset legislation, if that legislation were properly designed. For example, an agency could be forced to appear periodically *not* before its authorization committee but instead before a group of legislators on a sunset commission or on the Government Operations Committee. This group of individuals, none drawn from the relevant appropriations or authorization committees, could investigate agencies brought before them and determine whether their initial functions were being fulfilled and whether they should continue to exist. If such a group were independent of the authorization and appropriations subsystems and not prejudiced by preexisting commitments to an agency or its clientele group, then periodic review of an agency and its program might produce effective oversight.

AGENCIES AND STATUTORY REPORTS

Another mechanism Congress has developed to attempt to become more closely informed about the workings of the administrative state is the requirement for formal reports. The number of such reports has risen rapidly since the end of World War II, numbering nearly a thousand by the 1970s. These reports may be of several kinds—those requiring an agency to study a problem and recommend a solution, perhaps legislation; those, like the annual report, providing an ex post facto review of agency programs and activities; and with the development of the legislative veto, reports giving Congress and its committees advance notification of an intended action or decision.[36]

Responding to the increasing number of statutory reports, coming on top of the growing volume of case work referrals and other more informal communications, has added to the paperwork and burden of the agencies. However, such reports

---

[36]John R. Johannes, "Executive Reports to Congress," *Journal of Communications,* Vol. 26, No. 3 (Summer, 1976), pp. 55–56.

appear to have the potential for bringing problems and issues to the attention of agency officials as well as to members of Congress. It is not unknown, for example, for an agency's political executives to request the "burden" of a report in order to force consideration of issues its career cadres might wish to let lie dormant. And in addition to probing sensitive areas and sheding light on the inner workings of agencies, statutory reports, once completed, may provide reference points and guidance for agency officials.[37]

Evidence concerning the usefulness of statutory reports for congressional oversight is both scanty and mixed. The prevailing view—that these reports are paid little attention on the Hill—is reenforced by Ogul's findings. In his case studies, he found evidence that few if any congressional offices kept systematic track of agency reports; that in most cases, reports were only glanced at if read at all; and that though a staff specialist might read a report germane to his or her particular area of interest, required reports were of little use to members of Congress or their staffs as a whole. As one member suggested, "We have to keep the wastebaskets full to survive," intimating that many such reports found their way there.[38]

One of the reasons behind the mandating of formal reports appears to be the complexity, often a breakdown in the processes of informal communication between agencies congressional committees. It was hoped that such reports would help make communication more regular, as well as sensitize agency officials to congressional demands and perspectives—but there is little evidence that this has happened. One should also bear in mind that many if not most of these reports are required of agencies by the same legislative committees that are members of the policy subsystem of the agency or its bureaus, though on occasion a required report by an "outside" committee may reflect the latter's attempt to assert jurisdiction, especially where jurisdictional lines are unclear.[39]

[37]*Ibid.*, pp. 55, 60.
[38]Ogul, *op. cit.*, pp. 177–179.
[39]*Ibid.*, pp. 175–179; for a different perspective, see Johannes, *op. cit.*, pp. 57–60.

INFORMAL AND NONSTATUTORY CONTROLS

Over the years, the Congress has employed a number of informal controls over the agencies within its purview—communications or personal understandings that carry the intent of the legislature and its committees (or members) to the agencies and bureaus. Instructions concerning expected agency behavior may be found in committee hearings and reports, in debates and statements on the floor, and in personal meetings and phone calls. There have been relatively few studies of the role of informal controls as a device for linking Congress and federal agencies; personal contacts, especially, take place outside the glare of publicity and are rarely found in written records. Understandings between agency officials and members or staffs of Congress may be closely and privately held, known only to the intimates.

While it is difficult to measure the use of most informal and nonstatutory controls, committee hearings can be measured, as we saw in the preceding chapter. Two recent studies of committee hearings indicate that hearings have increased rather considerably since the passage of the oversight reforms. Joel Aberbach, in his study of the first six months of the 91st, 92nd, 93rd, and 94th Congresses (1969–1976) found that the number of all hearings increased over this time period by about 65 percent in the House and by about 48 percent in the Senate. The number of oversight hearings more than tripled in the House and more than doubled in the Senate. His statistical analysis indicates that one factor giving rise to this increase in hearings was the increase in congressional staff.[40]

A second study of hearings, by Robert Stein and James Regens, reinforces and expands on Aberbach's findings. The Stein-Regens study examined all hearings in the 91st and 94th Congresses, not just those held during the first six months of each. They found an even greater increase in oversight hearings than Aberbach did. Their statistical analysis indicates that, to varying degrees and under varying conditions, oversight activism is nurtured by having a decentralized committee, increas-

[40]Aberbach, *op. cit.*, pp. 17–29.

ing the size of staff, the existence of oversight subcommittees, and policy conflict between a committee and the president.[41]

In addition to examining the quantity of hearings, Stein and Regens analyzed the quality of hearings. They found that the quality of oversight hearings increased in both the House and Senate, but particularly in the Senate. They argue that "the Senate's less frequent oversight activity may be a function of more thorough and time consuming oversight activity." They conclude that the greater concern of the Senate with quality oversight is

> not altogether surprising. Senators hold office for a longer period of time and tend to have broader committee assignments than do their counterparts in the House. These differences may enable Senators to spend more time investigating entire agencies and issue areas. Representatives, whose time frame is restricted to a two year period, and whose committee assignments tend to be narrow and limited in number do not have the opportunity to develop the broad perspective necessary to sustain more focused, agency and issue area oversight activities.[42]

The development of nonstatutory controls by the appropriations committees was studied by Michael Kirst. The appropriations subcommittees, he finds, have fashioned to a fine art the wording of informal instructions to agencies concerning what they may and may not do with appropriated funds (instructions that would most likely be subject to a point of order if placed in the appropriations bills). If the subcommittee wishes to bind the agency, it "directs" or "instructs" the agency; if it allows the agency some leeway, it will "expect" or "urge" certain actions; weaker language includes such instructions as "desires" and "feels," language that the agency can often ignore. If the Senate and House Appropriations subcommittees, however, use different or opposing language, the agency can often choose the

---

[41]Robert M. Stein and James L. Regens, "An Empirical Typology of Congressional Oversight," a paper presented at the 1978 Annual Meeting of the Southwestern Political Science Association, Houston, Texas, April 12–15, 1978, pp. 13–26.

[42] *Ibid.,* p. 18.

interpretation it wishes, or, in some cases, ignore both sets of instructions.[43]

To disregard, however, a binding or strongly worded instruction is something not taken lightly by agency administrators; in the majority of cases, these instructions are heeded. The errant administrator or budget officer runs a risk of at least a severe tonguelashing the next time before the committee if not the possibility of stronger sanctions in the form of budget reductions. As Kirst summed up the reaction of agency officials to these informal controls, "disregard of nonstatutory techniques is rare. . . . The prevalent attitude of administrators with regard to nonstatutory directives is, 'we just have to live with them.'"[44]

Although the use of nonstatutory controls over administration by the appropriations committees may be an effective restraint on agency behavior, we would raise several issues regarding such procedures—issues similar to those raised earlier concerning the committee form of the legislative veto. The development of these techniques in the appropriations committees appears to result largely from the fact that appropriations committees are not allowed to "legislate." They can, of course, negate the intent of legislation passed by the authorizing committees by refusing to appropriate funds for certain programs. And the norms of restraint and parsimony that dominate much of their consideration of agency budgets reenforce such "negative legislation." There are, however, occasions where the appropriations committees wish to stimulate or influence agency actions in a positive or expansive direction or to "interpret" legislative intent. Here the resort to informal, nonstatutory controls over agencies may produce an effect similar to legislation.

One way in which the appropriations subcommittees may stimulate agency actions is to request the agency to report on a problem. On receiving the report, the subcommittee airs the report's implications with agency officials, and based on these discussions may mandate certain actions to be taken by the agency. Such procedures can also be used to block or prevent the

---

[43]Michael Kirst, *Government Without Passing Laws* (Chapel Hill: University of North Carolina Press, 1969), pp. 30–63.

[44]*Ibid.*, p. 73.

agency from moving in directions contrary to the wishes of the subcommittee, a kind of informal appropriations committee veto—where a statutory committee veto attempt might be ruled out of order.[45] The heavy reliance by the appropriations committees on these informal techniques—as opposed to statutory restrictions that must be reviewed and approved by the parent legislative body—is suggested by Kirst's finding that an appropriations act generally contains about five statutory restrictions on agencies, whereas the committee report accompanying the act generally has some thirty or more informal provisos that relate to other than financial or expenditure matters.[46]

We also observe that the use of nonstatutory techniques on the part of the appropriations committees is heavily concentrated in those subcommittees engaged in funding programs of a distributive nature. Some of the appropriations subcommittees that figure prominently in the pork barrel and in the appropriations subsystems—among them Public Works, Interior, and Agriculture—show a consistent preference for nonstatutory as opposed to statutory controls. In appropriations bills handled by the Public Works subcommittee, for example, there are generally some ten to fifteen new informal restrictions for every one new statutory proviso.[47] These observations lead us to the hypothesis that the development of informal controls by the appropriations committees may be linked to the struggle within Congress and among its committees and their subsystems over control of distributive policies. And they suggest that as the legislative committees have moved to increase their surveillance of the authorization subsystem through increased use of the committee veto, the appropriations subcommittees have moved to protect their interests in the appropriations subsystem through the development of nonstatutory controls.

Kirst's analysis, as we noted, suggests that agencies and their officials are generally responsive to the intent of the nonstatutory controls exercised by the appropriations subcommittees. Although administrators on occasion may "appeal" what they con-

---

[45]*Ibid.*, pp. 88–96.
[46]*Ibid.*, p. 115.
[47]*Ibid.*, p. 108.

sider a capricious use of informal techniques by the appropriations subcommittee of one house to that of the other, and in a
few instances attempt to avoid them altogether, the general pattern appears to be one of compliance. The risk of offending the
subcommittee that holds the agency's purse strings is one that
most officials appear not to wish to take. Indeed, there are
examples of administrators who prefer nonstatutory arrangements to formal statutory arrangements. Kirst concludes that
these nonstatutory techniques are generally an effective oversight device, a vehicle for stricter congressional control over
executive agencies.[48] We would question, however, how much
their development results from a desire for oversight and how
much from a reflection of the common interests of agencies and
appropriations subcommittees as they engage in subsystem politics.

The impact of such techniques on overhead executive control
of agencies raises an issue similar to that posed by the committee
veto. There is evidence that these techniques may be used by
agencies and appropriations subcommittees in making common
cause against the president and OMB. They allow agencies a
means of avoiding or negating regulations imposed by the
executive that bear on the administration or budget execution of
a program. An agency may on occasion "appeal" such regulations to its appropriations subcommittees and secure a report or
testimony that reflects the subcommittees' "intent" that certain
executive restrictions be ignored—a use, in short, of appropriations subsystem politics to end-run executive control. Kirst concludes that, "For a number of reasons, nonstatutory controls and
informal meetings are uniquely suited in circumstances where
an appropriations subcommittee and an agency want to impair
the effectiveness of central executive machinery."[49]

CONCLUSION
Overall, an examination of these four oversight techniques indicates that their use has increased significantly during the post-

[48]*Ibid.*
[49]*Ibid.*, p. 135.

war years, particularly during the era of congressional reforms. The significance of this increase is less clear. As we have noted throughout, these techniques often appear to be used more as weapons of conflict among committees, particularly between authorization and appropriations committees, than as instruments to influence bureaucratic decisionmaking. This problem is particularly true of the informal controls, since they can so easily be used by different subcommittees for different ends with respect to the same agency decision. This situation allows the agency to use congressional confusion as a justification for ignoring congressional direction altogether.

We have also found that even formal techniques such as periodic or annual authorizations and committee vetos have been used not to restrict agency discretion but instead to strengthen the hand of the legislative committees against the appropriations committees. Conversely, the latter have refined the use of nonstatutory techniques as a counterfoil to the encroachments of the legislative committees. And both appropriations and authorizing committees have used "oversight" devices to defend "their" agencies and programs against the overhead control emanating from the institutionalized presidency— weakening presidential surveillance of the federal bureaucracy without necessarily substituting their own. The struggle within the halls of Congress between legislative committees and their appropriations counterparts for control over the direction of agencies and programs—even where enhanced oversight is the apparent intent—allows the agencies considerable latitude in playing off one against the other. That the agencies have taken advantage of such tensions is clear.

Obviously, congressional *attention* to the agencies has increased in the past several decades. But it is not necessarily the case that the *impact* of congressional oversight has increased as a result. In fact, since the increased activism has not been accompanied by increased direction and coordination of oversight efforts, congressional influence on the bureaucracy may have decreased. The only congressional winners probably are those who want to maintain the bureaucratic *status quo,* since the primary consequence of oversight confusion within Congress is the maintenance and autonomy of the agencies.

As implied in previous chapters, this is due in no small measure to the dynamics of congressional developments and the rise of subcommittee government. So long as Congress attempts to conduct oversight through the current committee and subcommittee system, without serious mechanisms for coordination of oversight activity, the impact of oversight on the executive will probably remain minimal and the congressional committees will probably preoccupy themselves with intra-congressional struggles that leave the bureaucracy broad latitude.

The Resource Agencies of Congress

In part because of the problems associated with so many of its oversight techniques, and in part as a means of gaining and analyzing information for its oversight efforts, Congress has increasingly turned to its resource agencies. Such agencies are created by Congress to serve it and undertake specified actions in its name. They are largely independent of the committee system, though they do answer specific committee requests. In the past decade Congress has expanded the authority of two existing resource agencies, the Congressional Research Service and the General Accounting Office, and has created two new ones, the Office of Technology Assessment and the Congressional Budget Office. Consideration of the expanding role of these resource agencies can give us a better overall view of congressional oversight efforts.

CONGRESSIONAL RESEARCH SERVICE
The Congressional Research Service (CRS) is the oldest of the independent support agencies.[50] Its creation came in 1914, when the Librarian of Congress, acting on the authorization of Congress, established the Legislative Reference Service. The

[50]On the CRS, see James D. Carroll, "Policy Analysis for Congress: A Review of the Congressional Research Service," in *Congressional Support Agencies, Papers Prepared for the Commission on the Operation of the Senate,* Washington, D.C., 1976, pp. 4–30; and *Congressional Oversight of Regulatory Agencies,* pp. 68–69.

Legislative Reorganization Act of 1970 changed the name of the LRS to its current designation and expanded its responsibilities. In 1972 an authorized buildup of staff began; as a result the number of budgeted staff positions has almost tripled since 1967. The growth has occurred both with respect to research and reference positions, which are the heart of information gathering and analysis, and administrative and support positions such as clerical staff.

The range of Congressional Research Service responsibilities today is quite extensive. First, it provides traditional services that for decades had been its central activity. These roles, as summarized in a recent report for the Senate Government Operations Committee, include:

1. Assisting the hearing process by suggesting names of prospective witnesses, preparing questions, and analyzing testimony.
2. Preparing background studies, briefing papers, memoranda and draft reports.
3. Loaning specialized personnel to committees for temporary use.
4. Compiling bibliographies, developing pro and con arguments on topics.
5. Analyzing, summarizing, and commenting on judicial decisions.
6. Providing copies of issue briefs, reports, bibliographies, and special studies on a variety of public questions and problems.
7. Securing copies of or abstracting books, magazine articles, newspaper items, scholarly journal writing, or other publication.
8. Making charts, graphs, and maps.
9. Providing quick reference service for the retrieval of factual or statistical information.

In addition, recent increases in the staff size and statutory responsibility of the CRS allow it to work much more closely with congressional committees. Its traditional roles thus have been expanded to include:

1. Analyzing and evaluating legislative proposals.
2. Tracking major policy issues.
3. Submitting summaries of subjects for committee review and lists of program expiration dates at the beginning of each term.
4. Offering expanded consulting assistance.

The CRS considers these numerous roles to fall into three basic categories of responsibility: policy analysis and research; documentation and status of legislation; and information and reference service. Analysis of the agency's budget indicates that the most basic commitment of the CRS today is to policy analysis and research, followed distantly by its roles as an information and reference service. These services are provided to congressional constituents, to individual members of Congress, and to congressional committees. CRS also has a number of formal and informal relationships with the other resource agencies. The one major constraint on the CRS, as on the other resource agencies, is a restriction against formal involvement in the reelection efforts of members of Congress.

In spite of the increased responsibilities it has acquired over the past decade, the CRS has had difficulty shucking its image as an archive or a place where requests from high school students for help in writing term papers are forwarded. Although the upgrading and expansion of its services has increased congressional use of its resources, its activity only infrequently includes program evaluations or other analyses central to policy surveillance.

Yet CRS has recently begun to develop some activities that are geared to congressional oversight of administration. Studies provided to congressional committees have included a survey of the statutory development of the legislative veto and a report on oversight techniques available to them. CRS has also moved somewhat gingerly toward program evaluation and examination of individual agencies. Such reports, however, are rare and represent only a small fraction of its broad range of services.

Even though CRS may continue to develop a capacity to evaluate agencies and programs, it is possible that the utilization of its reports by the committees or members concerned may be limited. Neutral analysis may be discounted or distorted when it runs counter to the prevailing consensus of numerous policy subsystems. This problem is heightened because the CRS lacks the relative autonomy of the GAO and thus may be subject to greater buffeting by parochial interests inside Congress. Nor does the oversight potential of the CRS bulk large in the perceptions of agency officials; few if any of those to whom we talked felt that the work of the CRS contributed substantially to congressional oversight of their agencies or programs.

THE GENERAL ACCOUNTING OFFICE

The second oldest congressional resource agency, and by most accounts Congress' most valuable oversight support agency, is the General Accounting Office (GAO). This office was established by the Budget and Accounting Act of 1921 and is headed by the Comptroller General. "The basic intent of the Congress in creating the GAO and the Comptroller General was to enhance congressional authority and involvement with respect to fiscal matters both by assuring independence in the performance of the functions previously vested in Treasury officials and by furthering its ability to receive candid information."[51] In order to fulfill this role, the GAO has become the chief auditor of the federal government.

Today the GAO's multifaceted responsibilities encompass five distinct roles:

1. Assisting Congress in its legislative and oversight activities.
2. Auditing the programs, activities, and financial operations of federal departments and agencies.
3. Helping to improve federal agency financial management systems.
4. Settling claims and collecting debts.
5. Providing legal services.

While it is somewhat difficult to establish precisely the relative

---

[51]Quoted in *Congressional Oversight of the Regulatory Agencies,* p. 71.

emphasis placed within GAO on these various roles, a rough
estimate can be gleaned from a listing of estimated staff year
requirements for fiscal 1977 as presented in the House Appropriations
Committee hearings for that year. Based on these estimates,
it appears that approximately one-half of GAO's staff
years are devoted to the auditing function and one-fourth entails
direct assistance to committees and members of Congress.
The remainder of the time is spread among the other roles.[52]

Although it is true that these diverse roles performed by the
GAO vary in the extent to which they are responses to congressional
inquiries and requests, much of the activity of the GAO,
even its legal or auditing action, reinforces its supportive roles
for Congress. For example, "legal services and decisions" includes
"the tasks that the Comptroller General performs in an
adjudicative capacity when he rules on questions as to the availability
of appropriations," a task that serves to clarify congressional
intent. Similarly, the GAO itself may initiate audits. These
audits are far-reaching inquiries that include "not only examining
accounting records and financial transactions and reports,
but also checking for compliance with applicable laws and regulations;
examining the efficiency and economy of operations;
and reviewing the results of operations to evaluate whether the
desired results, including legislatively prescribed objectives, have
been effectively achieved."[53]

Clearly, the auditing activity of the GAO can uncover administrative
problems of which Congress was simply unaware; it
also provides an information base for Congress that is critical to
its conduct of oversight. The utility of these audits to Congress is
further increased by the fact that, while the reviews are self-initiated,
"the Comptroller General stresses the fact that, in
planning such work, the GAO looks first to the needs and interests
of Congress and, in that connection, maintains contacts with
committees."[54] This sensitivity to Congress can potentially have

---

[52]*Ibid.*, p. 72.
[53]Joseph Pois, "The General Accounting Office As a Congressional Resource," in
Congressional Support Agencies, p. 32.
[54]*Ibid.*, p. 33.

great significance for congressional-bureaucratic relations when one considers the extensiveness of GAO audits. During the fiscal year 1975, for example, GAO made 836 surveys and 1376 reviews of government programs and activities in the United States and in 78 other countries.

Just as Congress has moved in the 1970s to expand its resources in other areas, so it has moved to expand rather considerably the role that the GAO plays as a congressional support agency. In 1977 House Appropriations Committee hearings the Comptroller General estimated that when he joined the GAO in 1966, the direct assistance that the GAO provided Congress represented about eight percent of the effort of a professional staff of about 2400 people. By the mid-1970s, the Comptroller General estimated, GAO work for Congress constituted 34 percent of the effort of a professional staff of 3800 people.

This expansion in GAO service to Congress comes in part from an increase in requests by members and committees. It also stems, however, from expanded statutory authority given the GAO during the 1970s.[55] The Legislative Reorganization Act of 1970 mandated for GAO a significant responsibility for program evaluation. The 1974 Budget and Impoundment Control Act expanded the program evaluation responsibility of the GAO and extended even further its responsibilities. First, the Comptroller General was given the unusual role of assessing the needs and critiquing the activity of Congress. Second, the Act involved the GAO directly in the implementation of the new budget process and in the enforcement of the new impoundment procedures.

Although GAO reports to congressional entities often find their way into hearings and committee reports, there has been little systematic study of the influence of the GAO on individual agencies or of its contribution to oversight. Brown's analysis of the GAO's relations with the Tennessee Valley Authority (which as a government corporation is rather atypical of the bulk of administrative agencies) over a period of years found that, on the whole "the results of congressional follow-through, or cor-

[55]*Ibid.*, p. 35.

rective actions taken on GAO findings and recommendations have been mixed."[56] In some cases, the TVA had accepted GAO suggestions and recommendations for changes in procedures and policies, but in others fought the GAO position, even to the extent of securing amendments to its organic act to write into law its interpretation of issues in dispute—a procedure that entailed the cooperation of its legislative committees with which it made common cause against the GAO.[57]

The renewed push toward program evaluation urged on the GAO by Congress during the early 1970s has met with some resistance from the Comptroller General. There is only so far the GAO can move in this direction before evaluation begins to compete with its other ongoing responsibilities. The Comptroller General has recently taken the position that program evaluation should be primarily an agency initiative and has urged the committees of Congress to include in agency authorizations a statutory requirement that program evaluation be conducted by the agencies concerned. The Comptroller, one scholar has observed, "is obviously trying to stave off the deluge of program evaluation studies that could result if Congress construed the statutory provisions as making him primarily responsible for conducting such evaluations."[58]

In terms of its effect on agency programs and policy execution, it is possible that in many instances the GAO is more of a potential thorn in the side than a vigilant watchdog with teeth. This is especially the case where GAO findings or recommendations run counter to positions arrived at in the policy subsystems. GAO reports to committees and individual members are confidential by convention, with their dissemination dependent on their release by the committee or member who requested them.[59] Thus there is the potential for their use on a selective, even arbitrary basis—a potential that may diminish the impact of

[56]Richard E. Brown, *The General Accounting Office* (Knoxville: University of Tennessee Press, 1970), p. 71.
[57]*Ibid.*, p. 59.
[58]Joseph Pois, "The General Accounting Office as a Congressional Resource," in U.S. Senate, Commission on the Operation of the Senate, *Congressional Support Agencies* (Washington, D.C.: USGPO, 1976), pp. 40–41.
[59]*Ibid.*, p. 48.

the professional, nonpartisan review that is a hallmark of GAO's approach. Moreover, quite frequently a GAO report on an agency or program is not completed until sometime after the interest in its findings has diminished, thus detracting from its salience.[60]

Another factor involved in assessing the GAO's role in agency oversight has to do with its relations with the appropriations committees on the one hand and the legislative committees on the other. The core of the work of the GAO is still financial and expenditure analysis, subjects of considerable interest to the appropriations committees that provide the bulk of the funds spent by the agencies. And the relationship of the GAO with the appropriations subcommittees is often a close one. In spite of increased attention to program evaluation and analysis given GAO in recent years, it still assigns more professional staff to work with the appropriations committees than to any other set of standing committees,[61] and there is some evidence that GAO findings and recommendations surface more often in appropriations hearings and reports than in the work of the legislative committees.[62]

That there may be a "special relationship" between the GAO and the appropriations committees (moderating its ties to the Government Operations Committees) is suggested by the fact that the appropriations committees have strongly supported the GAO's reluctance to move toward greater program evaluation, fearing that this would detract from its primary responsibilities in examining the financial and expenditure aspects of agency activities.[63] The existence of close ties between the GAO and the appropriations committees were also suggested by several agency officials interviewed by the authors. They reported some tendency for appropriations subcommittees to rely on GAO studies more heavily than authorization committees do.[64]

[60]Joseph Pois, "Trends in General Accounting Office Audits," in Bruce L. R. Smith, ed., *The New Political Economy* (New York: Wiley, 1975), pp. 246–275.
[61]GAO, *Annual Report, 1975*, p. 2.
[62]Brown, *op. cit.*, p. 78.
[63]Pois, "Trends," p. 253.
[64]Authors' interviews.

Finally, the role of the GAO in activities supportive of oversight has also been constrained by a recent tendency on the part of Congress to add to its responsibilities in ways that may conflict with its oversight work. Recent additions to the GAO's perview have included expanded duties in approving accounting procedures used by agencies, establishing cost-accounting standards, and monitoring federal election and campaign finance laws. These and other new functions reflect congressional "proclivity for dumping responsibility upon the GAO regardless of their relevance to its fundamental mission . . . ,"[65] thus possibly decreasing its oversight effectiveness.

THE OFFICE OF TECHNOLOGY ASSESSMENT

Aside from its two traditional support agencies, Congress now has two additional ones. Congress authorized the first of these, the Office of Technology (OTA), in the Technology Assessment Act of 1972; the office began full operation a year later. Congress created the OTA to provide information about scientific and technological questions; it is authorized to undertake technology assessments and research projects either on its own initiative or at the request of any congressional committee chairperson. A 1977 Senate Government Operations Committee report on congressional oversight lists seven major roles of the office:

1. Providing unbiased information and technical expertise in the various applications of technology.
2. Securing, analyzing, and assessing data about the effects of technological development.
3. Identifying existing or probable impacts caused by new technology.
4. Ascertaining cause and effect relationships.
5. Exploring alternative technological methods for implementing programs.

---

[65]Pois, "Trends," p. 273.

6. Estimating and comparing the impacts that alternative technological methods and programs might have.

7. Reporting findings of completed analyses and identifying areas for further research.

The OTA has a regular staff of approximately 40 professionals, and is also authorized to draw on outside consultants and to contract out major portions of its research. Thus far the OTA has conducted major assessments in the fields of energy, health, food, materials, oceans, transportation, and world trade.[66]

The responsibilities and resources of the OTA provide additional potential for congressional oversight. It is intended to give congressional committees expertise and technical information that is independent of both executive agencies and the lobbies. Unfortunately, "the youthful OTA has not yet fulfilled its oversight potential."[67] Part of its problem may lie with its newness. It has also been overwhelmed with requests, receiving three to four times as many as it has the capacity to handle. In addition, OTA has an ambiguous task; analysis of its legislative history uncovered interpretations of technology assessments "varying from a definition that strictly implied the longrange forecasting of the economic, political and social side effects of new technological development, to a very broad concept that included analysis of any issue tht involved science and technology in any way, no matter how minor."[68] Clearly, such an ambiguous mandate and set of congressional expectations make it difficult for OTA to establish a strong role for technical and expert analysis of policy and administrative problems. It is quite possible for it to be overwhelmed by requests from congressional offices asking it to process constituent inquiries concerning science and technology.

OTA appears to have little direct contact with the federal agencies. Like the GAO and CRS, the work of OTA is also sub-

---

[66]On the OTA, see *Congressional Oversight of Regulatory Agencies*, pp. 69–70; E. B. Skomlikoff, "The Office of Technology Assessment," in *Congressional Support Agencies*, pp. 55–74.

[67]*Congressional Oversight of Regulatory Agencies*, p. 71.

[68]Skomlikoff, *op. cit.*, p. 58.

ject to the limitations of policy subsystems, especially those that have formed in the science and technology areas. A recent observer of OTA argues that:

> the strong political interests of congressional committees—who are the "clients" of OTA—render OTA reports, which strive for objectivity, vulnerable to political attack if their findings or implications conflict with deeply entrenched political currents in the Congress. The ability of OTA to survive in such a situation is not at all certain.[69]

THE CONGRESSIONAL BUDGET OFFICE
AND THE NEW BUDGET PROCESS

The newest of the staff agencies, the Congressional Budget Office, was created as part of the Congressional Budget and Impoundment Control Act of 1974. Mandated to assist Congress in creating a congressional budget, its fundamental responsibility is to provide budget data and analysis to the newly created budget committees of the Senate and House of Representatives. It is also mandated by law to furnish the Committees on Appropriations, Ways and Means, and Finance with information that they request and to assist them in fulfilling their legislative responsibilities. In addition, it is authorized to assist other congressional committees when time and resources permit. The utility of this office, with respect to oversight, depends on its ability to provide accurate, impartial financial data, to trace information from the executive, and to make budgetary information available to the Congress in an easily comprehensible, rapid, and intelligent manner.[70]

It is clear that the new budget process has altered the way that Congress goes about budget-making (and, through its rescission provisions, limited executive discretion in the use of appropriated funds). What has been rather neglected is the implications

---

[69]*Ibid.*, p. 61.
[70]On the Congressional Budget Office, see William M. Capron, "The Congressional Budget Office," *Congressional Support Agencies,* pp. 75–91; and *Congressional Oversight of Regulatory Agencies,* pp. 70–71.

the process holds for federal agencies and for the oversight role of Congress in the budgetary arena.[71]

One rather obvious effect of the congressional budget process has been to complicate the legislative environment in which agencies move. In addition to the authorizing and appropriating committees, they now face another set of committees—the Budget Committees—whose deliberations may affect them and their programs. In addition to facing the OMB, they now must deal with CBO. The resolutions offered by the budget committees and monitored by CBO have begun to influence the more familiar (and perhaps more stable) sets of committees that agencies have grown used to. A new set of congressional actors must be analyzed, a new set of member and staff relationships developed and cultivated. In addition to testifying before their legislative and appropriations subcommittees, agencies now may also appear on request before the Budget Committees and their task forces. Such appearances are especially likely if the agency is included in the major policy areas that the Budget Committees select for analysis. The House Budget Committee's task force on national defense matters, for example, has been particularly active.

The number of staff contacts between the House and Senate Budget Committees and the CBO on the one hand, and the agencies on the other, has steadily increased. Congressional staff appear to be soliciting information on budgetary matters directly from the agencies concerned, rather than requesting data from the Office of Management and Budget. Such requests for budget information have increased the workload of agency budget officers and legislative liaison officials—but coping with the stream of demands is seen by the agencies as necessary for

---

[71]Recent treatments of the congressional budget include Alan Schick, "The Battle of the Budget," in Harvey Mansfield, ed., *Congress Against the President* (New York: Praeger, 1976); Walter Williams, *Congress, Budget-Making, and Policy Analysis* (Seattle: Institute of Governmental Research, 1976); J. A. Thurber, "Clients and Analysts; Congressional Budget Reform and New Demands for Policy Analysis," *Policy Analysis,* Vol. 2., No. 2 (Spring, 1976), pp. 197–214.

maintaining good relationships with a set of new superiors on the Hill.[72]

Although the congressional budget has placed greater demands on the agencies, it has also given them new channels of communications to Congress in budgetary matters. An example of such reverse flow of information was offered by a staff member of the CBO. An agency in the functional area for which he was responsible approached the Office with what it felt represented an important new alternative to then-current programming. Agency officials visited the CBO, bringing along graphs, statistics, and slides—a "dog and pony show" in the words of the CBO official—that he and his staff found interesting. The division concerned later included this program in the analysis of alternatives in the functional budget area, and the proposal made its way into the deliberations of both Budget Committees. Other examples of agency initiatives being brought to the CBO and Budget Committee staffs are not uncommon.[73]

From the perspective of the agencies, the new Budget Committees and the CBO represent a kind of "third force" in budgetary matters, a force whose influence is difficult to predict in advance. And though this has complicated the agencies' relations with Congress, another quite important aspect of the process has helped "rationalize" the agencies' financial domain and allowed them to breathe somewhat more easily. This aspect concerns the mechanisms for controlling presidential impoundments that the Act provides. Under its provisions, the reader will recall, if the president wishes to "cancel" the budget authority (appropriations) passed by Congress, he may not simply block the obligation of funds (as the Nixon administration did in great measure) but must propose rescission legislation and secure its passage. And though the president may *delay* the commitment of appropriated monies until the end of the year, his request for such deferral is subject to veto by simple resolution of either house.

.As far as the agencies are concerned, these procedures for

[72]Authors' interviews.
[73]*Ibid.*

handling presidential restrictions on appropriated funds may be more important than those spelling out the new congressional role in budget formulation and approval. A common agency view is that the congressional budget is perhaps more important as a limitation of presidential and OMB powers in the realm of budget "execution" than as a restriction of presidential prerogatives in budgetary formulation. One budget office of an agency that had in the past been subjected to massive impoundments of its appropriated funds opined that the process had caused him and his colleagues to breathe a sigh of relief and had given a substantial boost to agency morale.[74]

An important set of questions revolves about the contribution of the congressional budget process to oversight of administration. Our tentative view is that as far as individual agencies are concerned, the process contributes only marginally, if that, to congressional surveillance of administration. True, the GAO has been granted expanded responsibilities under the Act for program analysis, and true, the legislative and appropriations committees have advanced their hearings to meet the burdens placed on them by the timetable the process necessitates. But few observers either on the Hill or in the agencies suggest that the congressional budget process has led directly to more intensive and enduring oversight.

However, there are several features of the congressional budget that may contribute to surveillance of administration more broadly construed. For one thing, the Congressional Budget Office and the Budget Committees represent two units of Congress that are not part of either the authorization or appropriations subsystems and at the same time are in a position to monitor agency activities; they represent another channel through which information concerning agency behavior may be fed into Congress. And the process tends to increase the visibility of the budget in nearly all its phases. The consideration of budget alternatives, especially, is placed squarely in the public domain for debate—a debate that previously was conducted

[74]*Ibid.*

largely in the relatively closed quarters of the White House, OMB, and agency budget offices.

The congressional budget, however, appears to be in danger of experiencing some of the same subsystem pressures that have surfaced in other aspects of congressional oversight. It has, indeed, the potential for affirming rather than threatening subgovernment dominance of policy. As a ranking official in CBO observed, the committees of Congress often have proved much more willing to make use of the analyses produced by CBO in the realms of evaluation of weapon systems, energy impacts, and health policies and problems than in those activities directly linked to the pork barrel. Here, he observed, "there is a limit to the amount of rational analysis the committees will buy."[75] Continued evidence that this may be the case is suggested by congressional reaction to the attempt by President Carter to eliminate a number of water development projects for the fiscal year 1978 budget—projects that "rational analysis" showed to be lacking in cost effectiveness. Although the budget process may help Congress regain a greater measure of control over the purse from the executive, it is not certain that it will tighten the purse strings around the distributive politics so firmly ensconced in many of its subsystems.

Casework and Congressional Liaison

The increased oversight efforts of Congress and the heightened attention of its members and committees to the federal bureaucracy have influenced bureaucratic structure and routine. Just as the rise of the administrative state has affected Congress—producing greater decentralization and enhancing subsystem politics—so have congressional efforts at policy surveillance affected departments and agencies. The extent of this impact is difficult to measure, yet two developments of the post-war years warrant special attention. They are the growth of congressional liaison within federal agencies and the latter's response to congressional requests for assistance with constituency problems—in short: casework.

[75]*Ibid.*

THE EMERGENCE OF CONGRESSIONAL LIAISON

The development of subcommittee government, as we have seen, has been accompanied by increasingly frequent use of new oversight devices and has hastened congressional demands for information and responses from administrative agencies. Congress has come to rely heavily on the agencies for information regarding proposed or existing legislation and for assistance in solving numerous casework problems forwarded by concerned committees and individual members. Casework, responses to congressional inquiries, testifying on the Hill, special reports and those required by statute, and other demands placed on the agencies have led to a vastly increased workload and the creation of more regularized channels for handling the flow of agency-congressional communications. One organizational response has been the development of the conduct of congressional liaison and its institutionalization in the congressional liaison office. The first of these offices began to emerge in the Departments of State and Defense in the late 1940s and had spread to all major departments by the early 1960s. The independent agencies of subcabinet stature were quick to follow suit, so that by the mid 1970s virtually all of them boasted a separate office charged with coordinating legislative relations.[76]

The typical congressional liaison office performs a variety of functions: coordinating testimony prepared for delivery before committees, providing a channel for agency responses to congressional inquiries, monitoring the development of the agency's programs and problems in Congress, providing such special services as speeches and tours for members, and so forth.[77] The workload of the congressional liaison offices is substantial and growing. During a recent fiscal year, even a relatively small agency such as the EPA testified nearly two hundred times be-

---

[76]General discussions of the development of the congressional liaison office may be found in G. Russell Pipe, "Congressional Liaison: The Executive Branch Consolidates its Relations with Congress," *Public Administration Review*, Vol. 26 (March, 1966), pp. 12–24; and Abraham Holtzman, *Legislative Liaison: Executive Leadership in Congress* (Chicago; Rand McNally, 1970), pp. 9–115.

[77]A study of the work of the liaison office on one agency may be found in Thomas P. Murphy, "Congressional Liaison: The NASA Case," *Western Political Quarterly*, Vol. 25, No. 2 (July, 1972), pp. 192–214.

fore 43 committees and subcommittees of the House and Senate.[78]

To an extent, the congressional liaison office represents a part of the congressional culture transplanted into executive departments and agencies. An interesting example of this phenomenon surfaced during a brief study of liaison offices made by one of the authors during the Ford administration. The example is drawn from the Department of Agriculture, one of the older departments and rather bureaucratic in its emphasis on the appropriate symbols of official position—carpeting, the appropriate executive-type wood desk, potted plants, and other perquisites of rank. Senior officials are generally accessible only through an anteroom guarded by senior secretaries or aides. The four departmental liaison officers in Agriculture—all high-ranking political appointees—had, however, violated most of the norms of officeholding. They had taken one large room together, each with one desk in a corner, and would shout across the room about problems, upcoming bills, and so on, often with feet on the desk, a phone in one hand—all while answering the questions posed by the interviewer. These men, all with previous experience on the Hill, had duplicated in the staid corridors of Agriculture a little microcosm of the crowded congressional staff office.[79]

It is clear that the creation of the congressional liaison office has helped increase the visibility of congressional activity within executive agencies and provided an institutionalized mechanism for dealing with congressional demands. But although it provides helpful services for members of Congress and enables the agency to track its fortunes on the Hill, the congressional liaison office was not created by the executive as a generous gesture of goodwill toward the legislature. (This is not to say that the goodwill it produces for the agency is not a factor in its continued development.) We view the creation of such offices essentially as one of the first attempts by the president and his senior officials to try to counter the growth of subsystem politics and its

[78]Authors' interviews.
[79]*Ibid.*

tendency to draw the executive agencies away from presidential control into the whirlpools of subgovernments. Through the creation of legislative liaison, the president and departments have been given an organizational weapon with which to try to combat subsystem politics. Several students of legislative liaison argue that its primary *raison d'etre* was to strengthen executive control over the growing interpenetration of agencies and bureaus on the one hand and committees and subcommittees on the other. As one scholar has suggested:

> *Responsible for advancing their department's legislative program within the context of the President's, departmental leaders were confronted in their own bailiwicks with well-established, traditional bureau-congressional relations, which were not necessarily receptive to White House or departmental priorities. The secretaries of departments found it imperative, therefore, to establish their own staffs, first for legislative programming . . . and finally for legislative liaison.*[80]

This attempt, however, to control the centrifugal tendencies of bureaus as they are pulled outward by congressional attraction has not, in our judgment, been particularly successful. Congress may have received more in the way of agency services and responsiveness than the executive has received in the way of a mechanism to influence and control subsystem politics. There are several reasons why this may be the case. One concerns the often conflicting roles of agency members working in congressional liaison. They not only represent their agency and its positions to Congress, but must also try to make known congressional perspectives and attitudes to their agency as it attempts to deal with its legislative masters. An effective liaison officer must possess empathy for both worlds to which he or she relates. Moreover, a number of these individuals have had considerable experience on the hill, either as members of Congress or as their aides. Holtzman's study of liaison officials in eight departments found that a majority had previously served as members of Congress or its staff. More than one of the liaison officials questioned expressed some ambivalence about their dual responsibilities. One went so far as to suggest that he would not push

[80]Holtzman, *op. cit.*, p. 6.

strongly legislation he felt the relevant committee opposed, as
this might damage his relationships with committee members. "I
am not," he asserted, "going to sell my friends in the Congress a
bill I do not agree on."[81]

In addition to the often ambivalent position of some congressional liaison officials is the fact of life that, as political appointees, they may be treated with suspicion, even hostility by the
agency's career civil servants and bureau chiefs—a suspicion en-
gendered by the conflict between the political and bureaucratic
cultures. Tension between liaison and career officials may be
exacerbated because part of the job of the liaison officials is to
attempt to loosen the bonds between congressional subcommittees and bureau heads that have been forged over the years. A
number of liaison officers in Holtzman's study viewed the career
bureaucracy with "a mixture of suspicion as to their motives;
contempt, in part, for its lack of political astuteness; fear for the
political deals it could arrange with an all too cooperative Congress."[82]

Animosity toward the career civil service on the part of liaison
officials was also uncovered by our own discussions with several
of those serving in the Ford administration. Here the tension
was increased by the fact that in many cases, the ideological
center of gravity of the bureaucrats was to the left of the Republican liaison appointees. The liaison officers in the Department
of Agriculture described above expressed a particular frustration with a civil service one of them called "eighty to ninety
percent Democratic-liberal," and complained that it was almost
impossible to "keep on top" of the dozen or so bureaus that
make up the department.

It should be added that bureaucratic resistance to the liaison
function may be stiffened by the congressional members of a
particular policy subsystem. Members are prone to maintain the
old established lines into the bureaucracy and are not often sanguine about attempts by political appointees of a particular administration to attempt to draw the reins into their own hands.

[81]*Ibid.*, pp. 89, 196.
[82]*Ibid.*, p. 123.

This does not suggest that bureaus and liaison offices are always at loggerheads. Cooperation is probably the rule rather than the exception, especially where bureau and departmental policy positions are similar or identical. But even though the liaison office may have made some impact on the authorization or legislative subsystem, it appears that the influence of liaison officials on the appropriations process, both within the agency and in Congress, is minimal. As a rule, agency liaison officials do not get involved in budget formulation or administration; budgetary matters are usually handled by a budget office or division (known colloquially as the "budget shop"), which is staffed almost exclusively by careerists. Liaison officials may often discover strong (perhaps inpenetrable) ties between bureaus and the relevant appropriations subcommittee, and on more than one occasion have been given the cold shoulder when attempting to cultivate members of appropriations subcommittees.[83] While agency congressional liaison, in short, may have made some impact (though minimal) in the agency's relations with legislative committees, it has yet to become involved effectively in the appropriations subsystem.

In sum, the congressional liaison office, perhaps the primary organizational expression at the agency level of executive response to developments in Congress, probably falls somewhat short of its intended mark. Although created to coordinate and monitor the flow of contacts between bureaus and agencies and congressional committees and individual members, the congressional liaison office has probably done more to rationalize a process for facilitating agency responses to congressional requests and to provide a convenient point of access for congressional needs for information and service than to weaken the traditional ties of subsystem politics or to enforce an "agency" (as opposed to a bureau) position on the Hill. The particular impact of the congressional liaison function, granted, depends on the complexity of an agency's legislative environment and on the multitude of factors discussed earlier that impinge on the relation-

---

[83]See Pipe, *op. cit.*, p. 20; Holtzman, *op. cit.*, p. 73; James Robinson, *Congress and Foreign Policy Making* (Homewood, Ill.: Dorsey Press, 1967), p. 131.

ship between an agency and Congress. But the effectiveness of the congressional liaison office as a device to gain policy and program leadership for the executive is certainly open to question. It is doubtful that a Congress dominated by subcommittee government would allow such an attempt to succeed if success threatened to endanger the congressional position in subsystem politics.

AGENCIES AND CONGRESSIONAL CASEWORK

The second major development within the administrative state during the post-war years is the rise of its role in assisting members of Congress in responding to inquiries and complaints from constituents—casework. A substantial proportion of constituent inquiries concerns problems an individual has encountered with federal agencies. Since an effective response by the legislator to such complaints is often crucial to his or her image and reelection, agencies involved in such complaints are central to the congressional caseload. From all accounts, complaints have exploded during the post-war years, leading members of Congress increasingly to seek help from the bureaucracy.

Congressional calls for assistance in casework are taken quite seriously by the agencies concerned. In most if not all cases, a constituent inquiry forwarded by a member of Congress is given priority attention; in some, it is automatically given high-level review.[84] Especially in agencies such as the Department of State that have little or no public constituency, there is a strong desire to be as responsive as possible to congressional case referrals. State, for example, places a high priority on such responses; in its corridors, one often sees a young Foreign Service officer hurrying by with a large, blue-bordered file marked "Congressional" to seek clearances from the bureaus concerned. Part of the emphasis placed on handling congressional inquiries in State comes from the (possibly mistaken) assumption that "the more satisfactorily it handles constituent-initiated requests, the more

[84]For case analyses of agency responses to such casework referrals, see Walter Gellhorn, *When Americans Complain* (Cambridge: Harvard University Press, 1966), pp. 57–130.

likely it is to obtain the support of members [of Congress] on policy."[85]

The burdens that congressional casework referrals place on the agencies are substantial. Normal routines may be disrupted while an official, or several, drops ongoing work to dig into the details of a particular case. As one student of the process observes:

> The artificially high priority accorded congressional . . . mail slows other business. Those aggrieved may then write the President or a Congressman to complain about delay in matters of interest to complainants—and thus the wheel is given another spin. Since a communication's importance seems to be appraised more by its source than by its content, the picayune often takes precedence over the profound.

Agency officials often view the effort devoted to casework as less than productive, feel the legislator concerned passes them the buck on a number of cases that are without merit, and consider the whole process more a distraction than a legitimate responsibility. As one liaison official complained: "This job would be the greatest ever if it were not for this constituent crap. I get buckets of it and have to handle it."[86]

Despite the burdens and disruptions that casework creates for executive agencies, the argument is often made that the ombudsman role inherent in the handling of casework plays an important role in the ability of Congress to monitor bureaucratic behavior and to discover incidents of maladministration that would otherwise go unchecked. It is true that agency responses to constituent complaints provide members of Congress with insights into agency activity they might otherwise not obtain. Moreover, there is some evidence that in processing casework, agencies become sensitized to problems occurring at the middle and lower levels of the bureaucracy (those levels that affect the citizen most directly) and even search for patterns behind the complaints.[87] And there is evidence that problems uncovered as

[85]Robinson, op. cit., p. 162.
[86]Quoted in Ogul, op. cit., p. 173.
[87]Gellhorn, op. cit., pp. 106–114.

a result of casework referrals occasionally provide a stimulus for the introduction of corrective legislation.[88]

On balance, however, it appears that casework referrals, as an oversight device, are largely ineffective. One reason is that agency responses to inquiries are usually handled at the same level of the agency (often by the same official) where the complaint arose in the first place. Supervisors may be reluctant to do much more than pass the answer back up the line for submission to the referring member of Congress. Moreover, agency officials may treat an obviously spurious complaint with the same insincerity as did the member who originally forwarded it. The member then may pass along the agency response to the complainant, content to have "processed" another case.

One experienced congressional staffer volunteered that only a third of congressional offices attempted to follow up the results of case referrals in any systematic way. Many cases, he asserted, "are just handled on a routine basis without any regard for political problems that emerge, simply with regard to handling the cases."[89] This may occur because occasions of actual maladministration are a small fraction of the referrals to agencies. Gellhorn estimated, for example, that of casework problems sent by members of Congress to the agencies, only about ten percent appeared to be serious enough to warrant a change in the agency's previous decision or action to one more favorable to the complainant.[90] Thus the fact that casework referrals only infrequently lead to hearings or the introduction of corrective legislation may be due not only to the modicum of attention paid to agency complaint patterns but also to the possibility that the agencies may be doing a better and fairer job than the volume of constituent complaints would suggest.

The chief drawback to using casework as a strong device for monitoring executive agencies involves the motivations of individual members. Casework is important because it is vital to the image of the member—that he or she is responding to con-

[88]Ogul, *op. cit.*, pp. 170–171.
[89]*Ibid.*, p. 165.
[90]Gellhorn, *op. cit.*, p. 79.

stituents, acting, getting something done. Here action tends to speak more loudly than the words agencies write in response to inquiries; getting the case processed is more important than the use of a number of cases in developing a pattern of agency performance or lack thereof. What oversight *does* result is often a kind of by-product rather than a calculated effort.

Conclusion

We come now to an assessment of the impact of congressional reforms and oversight techniques on the administrative state. In the previous chapter, we suggested that the rise of subcommittee government has exacerbated three problems that Congress faces in oversight of the executive: (1) a reduction in the bargaining power of Congress vis-à-vis agencies and bureaus; (2) the lack of adequate information about agency activities; and (3) the influence of special interest groups. Given that the oversight reforms of the 1970s and the development and expansion of various oversight techniques were designed in part to address these deficiencies, how effective have they been?

Overall, we find that although the amount of oversight activity has increased, its effectiveness is open to serious question. We would argue that the total impact of the use of the range of surveillance techniques discussed above is probably much weaker and less effective than generally assumed. Oversight has often been overridden by considerations quite external to the problem of agency control; and it is not surprising that the administrative state—though sensitive to new congressional attempts at control—has not come to view its legislative master(s) with fear and trembling. The "domain" of congressional concerns within agencies, their attention to them, and the importance of the institutional link provided by the congressional liaison function have of course increased in the past several decades, but it is not necessarily the case that the impact of congressional oversight has increased as a result. Indeed, perhaps the range of oversight techniques developed by Congress since

World War II has merely allowed it to stay abreast of (or cope with) the expansion of agency activities and programs rather than representing a step forward toward improved surveillance.

A basic reason for this situation is the inability (or refusal) of Congress to reorganize fundamentally its oversight function. Responsibility for oversight has remained scattered among a maze of committees and subcommittees and among a plethora of competing subsystems. Especially the struggle between the authorization and appropriations subsystems is a critical weakness in the congressional oversight process. We have found, for example, that both annual authorizations and committee vetos have been used on more than one occasion not to restrict agency discretion but rather to strengthen the hand of the legislative committees against the appropriations committees. Conversely, the latter have refined the use of nonstatutory techniques as a counterfoil to the encroachments of the legislative committees. And both appropriations and authorizing committees have used "oversight" devices to defend "their" agencies and programs against the overhead control eminating from the institutionalized presidency—making common cause in weakening presidential surveillance of the federal bureaucracy without necessarily substituting their own. Within the subsystems themselves, techniques commonly considered in discussions of oversight—annual authorizations, the committee veto version of the legislative veto, nonstatutory controls, and so on—have been converted to (or in fact applied as) mechanisms whose use suggests that agency surveillance may be only one (and perhaps a minor one) of the reasons why they are employed. As a result of the jurisdictional complexity typical of oversight efforts, the existence of competing committees and subsystems, and the lack of strong central oversight mechanisms, Congress has not been able to improve its bargaining position vis-à-vis federal agencies.

As regards the second goal of congressional reform efforts, there appears little doubt that Congress has succeeded in improving its system of information gathering. It has adopted statutes that force the bureaucracy to release information. And it has expanded the functions of the congressional resource agencies that gather and analyze information. But here, too, Congress has failed—not in upgrading its capacity to elicit information from the federal bureaucracy, but in failing to create a structure within Congress that can act on this information in a decisive and coherent manner.

The resource agencies of Congress cannot make up for the lack of coordination of subcommittee oversight. Nor can they draft and act on legislation that would address the deficiencies they uncover. We have seen, on the contrary, that the outputs of such staff agencies as the CRS, the OTA, and the GAO are largely informational in character and may be rather easily vitiated by actions (or the inaction) of committees and subcommittees hostile to them. The staff agencies, and the Committees on Government Operations as well, function largely outside the various subsystems, and their work can often be ignored or frustrated by subsystem members—especially where agencies and subcommittees make common cause against them. Tendencies for such alliances to be forged and maintained appear especially pronounced where the subsystems are heavily involved in policies that are primarily distributive in nature and where the pork barrel is an overriding concern. Even in the broader arena of regulatory policy, there is evidence of the continued endurance of subsystem alliances, especially where there is room for the interests and groups regulated to exert continuing pressure on the agencies that regulate them.

As we have observed, the reluctance of Congress to reform its oversight structure stems in large measure from the fear that such reform would weaken subcommittee government and thus the power positions it offers individual members. This reluctance appears reinforced by the play of special interests. Indeed, interest groups generally find subcommittee government to their advantage, and its rise over the past decades has strengthened subsystem politics and with it the access of lobbyists to the Congress.

The reforms of the 1970s, however, have done little to restrict the power of lobbies or to threaten their role in subsystem politics. The failure to strengthen the committees on government operations left responsibility for oversight in the hands of committees and subcommittees that are central actors in the various subsystems. The failure to pass stringent lobby laws, together with inadequate campaign finance and ethics legislation, have left the lobbies in a strong position.[91] We doubt that Congress will be able to reform its oversight structure in a meaningful way until it places responsibility for oversight in a committee or set of committees that are independent of subsystem politics and the access to special interests it provides.

Thus in each of the three problem areas facing Congress as it attempts to conduct oversight—its position in relation to agencies and bureaus, its access to information, and the influence of special interests—Congress has failed to provide meaningful and effective solutions. Nor is effective oversight reform possible so long as the pull of subcommittee government is stronger than the desire to assure effective implementation of public policy. Admittedly, we paint with broad strokes, and our rather skeptical view of recent oversight developments rests on generalizations that need further exploration and refinement. But we believe that more intensive work by other scholars in the area of congressional-administrative relations will bear us out. With those of a contrary persuasion, we would welcome debate.

The developments in Congress traced in this and previous chapters have made their influence felt in the corridors of the federal bureaucracy. The emergence of congressional liaison and the growth of a casework bureaucracy are two phenomena we have briefly discussed. The rise of subcommittee government, however, has affected not only the structure of administrative agencies but also their procedures for making and implementing public policy—in ways both subtle and profound. The shape of the policy process in the federal bureaucracy, as a result, is remarkably similar to Congress under subcommittee

[91]On the continued role of lobbyists, see Norman J. Ornstein and Shirley Elder, *Interest Groups, Lobbying and Policy Making* (Washington, D.C.: Congressional Quarterly, Inc., 1978).

government and exhibits many of the same characteristics and problems. Like Congress, it is highly decentralized and, in spite of a strong institutionalized presidency, it remains relatively uncoordinated.

The downward shift in the power centers of Congress from committees to subcommittees has apparently strengthened the position of bureaus and other lesser administrative units below the agency or departmental level. And, as we have seen, the proliferation of oversight devices may have weakened even further the already tenuous links between the career bureaucracy and its political leadership. We now turn to these and related issues.

7

Public Policy and the Administrative State

Introduction

In the preceding pages, we have watched Congress attempt to tackle some basic problems it has faced with the growth of national government—problems of congressional leadership, of accountability, of coordination and insulation. And we have examined at some length the range of issues that confront Congress in its role as overseer of the federal bureaucracy. We have argued earlier that for Congress to fulfill its constitutional role as a national legislature, it must be able to develop policy without undue influence from the bureaucracy and be able to ensure that the policies its adopts are in fact carried out. We have found, however, that the independence of Congress in these regards is far from assured; it has difficulty both in developing policy independently of the executive branch and in supervising its implementation.

How has the partial vacuum created by developments in Congress affected the role of the administrative state in the arena of public policy? Are the overhead controls that Congress has given the president sufficient compensation for the weakness of its own oversight mechanisms? Is the bureaucracy sufficiently responsive to Congress (and to the public), or are stronger oversight devices called for? And does the bureaucracy, in its approach to policy development and implementation, face problems of leadership, coordination, and insulation similar to those of Congress? The answers to such questions, tentative though they may be, are central to an evaluation of the relationship between Congress and the administrative state.

The intent of this chapter is to give the reader a broad overview of the policy process in the executive branch and of some of the major factors that condition it. We cannot examine this process as closely as we have with Congress, but we do hope to give the reader a feel for the policy dynamics of the administrative state—especially as they are affected by recent changes in Congress. We turn first to some general comments on the policy process in the bureaucracy and the context in which it occurs. We move next to examine how different "kinds" of policies may be handled in different ways and then to an analysis and evaluation of the effectiveness of overhead leadership and coordination of policy by the institutionalized presidency. We conclude with a consideration of how democratic the administrative state appears to be and the effectiveness of existing controls over it.

The Bureaucracy and Public Policy: Some Preliminary Observations

As Congress has expanded the scope and functions of national government, it has found it increasingly necessary to delegate substantial legislative powers to federal agencies. Statutes creating agencies and programs establish the broad parameters in which they operate, but the details of how policy is to be administered is generally left to bureaucratic discretion. Agencies refine and "translate" policy into action through rules, regulations, and procedures that themselves have the force of law. This "sublegislation" is essentially the unfolding of policy through administrative process. And in this respect, federal agencies probably make more "law" than Congress does.

With the growth of national government, Congress has entrusted agencies with this sublegislation not only out of necessity, but also because it is in the bureaucracy where the expertise and professional competence for program execution resides. That very expertise that is so valuable in implementing policy also shoves the bureaucracy into the arena of policymaking. Long experience and mastery of a particular policy area and its problems often lead officials to generate proposals for change, for new or different approaches to public problems. Offices, bureaus, even whole agencies, as well as individual bureaucrats, tend to become policy advocates, not merely policy executors.

Agencies of the administrative state also enter the policy fray by virtue of their representative functions. Indeed, as we saw in an earlier chapter, some departments and agencies have been purposely organized around certain economic or group interests and act as advocates or spokesmen for their constituents—the Departments of Agriculture and of Labor and the Office of Education are prime examples. This representative function of the bureaucracy, coupled with constituent advocacy, tends to thrust agencies foursquare into the policy process.

One must not draw too sharp a distinction, however, between policymaking on the one hand and policy execution or implementation on the other. The simple fact is that the "application" of policy very often involves shadings or refinements that are themselves interpretive or "policymaking" in nature. Indeed, one can visualize the function of the executive branch in the public policy arena as the successive refinement, interpretation, and application of policy mandates or guidelines—broad or narrow—emanating both from the Congress and from the president. Granted, there are some organs of the executive branch designed to *create* policy—the Council of Economic Advisors and the National Security Council come to mind. But for the most part, in its elaboration and ramification of policy, the administrative state is making a series of successive limited decisions that bring the overhead intent of the major policy bodies—Congress and the president—to focus on a single individual, group of individuals, or case. In so doing, policy is both tested and applied. As Paul Appleby suggested long ago, "executives do not sit at two different desks, treating policy at one and administration at another. Even intellectually, they more often deal with them as exclusively problems of policy or problems of administration. A detailed analysis of jobs at each hierarchical level would show, it is believed, the same close relationships between policy-making and policy execution at each level of administrative hierarchy."[1]

The administrative state is thus involved in policymaking by the very nature of administration itself. But there is another way in which the federal bureaucracy contributes to policymaking, flowing from the fact that the insights and experiences of seasoned bureaucrats often find their way into the upper echelons of the institutionalized presidency and into the committees of Congress. That is, *bureaucratic* initiatives and proposals often form a basis for legislative initiative, for the introduction of specific pieces of "agency legislation," or for presidential initiatives in the assembling of what eventually becomes the "administration's" program. But the reader should bear in mind that in the day-to-day work of the bureaucracy, policy implementation is often difficult to separate from policymaking; from the perspective of the individual bureaucrat, "policy" may simply be what goes on above him or her in the organization, while "administration" is that which takes place below.

The Policy Process in Context: Bureau Government

It is probably inaccurate to speak of "the" policy process in the federal executive branch. Instead, one might conceive more easily of a number of policy *processes,* each differing to some extent from the next. This results from a variety of reasons, including the "type" of policy involved, the nature of the organization or agency, the extent to which the policy is old and hoary or new and innovative, the number, kinds, and status of persons who may participate in a particular set of policy decisions, and so forth. We examine these factors and their influence on policy leadership and control later in this chapter, but the reader should guard against the assumption that there is any one

---

[1]Paul H. Appleby, *Policy and Administration* (University, Ala.: University of Alabama Press, 1949, 1975), p. 19.

paradigm or model that can apply to the implementation of all policies in all policy arenas at all times.

The policy process in the executive branch appears at times to be as truncated, disparate, and pluralistic as in our national legislature. Both Congress and the bureaucracy exhibit many of the same characteristics that surround their respective policy processes and, hence, many of the same problems. There are a number of parallels between the way Congress approaches policy formation and the way the executive branch approaches policy implementation. The executive branch is not really a strict hierarchy in which decisions at the top are passed down the chain of command, but is instead pluralistic, with a number of competing centers of power and expertise, each with their own institutional histories, norms, and outside power bases— analogous to the numerous power centers of Congress that have proliferated with the development of full subcommittee government. If the national legislature can be termed, as we suggest, "subcommittee government," then perhaps it is not too farfetched to suggest that the executive branch, in its implementation of public policy, may be conceived of essentially as "bureau government." Let us now turn to a closer examination of these and related themes.

For both members of Congress and the federal bureaucracy, government is a career—in contrast to the "in and out" patterns typical of the political appointees who head federal departments and agencies. Members of Congress, driven at least in part by the motive of reelection, tend to make their careers in one or two committees and (especially in the House) subcommittees. The committee, not the Congress as a whole, is the focal point for most members of the legislature. Likewise, officials in the bureaucracy, especially those near the top, are motivated by a combination of a desire for security and a drive for advancement, and *their* careers are generally developed in one agency, or more significantly, in one bureau of that agency. They identify with their agency or career service, not with the executive branch as a whole. Their career patterns are such that members of Congress and of the bureaucracy tend to become, over time, subject matter specialists (though granted that the specialization of the bureaucrat is much more intense). Longevity, organizational locus, and relative expertise tend to provide common bonds between members of Congress and senior public servants: they are generally better informed and simply around longer than the senior political appointees of any administration.

That "legislative work" that is one of the accepted folkways of Congress finds a corollary in what might be termed "bureaucratic work" in the executive branch. Although there are instances of bureaucratic careers being built on simple tenaciousness or on serendipity, those who aspire to the top levels of the bureaucracy must generally have proved to their superiors that they are capable of long hours, and of mastering the details of a particular substantive or functional speciality. And it is at the bureau level of an agency, not at its top, where bureaucratic careers are nurtured and controlled.[2]

Another similarity is the tremendous organizational variety found both in Congress and in the executive branch. Each congressional committee and subcommittee is often a world into itself, guided by distinctive norms and values, and attracting certain kinds of members to it. Subcommittee government, as we have observed, is characterized by decentralization and pluralism. It goes almost without saying that organizational diversity and complexity is also characteristic of American bureaucracy. This diversity is, of course, largely a result of congressional action. The way in which a department or agency has been structured by the Congress helps one understand why certain policies are developed and administered as they are, as well as the relative importance of the roles of Congress and the president in their supervision.

In terms of organizational structure, one can conceive of a continuum of executive branch agencies based on their proximity to the president at the one end and the Congress at the other. Closest to the president and generally under his more or less direct control are the elements of his Executive Office. Although some of these units, such as the Council of Economic Advisors,

[2]See, among others, Hugh Heclo, *A Government of Strangers: Executive Politics in Washington* (Washington: Brookings Institution, 1977), p. 116.

are statutory creations, Congress has generally allowed the president relatively free reign in structuring the Executive Office. Most of the Executive Office elements, unlike the major departments and agencies, have no real constituency apart from the president and his own immediate advisors. For the most part, these units are designed to provide expert advice to the president (the Council of Economic Advisors), to coordinate high-level presidential decisionmaking in certain policy areas (the National Security Council), or assist him in the overall management and policy guidance of the executive branch (the Office of Management of Budget).

The workhorses of the administrative state are, of course, the main line departments and agencies, which employ the vast bulk of federal officials. The lines of control over these agencies run from the president to a single agency head at the top. Presidential policy directives are supposedly carried down the chain of command and into the career bureaucracy by the several layers of political appointees under each agency head or departmental secretary.

A third category of executive branch units is the regulatory commissions, which are multi-headed rather than single-headed agencies. These commissions are traditionally considered by Congress to have a special relationship with that body. Because they perform functions that are quasi-legislative and quasi-judicial in nature, Congress, by providing for a plural executive structure and for commissioners from both major parties, has decoupled the commissions from overhead presidential control—in contrast to the more traditional hierarchial structure exhibited by the departments and agencies. The multi-headed executive form is also used in cases where Congress has, for special reasons, decided to place executive units somewhat outside the immediate chain of command leading up to the president; the National Science Board of the National Science Foundation and the boards of various governmental corporations are examples. By determining the leadership structure of bureaucratic organizations, in sum, Congress may prescribe the extent to which they are subject to or partially immune from overhead presidential control as well as from the constituencies and clientile that they serve.[3]

Given the organizational diversity of the executive branch and of the congressional committee structure, there may be certain broad parallels between them. One recalls Richard Fenno's typology of congressional committees, which distinguishes among those whose members are concerned largely with ideology, those which attract members seeking power and position, and those that attract members because they can serve important constituency groups.[4] Although the typology is not immediately applicable to the executive branch, one can, for example, point to departments like Labor and Agriculture that are largely constituency agencies; to the Office of Management and Budget, the White House office, and the Justice Department, which often wield substantial power; and to such units as the Office of Education, the Community Services Administration, and HUD, where policy concerns run high. This is not to argue that typologies of congressional committees can be applied directly to an analysis of the executive branch, but it does serve to underscore the substantial variety in the organization and culture of both Congress and the bureaucracy. Like those surrounding committees of Congress, such cultures and norms can and do affect the way in which bureaucratic officials view their jobs, plan their strategies, and make basic decisions.

Another characteristic common to the way in which Congress and the executive branch approach policy, and one whose influence is probably underestimated, is the conflict among organizational units or subunits and, as one result, the amount of decisionmaking that occurs through bargaining and compromise rather than by fiat. We have discussed earlier conflicts over jurisdiction that have accompanied the rise of subcommittee government. Tension and conflict over decisions and policy

[3]These basic differences of organizational type are discussed in Harold Seidman, *Politics, Position and Power* (New York: Oxford University Press, 1975), pp. 221–263.

[4]Richard Fenno, *Congressmen in Committees* (Boston: Little Brown, 1973), pp. 1–14.

jurisdictions are also typical of the executive branch—largely because Congress has often been reluctant to consolidate all aspects of a given policy area within one executive branch department or agency. Pieces of the action are often spread out among numerous agencies of the federal government, and stories of conflict over "policy space" and protection of one's turf are rife in the literature of bureaucracy.

Congress has often contributed further to this competition by requiring that agencies, before they act, take into account positions held by other agencies. Numerous statutes provide for consultation and review by designated agencies before major policy decisions can be made. The amount of *lateral* decisionmaking that takes place in the executive branch is substantial. And overlaping agency jurisdictions, in a way reminiscent of Congress, suggest that bargaining, coalition-building, and consensus are often the way in which the administrative work of the public gets done. One of the leading scholars of the federal bureaucracy argues that "in many ways policy making within the executive agencies is indistinguishable from the process which takes place within legislative assemblies . . . bargaining or the adjustment of conflicting interests is as constant a feature of administrative politics as it is of relations among legislators and legislative committees."[5] In sum, the organizational variety and complexity of the executive branch, and the multiplicity of agencies involved in policy implementation, implies that bargaining—and not administrative fiat—is as much a hallmark of the bureaucratic process as of the legislative.

Equally important to an understanding of the context of policy is the variety of bureaucratic subcultures that exist in federal agencies. It could be argued that these subcultures and their interactions help shape and determine the output of federal administration as much or more than does a particular organization design. To a large extent these subcultures are based on the functional specialities of administration—program management, budgeting, administrative law, personnel management,

[5]Francis E. Rourke, *Bureaucracy, Politics and Public Policy* (Boston: Little Brown, 1976), p. 127.

and so forth. The common designation given to many of these units is the "shop"—for example, the "budget shop" or the "personnel shop" or the "planning shop." These various occupational subcultures, often reinforced by the professional specialities of those involved, appear in nearly all agencies of the executive branch. To a substantial extent, the conflict within organizations and bureaus over policy implementation reflects a jockeying for position among those groups.

A basic potential conflict is that between program managers on the one hand and agency budget officials on the other. Program officers, responsible for the management of various federal activities, often tend to push for an expansion for their programs, while the budget officials caution restraint and parsimony and often urge a narrower or stricter interpretation of which activities are consistent with legislative intent. (This phenomenon is often a reflection of the tension in Congress between the authorization committees on the one hand and the appropriations committees and subcommittees on the other.) The legitimate lines of control over program direction, from the program managers' point of view, run upwards into the political echelons of agency leadership and into the authorization committees of Congress; indeed, it is here that "bureaucratic imperialism" is often most evident. The agency budget officials, on the other hand, see their lines of authority running upwards to the budget offices at the agency or department level, and ultimately into the recesses of the Office of Management and Budget and to the appropriations subcommittees of Congress.

Agency budget officials are often perceived by program managers as green-eyeshaded misers, whereas the program officials are seen by the later as wild-eyed spenders who have little regard for the public purse. In many executive departments, an office of grants and contracts acts as a buffer between program officials seeking expansion and budget officers emphasizing restraint. Thus the funding decisions proposed by program managers must often pass through several layers of contract and grant review before they become a reality. The power of the budget subculture is given additional clout because in many programs the right to "obligate" federal funds lies not with the program managers but with the budget staff. It is not uncommon, however, for an agency program official, overruled on an item of expenditure by "his" budget shop, to appeal to program officials above in his chain of command with the hope that "their" budget officials will overrule their inferiors and allow the necessary obligations. Thus many policy and program decisions in the federal bureaucracy are the outcome of bargaining and negotiating between these two basic agency subcultures.

In addition to the competition between the program and budget subcultures, there are the perspectives and positions taken by the legal shops, most commonly housed in an office of the General Counsel, but in many cases dispersed among various operating units and divisions. It is generally here where early interpretations of relevant statutes are made, and certainly here where rules and regulations to be proposed by the agency (i.e., sublegislation) receive their initial review and clearance. Legal sections are relied on heavily for interpretations of congressional intent and on occasion act as in-house referees between program and budget officials when a proposed activity may be of hazy legality in either the authorization or appropriations legislation to which the agency is subject.

With the continued increase in regulation and rule making, and especially the creation of additional regulatory agencies, the role of the legal profession in the administrative state has increased substantially. It has been further augmented by the requirements for due process in administrative proceedings required by the Administrative Procedure Act and as well by "government-in-the-sunshine" provisions and the rights of citizens to records and documents of the agency under the Freedom of Information Act and its amendments. Attorneys, faithful to their training and the law, may tend to lean against a "flexible" interpretation of statutes, and are probably an important source of that incrementalism that seems to pervade the administrative process so thoroughly.

Another subculture within administrative agencies is based on the personnel shop. Since the individuals recruited to an agency bring with them biases and perspectives on policy and its implementation, personnel office control over who is hired (and fired) represents yet another policy force within administrative agencies. Although personnel offices conduct their work under civil service rules, they are generally allowed wide discretion. In numerous agencies in which professionals bulk large, the personnel operations have been "captured" by the professions in question;[6] they thus have a substantial influence on what kinds of individuals are recruited and, consequently, the approach their agencies take to policy implementation. In addition to the personnel subculture are others—among them units associated with program evaluation, audit, and public information, and, as we have discussed in the previous chapter, congressional liaison.

Complicating this already complex mix of bureaucratic subcultures is the fact that most agencies are not only part of the Washington bureaucracy, but have regional and district offices spread throughout the country. That nearly 90 percent of federal civil servants are employed outside Washington, D.C., suggests an almost rampant geographic decentralization of the federal executive branch. Compounding the problem of policy coordination and control within an agency's Washington office is the myriad of perspectives and regional pressures that the field elements of an agency may bring to bear. Such federal domestic programs as education, community development, housing, and transportation are administered largely in the field. And as the federal government has turned increasingly to the states and local governments as instrumentalities of policy implementation, the role of district and regional offices has grown commensurately. These geographical subdivisions of agencies and departments, subject as they are to local and regional pressures, add their own peculiar flavor to the already complex problem of administration.

Bureaucracy and the Policy Process

Keeping in mind the caution made earlier that the role of the bureaucracy in policymaking is seldom completely distinct from its role in policy implementation or administration, it is

[6]See Frederick C. Mosher, *Democracy in the Public Service* (New York: Oxford University Press, 1968) pp. 124–125.

nevertheless helpful for purposes of analysis to examine these roles separately. For purposes of discussion, let us visualize first the part that bureaucracy plays in the development of policy, then turn later to its role in the implementation of policy.

Figure 7-1 is a simple model of the place of bureaucratic agencies in policy development and formulation. The solid lines in the figure represent the flow of legislative proposals and actual legislation; the dotted lines represent the transmission of advice and information related to the development of policy but not actually legislation per se. The bureau, as the model suggests, is often a rich source of legislative proposals both upwards into the political echelons of agency leadership and laterally into the Congress. Those forwarded upwards may actually come at the request of the agency leadership (possibly at presidential urging) or may be initiatives from the bureaucracy for new legislation or amendments to existing authority. They may be part of a developing presidential program or, as "agency bills," be the result of bureaucratic stimulus.

Agency bills or proposals which are initiated by the bureaus

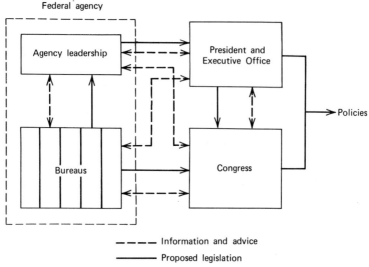

Figure 7-1. The role of federal agencies in policy development.

are usually reviewed by the agency leadership and if acceptable, are forwarded to the Office of Management and Budget in the Executive Office. The OMB examines the proposal, consults with other agencies affected, makes a determination whether the proposal is consistent with the president's programme, and either holds it back or consents to its being sent to the Hill.[7] Agency legislative proposals that are produced at presidential request follow largely the same route as agency bills. As the solid line between the president/executive office box and Congress suggests, they are generally forwarded formally to Congress as part of the administration's program.

As the line in the figure running from the bureaus to Congress indicates, legislative proposals can also flow laterally between the two institutions. Part of this flow may represent bureau proposals that are blocked at the agency or OMB review level, and there are instances of bureau proposals that have been turned down "upstairs" appearing mysteriously on the desk of a member of Congress or surfacing as a staff suggestion. These "end runs" are not looked on with favor by agency leadership or the OMB; but especially in the subsystem arena, there are few sanctions that can be brought to bear against an offending bureau. Other proposals flowing between bureaus and Congress may be stimulated by a direct congressional request for legislation—sometimes with, sometimes without agency sanction.

There are, however, other policy instruments than legislation. The president may, for example, request an agency or interagency task force to draft an executive order or presidential reorganization plan, and stamp what is produced by the agency with his imprimatur. Executive orders, though they create policy, do not pass through the congressional process. In the model, they flow along the line from agency to presidency to policy. The same can be said for presidential reorganization plans that do not encounter a congressional veto.

---

[7]See the discussion by Robert S. Gilmour, "Policy Formulation in the Executive Branch: Central Legislative Clearance," *Public Administration Review*, Vol. 31, No. 2 (March/April, 1971), pp. 150–158.

All policymaking is not, however, expressed in legislation or formal policy documents, but rather results from high level decisions—and the bureaucracy is often a source for the information on which such decisions are made. The field of foreign policy is replete with instances where presidential decisions are based on information developed and processed by the foreign affairs agencies (the discovery of missles in Cuba, the Mayaguez). Although much of this information passes up the chain of command through the political leadership of an agency and into the Executive Office, there are occasions when information reaches the president and Executive Office officials without going through channels.

One reason for such short-circuiting of the normal chain of command may stem from bureaucratic initiative, a frustration on the part of certain career officials that their perspectives are not being given adequate consideration upstairs. It is not unusual for the president, when facing a major decision, to have available "bootleg" copies of memoranda that have been produced in the bureaucracy.[8] Another reason for avoiding the chain of command has to do with the fact that information passed upwards in a hierarchy is subject to distortion—a severe example being the practice of the Defense Intelligence Agency to change intelligence figures and estimates at the behest of an affronted field commander.[9] For this reason, White House officials, and occasionally the president, sometimes get in touch directly with bureau chiefs or office heads to gather information closer to its source. John Kennedy was particularly noted for such techniques and on more than one occasion placed phone calls directly to startled State Department desk officers to get their opinions and judgments on a pending foreign policy decision.

Agency views are generally solicited by the presidency not

---

[8]Morton Halperin, *Bureaucratic Politics and Foreign Policy* (Washington: Brookings Institution, 1974), p. 108.

[9]Charles Peters and Taylor Branch, eds., *Blowing the Whistle: Dissent in the Public Interest* (New York: Praeger, 1972), p. 115.

only during the development of executive policy decisions but also as part of presidential response to congressional legislation. It is common practice for the Office of Management and Budget to ask for agency views as to how certain bills awaiting the president's signature may affect agency operations and for advice as to whether a particular bill should be vetoed.

We have examined in previous chapters the exchange of information between bureaus and agencies and congressional committees and staff. And we have suggested that on a day-to-day basis, the bureaucracy is a more frequent, often more important source of information than the White House. Although not all the data provided by bureaus and agencies makes a contribution to development of congressional policy, bureau testimony at hearings, official reports, responses to constituency problems, and informal contacts have a substantial cumulative impact on congressional policy deliberations.

The above picture of the role of federal agencies in policy development is admittedly simple. We have not examined, for example, the numerous factors that condition the position a bureau, agency, or individual official may take on a particular policy—such factors as the role of interest groups and agency clientele, court decisions, the influence of professional groups, technical considerations, press publicity, public opinion, and the like. These various "inputs" that affect the policy development role of a bureau or agency, while not our immediate concern, should be kept in mind.

Equally complex is the role of agencies and bureaus in *implementing* a policy once established—be it a piece of legislation, an executive order, a presidential decision, or congressional directive. However, the main outlines of the agency role in the implementation of policy can be visualized along the lines suggested in Figure 7–2.

For our purposes, it is helpful to distinguish between the agency role in refining policy on the one hand and in applying it on the other. Policy *refinement* is the process whereby an agency or bureau interprets congressional (or presidential) intent and provides the context in which the policy will be carried out. The

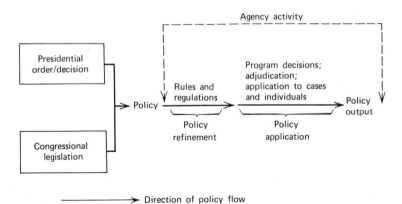

Figure 7-2. The role of federal agencies in policy implementation.

broader or more general the policy guidelines—such as the mandate of some regulatory commissions to provide for the "public convenience and necessity" or to prevent "combinations in restraint of trade"—the greater the attention and effort that must be given to this initial stage of policy implementation. The most common feature of this stage is the drafting and adoption of rules and regulations that define further the intent of the policy and guide administrators in its eventual application to specific cases and programs.

The process of rulemaking and regulation-writing generally begins with a first draft of proposed rules, usually written by an agency career official with an intimate knowledge of the area concerned. Also involved is the legal office or general counsel's staff, often the bureau chief, and occasionally the agency head and groups affected by the proposed regulations. Draft regulations or announcements of proposed rulemaking are published in the *Federal Register* and a certain period of time, generally 60 to 90 days, reserved for comment by the public or affected parties. Occasionally, a congressional subcommittee or staff, or the Executive Office of the President may become involved if the matter is especially controversial—as witness the requirement during the Nixon administration that the OMB review draft regulations proposed by the Environmental Protection

Agency.[10] During the time the draft regulations are being considered, agency officials may hold public hearings, consult informally with affected groups, and receive advice from advisory committees, some with a statutory mandate to review agency regulations. After the review and comment period and consultations, the final regulations, the rule, or program guidelines are published in the *Register* and later become part of the *Code of Federal Regulations*, the massive compendium of agency "legislation."[11]

Based on the rules, guidelines, and regulations thus adopted, agency officials then apply or administer the policy. Much application involves adjudication, that is, decisions regarding claims of individuals—a retiree claiming social security benefits, a corporation requesting a television station license—or decisions concerning compliance with regulations, whether a company has complied with the safety and health guidelines of OSHA, whether the National Labor Relations Board judges certain labor practices as unfair, and so on.

Program administration looms large in the application of policy by federal agencies. Some programs naturally involve adjudication. Others dispense a variety of funds and services—the construction of physical facilities; the procurement of weapons systems; support to institutions of learning; building airports, river improvements, and water projects. A substantial amount of federal funds goes to scientific research and development, both for basic research (the province of the National Science Foundation) and for more applied research that is directly related to the missions of various agencies. And of course policy is "applied" through enforcement of federal law by the Department of Justice, the Equal Employment Opportunity Commission and other law enforcement agencies.[12]

---

[10]Kenneth W. Kramer, "The President, Bureaucracy, and Environmental Policy," a paper prepared for delivery at the annual meeting of the Southwestern Political Science Association, Houston, Texas, April, 1978, p. 16.

[11]An extensive review of the regulation and rule-making process may be found in William L. Boyer, *Bureaucracy on Trial: Policy Making by Government Agencies* (Indianapolis: Bobbs Merrill Co., 1969).

[12]For a general discussion, see James E. Anderson, *Public Policy-Making* (New York: Praeger, 1975), pp. 113–120.

The Influence of Policy Type

Having sketched briefly the role of the federal bureaucracy in policy development and policy implementation, let us turn to consider how the particular type of policy under consideration may influence or condition that role. For convenience, our point of departure is the familiar typology—developed by Theodore Lowi—of distributive, regulatory, and redistributive policies. As the reader will recall, distributive policies spread benefits or subsidies among certain groups and interests, are of low visibility, and generally associated with subsystem politics. Regulatory policies are somewhat more visible and contentious and control or regulate a group (or groups) for broader public benefit. Redistributive policies, which are generally quite controversial, take resources from one element or sector of society and redistribute them to others.

Variants of the Lowi typology have been developed for application to the foreign affairs and foreign policy arena, where a key distinction is between policies with a domestic component and distributive flavor (the siting of military bases, weapons procurement, etc.) and those concerned with crisis decisionmaking or that are strategic in nature—commitment of troops, rescue of a captured naval vessel, and the like.[13]

As we have seen in previous chapters, executive branch bureaus are the handmaidens of subsystem, distributive politics, cooperating with congressional subcommittees and concerned interest groups in spreading benefits among the latter. Among such bureaus are the Army Corps of Engineers, the various commodity divisions (for cotton, tobacco, rice, etc.) of the Department of Agriculture's Agricultural Stabilization and Conservation Service, the Department of Interior's Soil Conservation Service, and a host of others.

Although they are intimately linked with distributive politics, such bureaus are not necessarily heavily involved in policy development. They do exercise considerable influence through the

[13]See the discussion in Randall B. Ripley and Grace Franklin, *Congress, the Bureaucracy and Public Policy* (Homewood, Ill.: Dorsey Press, 1976), pp. 143–164.

administration of policies developed in the subsystem itself. Ripley and Franklin cite several examples where attempts by bureau officials to modify subsystem procedures or bureau activities were stymied by the congressional subcommittee concerned. They suggest that if conflict between the bureau and subcommittee persists, "the congressional position taken by the subcommittee is more likely to prevail than the bureaucratic position."[14]

Instances of bureau initiatives in subsystem politics, however, do exist—especially where they are protective of clientele interests. When the Food and Drug Administration in 1959 officially warned the public not to eat cranberries that had been contaminated by a weed killer, the cranberry industry lost substantial profits as a result. Enterprising attorneys in the Department of Agriculture found a neglected statute that allowed the Department to indemnify, through administrative action, the cranberry producers to the tune of $10 million.[15] Such initiatives, however, appear to be the exception rather than the rule.

One should bear in mind, however, that not all distributive programs of the federal government are administered through tight subsystems. Such programs as revenue sharing and grants to state and local governments may be on a formula basis, with the formula determined in legislation or in administrative regulations. Administration of these programs may involve rather routine calculations or an almost automatic distribution of funds, rather than leaving such judgments to the discretion of administrative officials. Further, "entitlement" programs, such as unemployment insurance, veterans' benefits, social security, and the like, call for payments to individuals who meet certain criteria. Granted, the determination of elegibility for such programs is a matter of judgment by an official or caseworker, and some measure of discretion is involved—but the comprehensiveness of the criteria often leaves only narrow scope for

[14]*Ibid.,* p. 94.
[15]Eugene Feingold, "The Great Cranberry Crisis," in Edwin A. Bock, ed., *Government Regulation of Business: A Casebook* (Englewood Cliff, N.J.: Prentice-Hall, 1962), pp. 1–31.

bureaucratic initiative; indeed, from the point of view of the caseworker, the guidelines may be too strict and inflexible.

Another mechanism for conducting distributive programs is the competitive grant or contract, a process that may take place largely outside subsystem politics. Funds for research, both basic and applied, are awarded by nearly every major federal agency—and several agencies, such as the National Science Foundation and the National Foundation on the Arts and the Humanities, have as their primary function the awarding of grant monies for research. Many funds so spent are awarded at the advice or instruction of panels of experts knowledgeable in the field of research concerned, and incoming proposals are evaluated by the peers of those applying for funding. Although there is some element of conflict-of-interest possible, this peer review system does place substantial powers in the hands of panels of outside experts instead of in the officials of the administering agency. This is not to suggest, however, that bureaucratic initiative in federal research and development efforts is a function beyond the reach of subsystem politics, as witness the subgovernment for health research as conducted during the 1950s and 1960s, with the National Institutes of Health and the relevant appropriations subcommittees of the House and Senate as the major governmental actors, or the subsystem pressures on some programs of the National Science Foundation.[16]

An especially interesting example from the foreign policy distributive arena comes from the attempt by the Air Force to build a nuclear-powered airplane in the period following World War II. Here air force officers, fascinated by the possibility of atomic-powered flight, pushed hard for the immediate development of an atomic plane. Backed by the highest career echelons of the Air Force, by bureaucratic allies in the Atomic Energy Commission, by a subcommittee of the House Armed Services Committee, and the Joint Committee on Atomic Energy, Air Force careerists were able to keep the project alive

---

[16]See the discussion in Daniel Greenberg, *The Politics of Pure Science* (New York: New American Library, 1967).

for over a decade—despite the opposition of several Secretaries of Defense and the president's science advisors. It took the personal intervention of President Kennedy (plus the growth of missile technology) to finally kill the nuclear plane effort in the 1960s.[17]

Although the influence of the bureaucracy in distributive policy may be varied and sporadic, in the arena of regulatory policy—especially its implementation—the role of career officialdom is substantial. A major reason is that Congress has intentionally delegated to the regulatory agencies significant powers of both a quasi-legislative nature (the rule-making process) and of a quasi-judicial nature (adjudication). More "law" is made in the regulatory commissions than in Congress, and more "cases" decided than in the federal courts. Further, their knowledge of matters under their purview and long experience with issues of rather narrow range give career officials in the regulatory agencies substantial power of expertise. This power, backed by statute, gives regulatory agencies the authority to order commercial goods withdrawn from the market, a broadcasting station to cease transmitting, a security to be suspended from trading on the stock exchange.

To assist in the exercise of their adjudicatory functions, the regulatory agencies have developed, with congressional approval, a special cadre of officials called administrative law judges (a more distinguished term than their former title, hearing examiners), who are relatively immune from political interference in their decisions. They sit essentially as trial judges in various proceedings brought before the agencies, and their decisions (though on occasion subject to judicial review) are generally binding on the parties concerned.

Although the regulatory agencies wield considerable power, there is evidence, as we have suggested previously, that this power is not always used impartially. Most regulatory commissions, or certainly large areas of their activities, are subject to the same subsystem pressures as distributive politics. Indeed, many

---

[17]W. Henry Lambright, *Shooting Down the Nuclear Plane* (Indianapolis: Bobbs Merrill Co., 1967).

of the classic examples of subgovernments—in airline regulation, in trucking—are drawn from the regulatory arena. And the problem seems especially acute where the number of regulated interests (and representatives of those interests) is relatively few. A common charge is that the regulatory commissions, and hence much regulatory policy, have been captured by the groups they are supposed to regulate; but it is also true that cozy relationships between the regulated and the regulators have been encouraged by the continued development of subcommittee government in Congress—and by disputes over regulatory policy within the executive branch itself.

Two examples are instructive here. The first concerns the efforts of the Federal Trade Commission to bring its rulemaking powers to bear against deceptive advertising in the cigarette industry. Frustrated in its attempt to regulate advertising by cigarette companies on a case-by-case basis, the FTC moved in 1964 to adopt a rule requiring a statement in advertising and on cigarette packages warning of the health hazards of smoking. The reaction of the well-financed tobacco lobby was intense. Its pressure on the Commerce committees (and tobacco growers' pressure on the Agriculture committees) was strong enough to cause Congress to intervene on behalf of the subsystem clientele. In 1965, it passed a bill that stripped the FTC of rule-making power over cigarette advertising for a period of years, prohibited other federal agencies from requiring health warnings, and prevented states or local governments from doing so.[18] Such direct and blatant congressional involvement in regulatory policy is rare but much more than symbolic of the interest that it may take in policies that adversely affect strong constituencies.

Another case involving the regulatory powers of the FTC, and one showing the power of the bureaucracy in regulatory administration, concerns the controversy over a battery additive that had been developed in the 1950s by one Jess Ritchie. To scientists at the National Bureau of Standards, which had conducted

---

[18]A. Lee Fritschler, *Smoking and Politics* (Englewood Cliffs, N.J.: Prentice-Hall, 1975).

numerous tests on similar additives and found them worthless, Ritchie's "new" AD-X2 was just another in a series of fradulent products—and it so advised the trade publications that had been carrying his advertisements.

Ritchie, however, took his case to the Senate Small Business committee and to a new Republican Secretary of Commerce— appealing outside the normal routines of regulation. After considerable controversy surrounding the scientific merits of the product (which chemically was found to be about as potent as distilled water), the Federal Trade Commission finally moved to ban Ritchie's advertising as false. But its attempts were blunted by one of its own hearing examiners who argued that FTC attorneys bringing the case against Ritchie had not met the burden of proof required of them—given the number of users who testified that AD-X2 had brought their old batteries back to life. The hearing examiner dismissed the case, and Ritchie was soon advertising that his product had been "proved" before the Federal Trade Commission.[19]

In the arena of regulatory policy, these two cases are rather exceptional. Most implementation of regulatory policy goes on without the intervention of agency heads or congressional committees. But as the examples suggest, there is substantial potential both for the involvement of the congressional components of subsystem politics and for substantial independence on the part of individual officials in the regulatory agencies.

In the arena of redistributive domestic policy and strategic (or crisis-level) foreign policy, on the other hand, the scope for bureaucratic input—especially in policy development—appears rather narrow. A contributing factor in the domestic arena is that the battles over such redistributive issues as a progressive income tax, a voting rights act, or Medicare tend to be fought at the institutional levels of the federal government—involving the president, the Congress, and "peak" associations of interest groups. Once redistributive issues have been decided, the resulting program is often administered with a quiet technicality. Im-

---

[19]Samuel Lawrence, *The Battery Additive Controversy* (Indianapolis: Bobbs Merrill, 1962).

plementation of redistributive policies may be surrounded by complex regulations and procedures—as witness the Internal Revenue code and criteria for Medicare eligibility—that tend to limit bureaucratic discretion. This is not, however, always the case in redistributive policies, as exemplified by the struggle over the administration of the programs of the Office of Economic Opportunity.

In crisis or strategic foreign policy matters, the likelihood of strong input from the bureaucracy is again, rather low—though intelligence developed through bureaucratic channels (as in the discovery of the Cuban missile sites) may occasionally play a crucial role. This is partly because of the closely held nature of much crisis foreign policymaking and the desire on the part of the president and top advisors to restrict sensitive information to as small a circle of persons as possible. During the planning stage of the ill-fated Bay of Pigs invasion, for example, even such key officials as the head of the U.S. Information Agency and the director of the State Department's Bureau of Intelligence and Research were kept ignorant of the planning—even when they had heard rumors of the invasion and confronted their superiors.

In decisions of less than crisis importance, the voice of the bureaucracy is still rather muted—relegated to a "second circle" of influence removed from the president and his key advisors in the National Security Council and the foreign affairs agencies. As Spanier and Uslaner suggest, "The function of the second circle is to provide ideas and information or policy alternatives and to make policy recommendations that the members of the inner circle can discuss among themselves. . . . It does not play a direct role in crisis decision-making or even in most foreign policy decisions, but it serves the members of the inner circle by providing background information and analyses to decision-makers."[20]

Moreover, a certain bureaucratic reluctance to become overtly involved in foreign policy issues in general has been identified

[20]John Spanier and Eric Uslaner, *How American Foreign Policy is Made* (New York: Praeger, 1974), p. 64.

Table 7-1.
Relative Importance of Bureaucratic Policy Role by Type and Stage of Policy

| | DOMESTIC POLICY | | | | | | FOREIGN POLICY | | | |
| | Distributive | | Regulatory | | Redistributive | | Distributive | | Crisis/Strategic | |
	Dev.	Imp.	Dev.	Imp.	Dev.	Imp.	Dev.	Imp.	Dev.	Imp.
Strength of bureaucratic influence	Low to medium	Medium	Low to medium	Medium to high	Low	Low	Low to medium	Medium	Low	Low

Dev. = Development.
Imp. = Implementation.

by, among others, Morton Halperin. The elite bureaucratic cultures of most foreign affairs agencies are career systems (the foreign service, the military services) where promotions are dependent on favorable reviews of performance by one's superiors and aberrant or innovative behavior is generally looked on with disfavor. Moreover, as Halperin notes, these careerists identify rather strongly with their career service and are generally not inclined (or encouraged) to push for new policies or to rock the boat. In most foreign policy, Halperin argues, "The bureaucratic system is basically inert. . . . The majority of bureaucrats prefer to maintain the status quo, and only a small group is, at any one time, advocating change. . . . Most policy issues are not new; they have arisen time and time again."[21]

From this brief discussion of the role of the federal bureaucracy in policy development and implementation in various policy settings, we find that the importance and intensity of this role does appear to vary with the type of policy under consideration. Table 7-1 summarizes the tentative findings explored in the previous pages.

Problems of Policy Leadership and Coordination

Earlier in this chapter, we discussed briefly some apparent similarities between Congress and the federal bureaucracy—in their decentralized structure, their pluralism, their approaches to the making of decisions, and so forth. Here we pause to explore some further similarities in these two institutions, namely, the problems of institutional leadership and of control of the policy process that appear to plague both. There seem to be a number of parallels between the congressional response to problems of policy coordination, discussed at length in previous chapters, and that of the executive branch.

It appears that effective policy leadership of the executive branch by the president and the institutionalized presidency is extremely difficult. In some respects the "leadership" exercised

[21]Halperin, *op. cit.*, pp. 85–89, 99.

by the presidency has proved as weak as that coming from the Congress. A new president taking over the helm often comes into office with only vague policy ideas and notions, many of them developed during the campaign and lacking specificity or concrete program objectives. Making broad policy pronouncements is one question; translating them into executive action is another. Moreover, from the vast range of problems and issues that may confront an incoming president, there are only relatively few that may become really central or "strategic" to his administration. It is simply impossible for a president to follow all policy areas at all times; he is forced to focus on those he deems particularly important, leaving leadership or control of other areas to his subordinates or in many cases, by default, to the career bureaucracy. As Hugh Heclo has suggested, "Presidential leadership is like a spotlight that can sweep across a range of executive activities but can concentrate on only a few at a time."[22]

Another problem, and one discussed more fully below, concerns the responsiveness to the president of the top level political appointees who form the leadership cadre of any administration. Few executives may really know what presidential "policy" in a particular area is. Further, as they are gradually socialized to the views and perspectives of the agencies that they head, they may come to hold opinions substantially different from those of the president himself. Then of course an incoming president faces one of the basic constitutional facts of life of American government, namely, that ours is a system of shared powers and that other elements of the body politic—notably the Congress, the courts, interest groups, and the bureaucracy—all have claims to a major say in those policies over which the president may be attempting to exercise leadership. This observation holds for the presidential role in policy formulation as well as for the implementation of enacted legislation. Given these constraints, it is hardly surprising that such observers of presidents as Richard Neustadt have suggested that persuasion and bargaining, rather

[22]Heclo, *op. cit.*, p. 12.

than raw exercise of power, are the way in which presidential initiatives and policies are translated into action.

Even in the arena of foreign policy, where the constitutional prerogatives of the president are substantial, implementation of presidential directives is, as Morton Halperin has pointed out, often extremely difficult. Halperin concludes that "it is true only in very special cases that presidential decisions [in the foreign policy arena] are self-executing. Usually, in fact, they begin a process."[23] Foreign policy officials directly under the president may not completely understand him and thus fail to carry out his instructions explicitly. They may simply not be able to do what the president has ordered, or in some cases may feel strongly that the decision is inappropriate and refuse to implement it. Even such a straightforward directive as President Kennedy's order to remove missiles from bases in Turkey were not carried out (thus complicating his bargaining position during the Bay of Pigs) because military officials felt that the order was in opposition to the basic policy of strengthening the NATO alliance. As George Kennan has suggested:

> Anyone who has ever had anything to do with the conduct of foreign relations knows that policies can be correctly and effectively implemented only by people who understand the entire philosophy and world of thought of the person or persons who took the original decision. But senior officials are constantly forced to realize that in a governmental apparatus so vast, so impersonal, and lacking in any sort of ideological indoctrination and discipline, they cannot count on any great portion of the apparatus to understand entirely what they mean.[24]

Given the restraints on presidential policy leadership at the highest level of the executive branch, one might take comfort in the assumption that certainly at the second echelon of political power (the department and agency heads) effective policy leadership of the bureaucracy is maintained. These officials, so the theory goes, are appointed by the president to carry out his policy initiatives. They become a potent force for ensuring that presidential perspectives are carried into the routines and deci-

[23]Halperin, *op. cit.*, p. 238.
[24]Quoted in *ibid.*, p. 240.

sions of their respective organizations. Often, however, an agency head faces (from his or her perspective) the same cotorie of problems of policy leadership facing the president.

The activities and organizational units of most departments and agencies are themselves quite diverse, and it is impossible for any department or agency head, especially in such behemoths as the Departments of Defense and Health, Education and Welfare, to keep on top of the many developments at lower organizational levels. "Their" bureaus and offices, moreover, may have many sources of independent power. Further, the political appointee cadre of an agency or department is thin indeed, a minute percentage of agency personnel. The executive branch has only about 600 top level political officials appointed by the president and confirmed by the Senate, and an additional five or six hundred at the second layer (those appointed by agency heads), thus creating a political leadership group of eleven or twelve hundred individuals over a federal bureaucracy of two and one-half million. Presidential appointees are certainly outnumbered (and often outgunned) by the federal bureaucracy they supervise. Thus much of the policy leverage an administration posseses depends on the extent to which it is able to press its goals and directions on career officials.

The basic tensions between the career bureaucracy and presidential appointees have been discussed at some length in an earlier chapter.[25] The basic complaint that the political leadership of the administrative state has against the career civil service was summarized aptly by a reflective Harry Truman: "The difficulty with many career officials in the government is that they regard themselves as the men who really make policy and run the government. They look upon elected officials as just temporary occupants. Every President in our history has been faced with this problem: how to prevent career men from circumventing presidential policy. Too often career men seek to impose their own views instead of carrying out the established policy of the administration. Sometimes they achieve this by influencing the key men appointed by the President to put his policies into

[25]See pp. 50–54.

operation".[26] The political appointee enters a bureaucratic culture that has its own values, institutional history, and inertia. As Harold Seidman has suggested:

> Department heads seldom start with a clean slate. Generally they must adapt to the institution rather than the institution to them. There are likely to be daily reminders that they are merely temporary custodians and spokesmen for organizations with distinct and multi-dimensional personalities and deeply ingrained cultures and subcultures reflecting institutional history, ideology, values, symbols, folklore, professional biases, behavior patterns, heros, and enemies. . . . Most department heads are free only to be as big men as the president, the bureaucracy, the Congress, and their own constituencies allow them to be.[27]

There are only relatively few sanctions that even the most powerful political appointees can bring to bear against recalcitrant senior-level career officials. Those who fail to cultivate the sympathies and sentiments of the career bureaucracy in a constructive way may find themselves isolated or cut off from that flow of information and expertise that is one of the primary sinews of bureaucratic power.

Implementation of policies originating in the political leadership of an agency is highly sensitive to and dependent on the cooperation of senior career officials. It is extremely difficult to push through programs or directives that are at loggerheads with the career bureaucracy. While cases of outright bureaucratic sabotage are rare, the senior bureaucracy does, as Heclo suggests, have a kind of veto power over the intentions of agency political leadership. "Unlike the 'legislative veto' (in which executive actions take effect unless disapproved by Congress), the 'bureaucratic veto' is a pervasive constant of government, for without higher civil service support almost nothing sought by political executives is likely to take effect. It is a power that can consist simply of waiting to be asked for solutions by appointees who do not know that they have problems."[28]

[26]Harry S. Truman, *Memoirs: Years of Trial and Hope* (Garden City: Doubleday and Co., 1956), p. 165.
[27]Seidman, *op. cit.*, pp. 121–122.
[28]Heclo, *op. cit.*, p. 172.

The difficulties of policy leadership, Heclo suggests, result because many of the requisites for effective political leadership—program commitment, strong outside political support, the ability to coordinate and manage effectively, and a sensitivity to the ambiguity of their positions—are lacking in many of those holding top level positions of political leadership. There appears to be a considerable gap between the requisites of effective policy leadership and the abilities and experience of many of those appointed to political positions. This mismatch "often prompts experienced appointees and civil servants alike to observe that the problems ascribed to unresponsive bureaucracies are commonly due to the inadequacies of political leadership. Possibly some governments, like some musical instruments, might respond well to amatuers, but unfortunately the U.S. executive branch is a place for violinists, not kazoo players."[29]

But the problems of policy leadership do not lie soley with those who occupy positions of strategic political leadership, but also with the changing nature of federal public service itself. As Frederick Mosher, among others, has argued, recent trends in the public service have served to isolate even further many bureaucratic agencies from overhead policy leadership of the executive. Of primary import has been the increasing number of career officials who are trained as professionals, both those from the "general professions," such as attorneys, physicians, and economists, and as well from the "public service professions" such as the military, the Foreign Service, and the Public Health Service.[30]

The world view of politics held by the professions tends to denigrate the validity (if not morality) of much of the political system. Professionals disparage and are often suspicious of "political" leadership, especially where the goals of the political cadre may conflict with the norms of professionalism. The professional relies on scientific, rational, and technical judgments in arriving at decisions rather than the compromise and negotiation typical of the political process. Politics, moreover, is at odds

[29]*Ibid.*, p. 239.
[30]Mosher, *op. cit.*, pp. 99–133.

with some of the core assumptions of professional practice—among them professional autonomy, an emphasis on individual clients, and professional self-control—which often leads to a built-in hostility between the professional estate and the world of politics.[31]

Although it is true that, in a number of cases, professional practice may be consistent with the goals of public organizations—forestry, the military services, and public health come to mind—the fact that professional perspectives can reinforce those goals does not necessarily increase the receptivity of the professions to broader policy control at the highest echelons of government. As Mosher observes, "For better or worse—or better *and* worse—much of our government is now in the hands of professionals (including scientists). The choice of these professionals, the determination of their skills, and the content of their work are now principally determined, not by general governmental agencies, but by their own professional elites, professional organizations, and the institutions and facilities of higher education."[32] And though Mosher recognizes the positive contributions the professions have made to governmental activity, he fears that government, through its importation of professionals, may have lost control over the substance of their work.

Closely allied with the increased reliance on professionals has been the growth of *career* systems. Here persons are brought in at the bottom of a tight hierarchical structure and move upward through a system of promotions (the military, the foreign service, and others). Based on rank in the individual rather than in the job, these career systems often form semiautonomous units within a number of agencies and departments. The ramification of these career systems has been accompanied by a certain insensitivity of many of their members to the requisites of overhead political leadership. As Mosher observes, "Large and important areas of policy are of course within the purview of individual agencies that are largely dominated by members of career sys-

---

[31]For an elaboration of these themes, see Don K. Price, *The Scientific Estate* (Cambridge: Harvard University Press, 1965), pp. 208–269.

[32]Mosher, *op. cit.*, p. 132.

tems. The development and effectuation of changes in policy thus inevitably depend upon the abilities, perspectives, values, and strategies of political leaders who are not themselves 'of the career.'"[33]

In addition to these issues is another set of factors that reduces the potential for overhead leadership and policy control over much of the bureaucracy. The fact is that most agencies and bureaus have sources of power separate from (and often in conflict with) those at the "political" levels of the executive branch. One major contributing factor, often a concomitant of professionalism, is the expertise agencies possess in the policy arenas in which they operate. The intense, sustained attention that an individual bureau or office can devote to a particular issue or problem provides it a reservoir of understanding and knowledge that an agency's political officials (not to mention the institutionalized presidency) find difficult if not impossible to match. Political leaders are increasingly dependent on these reservoirs for their own information, if not on occasion hostage to them. The closely held nature of much of this information permits bureaus substantial leverage over those wishing to acquire this information for their own ends.[34]

Another source of agency power stems from the fact that they do not exist in a political vacuum, but rather interact with various elements in their political environment—the public at large; interest or clientele groups that may affect or be affected by agency activity; the Congress with its various committees and subcommittees; the courts; and, of course, other agencies of the executive branch itself. Although general public support for an agency may on occasion be rather fickle (NASA appears to be an example), special interest groups play a major role in augmenting the power base of many agencies vis-à-vis both the Congress and the institutionalized presidency. Especially where an agency distributes benefits to a broad and organized clientele, as does the Veteran's Administration, this outside support may make

---

[33]*Ibid.*, p. 163.

[34]For a general discussion of the power of bureaucratic expertise and routines, see Francis Rourke, *op. cit.*, pp. 14–41.

the agency virtually unassailable by its purported executive branch masters. In other cases, interest groups can become so entwined with an agency's activities as to produce a "capture effect," whereby interests supposedly regulated may actually be in a position to influence substantially policy directions taken by an agency. The regulatory commissions are classic examples. But even those agencies that are not primarily regulatory in nature may be subject to strong influence by groups they serve, as demonstrated in the classic study of the Tennessee Valley Authority by Phillip Selznick.[35]

We have already noted in previous chapters the considerable influence that congressional committees can exercise over the day-to-day routines and decisions of administrative agencies. We have also suggested that agencies with strong interest group constituencies as well as strong congressional support can use these sources of power to play off one against the other, and both against attempts at presidential control. As Francis Rourke has observed, "through the assiduous cultivation of legislative and public support, it is possible for an administrative agency to establish a position of virtually complete autonomy within the executive branch. . . . Historically . . . the quest for outside support has often been a divisive force within the organizational structure of American national bureaucracy, weakening the identification of departments with the president or of bureaus with their department."[36] This phenomenon does not hold for all agencies, however. There are a number with little or no potential to mobilize constituency support—the Agency for International Development and its predecessors, for example. Such agencies are more amenable to presidential direction and control. Then, too, agencies vary greatly in the extent to which they develop reservoirs of expertise, and as well the extent to which they have strong ties to congressional committees. There are thus substantial differences in the relative outside power positions held by agencies and thus the degree to which they are

[35]See his *TVA and Grass Roots* (Berkeley: University of California Press, 1949), *passim.*
[36]Rourke, *op. cit.,* p. 65.

subject to policy pressure flowing downward from the presidency.[37]

Another major factor in the degree of responsiveness of federal agencies to overhead policy direction and its eventual implementation is the increasingly greater proportion of federal programs that are administered directly not by federal agencies themselves, but by those of other governmental jurisdictions. Just as the center of gravity of program administration has drifted downwards within the federal executive branch over the past decades, so have increasing proportions of the federal budget been spent by agencies that are outside the boundaries of the federal government. This is particularly pronounced in the awarding of grants-in-aid and contracts to state and local governments.

As noted in Chapter 2, the increased reliance on program administration by other jurisdictions has been a hallmark of the growth of the modern administrative state. The federal government has increasingly turned to the states and local governments for a variety of administrative tasks, including those relating to the construction of airports, for transportation, pollution control, welfare, community development, and a host of others. This trend has implications for overall leadership and coordination of federal policy and programs. Today, as much as one-third of the national budget devoted to domestic programs is administered not directly by Washington but rather through the intervening delivery systems of state, local, and special district governments.

One motivation behind these developments is that in many policy areas, conditions vary widely, and effective solutions to many of the problems these programs address must be applied in the context of a particular region or locality. Further, there is the advantage of such programs being delivered by governments that are somewhat "closer" to the people than the federal bureaucracy is often perceived to be. In a number of the newer

[37]For a discussion of these differentials in agency power, see Rourke, *op. cit.,* pp. 81–106.

grant-in-aid programs, the national government is more of a partner with state and local governments than it is a sovereign.

The implications of these trends for overhead policy coherence are suggested by one of the leading students of intergovernmental relations, Arthur MacMahon. These programs, he suggests, have "already brought new administrative problems, since such programs usually require action by several national agencies rather than by a single one as had been the case in the early grants-in-aid schemes. An attendant feature is the fact that the emerging programs can not depend upon clear lines of authority from superior to subordinate. . . . An accompanying trend is the shifting of operating decisions into the field."[38] The intergovernmental system of grants-in-aid has to some extent traded off strong federal control for the increasing influence of state and local governments over federal policy. And though federal regulations, audits, and other mechanisms provide for some consistency and checks on the implementation of these politics within a local context, this "indirect administration" has dispersed and decentralized the implementation of public policy in a number of areas.[39]

Fiscal federalism has, moreover, increased the interest in and influence over the execution of federal policies by political officials at other levels of governments—governors, state legislators, mayors, city councils, and elected officials of special purpose districts. Especially in the area of categorical grants, the scope of nonfederal involvement is substantial. Public welfare and assistance programs, especially aid to families with dependent children (AFDC), are prime examples. While the federal government provides half of the funds for such activities administered by the states, it has allowed them to make such crucial program decisions as the level of benefit payments. As Michael Reagan has suggested, "While it is true that the federal government has over the years has exercised a good deal of influence over state public assistance programs . . . most of that influence has been

---

[38]Arthur W. MacMahon, *Administering Federalism in a Democracy,* (New York: Oxford University Press, 1972), p. 89.
[39]See the discussion in *ibid.,* pp. 172–190.

on the periphery of the program and mainly on administrative aspects. . ."[40] Although the federal government spends substantial amounts on categorical and other grant programs, this does not necessarily imply federal control of the distribution of such funds. As Reagan observes, "the saying is that 'he who pays the piper calls the tune.' The truth in the saying is that he who pays the piper has a leverage for potential say regarding what tune is played, but the leverage may not be exercised, the potential may not become actual."[41]

This delegation of fiscal and policy decisionmaking to the states and local governments is not complete, but the stage has been set for state and local initiatives to produce policy outcomes that may be in conflict with the broad outlines of national policy. Among the more extreme examples of the potential distortion implied by local control of national policy was the Selective Service System. Davis and Dolbeare's study of its administration found that local control through draft boards had created "an intricate meshing of deferment policy and organizational characteristics which has the combined effect of offering alternatives to military service to the sons of the higher socioeconomic strata while conferring the management of deferments and inductions upon community influentials drawn from the same strata."[42] And those who are concerned with the carefulness and efficiency with which fiscal federalism is administered can find little comfort in Martha Derthick's study of social services grants.[43]

A final development that limits policy leadership lies neither in the constitutional framework of the federal bureaucracy nor in the conflicts among various bureaucratic cultures or between federal and local governments. This development is typical of organization and bureaucracy in a modern, post-industrial

[40]Michael D. Reagan, *The New Federalism* (New York: Oxford University Press, 1972), p. 109.

[41]*Ibid.,* p. 108.

[42]James W. Davis and Kenneth M. Dolbeare, *Little Groups of Neighbors* (Chicago: Markham, 1968), pp. 4−5.

[43]Martha Derthick, *Uncontrollable Spending for Social Services Grants,* (Washington: Brookings Institution, 1975).

age—the decline of hierarchy as *the* major control mechanism for the administration of large and complex organizations. Subtly but surely the lines of control, the "chains of command" of most large organizations have become weakened, the power of hierarchial routines diminished.

The classical Weberian characteristic of hierarchial control appears to be on the wane in much of modern organization. Although those who have predicted the "death" of hierarchy and its replacement with ad hoc, fluid organizational forms have been premature in their predictions,[44] recent developments do suggest the continued weakening of hierarchy. Part of this trend in government organizations undoubtedly results from the professionalization of the public service and the greater emphasis placed on collegial as opposed to subordinate-superior relationships. Moreover, the increased educational level of public servants has perhaps lowered their willingness to accept orders from above without question. The "zone of tolerance" for overhead authority, described years ago by Chester Barnard[45], has narrowed. This phenomenon has extended even to the career military services, where dissent from a superior's views appears to have become somewhat more acceptable.

Another phenomenon that may have contributed to the decline of hierarchial authority is the fact that development of modern public organizations has brought greater scope for staff and analysis functions, instead of an increase in the number of positions actually in the "line." That is, increasing numbers of federal officials are in positions of observing, analyzing, and giving advice rather than actually "administering" or carrying out orders. Their impact on the organizational structure may further augment the pluralistic and consensual nature of much of modern-day organizational decisionmaking. In his study of federal organization, Herbert Kaufmann discovered that since

---

[44]See, among others, Warren G. Bennis and Philip E. Slater, *The Temporary Society* (New York: Harper & Row, 1968) and Alvin Toffler, *Future Shock* (New York: Random House, 1970).

[45]See Chester Barnard, *The Functions of the Executive* (Cambridge: Harvard University Press, 1938, 1968), pp. 161–184.

the 1920s, staff units in the major departments in the federal executive branch have demonstrated a "rising birth rate while line units were falling off sharply." The ratio of federal staff units to line units had grown by 1973 to 1.5 to one.[46] Although the distinctions between staff and line can be overdrawn, it is a safe assumption that the continued growth of staff units within bureaucratic organization may tend to limit even further the potential of hierarchy as a device to secure policy leadership from above.

Problems of Insulation and Responsiveness: Bureaucracy and Democracy

The preceding discussion has suggested some reasons why policy leadership in the executive branch—from the institutionalized presidency and from agency and department heads—is difficult. We find that strong overhead policy direction, which is problematic for Congress, is a challenge to the executive branch as well. Like Congress, the federal bureaucracy also faces the dilemma of insulation from effective democratic control. Especially in a democratic form of government, where national policy initiatives at least claim to reflect the will or consensus of the people, democratic checks on a bureaucracy are of paramount importance. If the bureaucracy is out of control, its actions may bear little resemblance to the intentions of its elected and appointed leaders.

In one sense, control of the bureaucracy by the overhead executive means control of bureaucrats by political officials—an issue we have explored in some depth above. But it also means, often crucially so, control of bureaucrats by other bureaucrats and the wielding of hierarchy in the name of the public or general interest. How to monitor individual officials, their decisions, and their discretionary power, has been a long-standing issue in the literature of political theory and public administration.

---

[46]Herbert Kaufmann, *Are Government Organizations Immortal?* (Washington: Brookings Institution, 1976), p. 39.

The problem of controlling administrative behavior, as Chester Barnard pointed out, is closely linked to the notion of authority itself. As he observed, authority is as much a function of the individual responding to an order or directive as it is of the individual who is giving that order or the order itself. Barnard suggested that most individuals in organizations have a sphere or zone of "indifference," within which they accept rather easily orders given from above. If, however, a directive is judged unreasonable by its recipient and falls outside of this zone, the chances are good that the individual will ignore or distort the order.[47] This zone of indifference may vary both with the individual concerned and the type of organization in which the order is given, as well as with the kinds of sanctions an organization can bring to bear on its members for refusal to follow directives. The emphasis on unquestioning obedience to orders from superiors is, for example, greater in the various elements of the Department of Defense (not to mention an actual battlefield situation) than it is in many of the domestic agencies of the federal government.

Responsiveness to overhead authority is also a function of the legitimacy with which the receiver of an order views its giver. Professionals in most organizations, for example, are generally reluctant to follow orders from those above them in the chain of command who do not possess the same credentials or expertise as the professionals themselves.[48] Indeed, the reluctance of professionals to accept directives concerning their immediate work from those not trained in their fields has been one of the major forces behind the rapid movement of professionals into the upper levels of the bureaucracy. To fill their highest administrative ranks, many agencies have turned to those in the professions. Administrators from professional backgrounds tend to be more effective managers of their former peers, for the authority

[47]Barnard, *loc. cit.*
[48]See, for example, the discussion in Victor Thompson, *Modern Organization* (New York: Knopf, 1961).

of their formal position is reinforced by the authority of their expertise.[49]

The individual in an organization may also be more or less inclined toward adhering to directives and instructions depending on the sense of attachment to or identification with the organization. There exists, for example, in most large organizations a group of individuals, generally highly motivated and career oriented, who desire to rise rapidly. These individuals are often strongly identified with the organization, if not its goals, and have been typed as "climbers" by Anthony Downs[50] and as "upward mobiles" by Robert Presthus.[51] Their orientation may lead to substantial if not complete acceptance of orders from superiors in an attempt to curry their favor and obtain rapid promotion. On the other hand, those individuals who are indifferent to the organization or perhaps ambivalent about it, may be less inclined to follow the dictates of superiors. It is at least suggestive that Presthus, in his research, has found that the "indifferent" orientation is widespread in modern organizations.[52]

Numerous remedies have been proposed to check arbitrary bureaucratic decisionmaking and noncompliance with orders from above. Opposing views held by two early observers of the problem of bureaucracy in a democracy—Herbert Finer and Carl Friedrich—are illustrative. Friedrich argues, perhaps somewhat optimistically, that checks on bureaucratic power must come essentially from the bureaucrats themselves, from a special sense of obligation to the view that they represent the broader public interest. Legal and administrative prescriptions against certain kinds of bureaucratic excess are probably

---

[49]Richard L. Schott, "Public Administration as a Profession: Problems and Prospects," *Public Administration Review*, Vol. 36, No. 3 (May/June, 1976), pp. 256–257.

[50]Anthony Downs, *Inside Bureaucracy* (Boston: Little, Brown, 1967), pp. 92–95.

[51]Robert Presthus, *The Organizational Society* (New York: St. Martin's Press, 1978), pp. 143–183.

[52]*Ibid.*, p. 184.

doomed to failure. The individual official, he argues, carries a responsibility to the technical and professional standards of his work as well as to broad popular sentiment. Although these "inner" checks are more effective than statutes or administrative regulations, Friedrich cautions that "even under the best arrangements a considerable margin of irresponsible conduct of administrative activities is inevitable."[53]

Herbert Finer, in contrast, places greater emphasis on the importance of administrative rules and procedures that limit bureaucratic discretion. He argues that the kinds of internal checks referred to by Friedrich actually work only because they exist within the context of legal sanctions. The history of administration, Finer suggests, "has demonstrated without the shadow of a doubt that sooner or later there is an abuse of power when external punative controls are lacking."[54] Control over bureaucratic policy, he concludes, necessitates stricter control over bureaucrats themselves, both by the legislative branch and by the upper echelons of the executive branch itself.

However, the assumption that bureaucratic officials at the supervisory levels are actually interested in strict oversight of their subordinates may be open to question. An interesting study by Herbert Kaufmann of the process of "administrative feedback" in organizations suggests that superiors are often disinclined to monitor their subordinates' activity, even when they have adequate time and resources. In many cases, "Subordinate non-compliance with the wishes of leaders of large organizations," Kaufmann concludes, "is . . . virtually inevitable."[55]

One of our most astute observers of federal bureaucracy, Francis Rourke, has argued that there are two broad categories of bureaucratic organizations for which the problem of democratic control is especially pressing. The first of the two groups

---

[53]Carl J. Friedrich, "Public Policy and the Nature of Administrative Responsibility," in Francis E. Rourke, ed., *Bureaucratic Power and National Politics* (Boston: Little Brown, 1972), p. 316.

[54]Herbert Finer, "Administrative Responsibility in Democratic Government" in Rourke, *Bureaucratic Power,* p. 329.

[55]Herbert Kaufmann, *Administrative Feedback* (Washington: Brookings Institution, 1973), p. 67.

he has termed broadly, "constituency agencies." These are agencies that are especially close to a particular clientele or interest group, so much so that effective control over their implementation of policy by either Congress or the president is often difficult. Among constituency agencies are those that represent certain clientele within the federal executive branch, such as the Veterans' Administration, Department of Agriculture, Department of Labor, and so forth. In addition to these are the regulatory agencies, whose tendency to be captured by the groups they were created to regulate has been documented in numerous studies over the past decades. Also among the clientele agencies, Rourke suggests, are such public works agencies as the Army Corps of Engineers and the Bureau of Reclamation of the Interior Department, the "porkbarrel" agencies that are highly susceptible to pressures from congressional committees and subcommittees. Rourke argues that these constituency agencies are not really out of control. "Indeed, the problem is that [such an agency] is too well controlled by the group that it serves—the partners with which it is joined."[56]

A second category of agencies in Rourke's typology are the "autonomous" agencies, which are often controlled by the career agency officials who direct their activities. Among these are "charismatic" organizations, such as the CIA, which see themselves as relatively immune from the normal channels of political control and subject to a "higher authority" such as national security. Other autonomous agencies are those involved in law enforcement and such technical agencies as the National Science Foundation, the National Institutes of Health, and NASA, whose ranks are filled largely by those from science and professions. The key to the problem of control in autonomous agencies lies with those who form their career cadres rather than with their constituencies.[57]

Rourke is rather sanguine about the possibilities of establish-

[56]This discussion is taken from comments made by Francis Rourke at a conference on the Presidency and Congress sponsored by the Lyndon Baines Johnson Library and the Lyndon B. Johnson School of Public Affairs, Austin, Texas, November 15–17, 1977.

[57]*Ibid.*

ing a broader, public control over the policy processes of both constituency and autonomous agencies. In the case of the former, this is partly due to the rise of certain latent elements of the public—the consumer public, the environmental public, the feminist public—that appear to be mobilized with increasing frequency, and as well to the rise of "public interest" organizations. Thus the clientele of constituency agencies may be increasingly offset by the rise of "counter" constituencies with a somewhat broader view or mandate. In the case of the autonomous agencies, Rourke argues, a decline in the general deference toward expertise and arcane knowledge has led to a weakening of the professional mystique and thus in some cases to a declining influence of professional cadres. "There seems to be strong evidence," Rourke concludes, "that public control is today in a period of ascendency—partly, I think, traceable to certain changes that have taken place in Congress, partly attributable to the rise of public interest groups and to the growing role of the media. The two other forms of control, constituency control and bureaucratic control find themselves increasingly on the defensive."[58]

A final perspective on the problems of controlling bureaucracy in a democracy is provided by Emmette Redford's study, *Democracy in the Administrative State*.[59] In his analysis, Redford makes a helpful distinction between micropolitics, "in which individuals, companies, and communities seek benefits from a larger polity for themselves," and the subsystem politics we have analyzed in preceding chapters. In micropolitics (an individual or company seeking a grant or license, a local government desiring public housing funds), there is a high level of involvement and interest on the part of those applying for the privilege or benefit, and a relatively narrow, usually dimly exposed decision process on the part of the bureaucracy responding to such requests.

The danger at the micropolitical level is that all comers will not be treated impartially. This danger results from the possible association of bureaucratic decisionmakers with the same indi-

---

[58]*Ibid.*
[59]New York: Oxford University Press, 1969.

viduals or groups who are making the request, and the special interests of party officials, the president, and especially members of Congress in the outcome of the decision. The attempt to limit outside "political" influence on such decisions has, Redford suggests, been to increase the neutrality and impersonality of administrative process itself. This is done by creating rules and standards for handling cases, by sinking the decision process in routine administration, and by involving in such decisions persons from a professional or technical background whose judgment may be less sensitive to political favoritism. "In sum," Redford concludes, "the primary route to reduction of micropolitics is bureaucratic administration—administration according to rule, immersed in process and protected by impersonal judgement."[60]

A second major problem of overhead democratic control of bureaucratic institutions that Redford considers is subsystem politics. Redford holds that, in spite of their defects, subsystems do provide for a certain balance among competing interests, as well as access for group interests that might not otherwise be represented. Redford grants that the subsystems are "imperfect instruments of democratic government."[61] Yet he suggests that as reflections of the broader national political system, they are subject to that system for their structure and rules. Thus one must turn to the Congress and the presidency for restructuring subsystems to make them more accountable to democratic morality. Our analysis, however, suggests that certainly as far as Congress is concerned, the development and endurance of subcommittee government holds little promise for changing subsystem politics as traditionally played.

Assessing the Administrative State: The Persistence of Bureau Government

The numerous factors discussed in the preceding pages place severe restraints on the ability of the presidency to lead and

[60]*Ibid.*, pp. 83–96; the quotation is from p. 88.
[61]*Ibid.*, p. 106.

orchestrate policy implementation by the federal bureaucracy. The transitory nature of political leadership, the entrenched position of an increasingly professionalized public service, the expertise and outside power bases developed by agencies and their bureaus, all serve to undermine the already limited capacity of the president to function as "administrator-in-chief" of the modern administrative state. Limitations on presidential leadership are enhanced by the constant outward tug of other actors in an agency's political environment. Committees of Congress, clientele and interest groups, the media, the courts, and the public at large draw an agency into a broader public arena, away from the rather tenuous lines of authority extending downwards from above. Indeed, the recent focus on the institutionalized presidency as an agent of macropolitical control and policy leadership is probably misplaced. Although the presidency may have become more imperial, it has not succeeded in translating the trappings of imperialism into effective policy control of the federal bureaucracy.

Extremely important from our perspective, of course, is the influence of those historical developments in Congress that we have traced in some detail. The growth of committee and then subcommittee in Congress has stimulated the development of its executive branch analogue, bureau government. Broadly speaking, the real power centers of the federal bureaucracy are and continue to be individual agencies and the bureaus within them. The limitations on overhead executive control and the strong and consistent press of subcommittee government suggest that real influence over policy elaboration in the executive branch will continue to be exercised in the main by agencies and bureaus closely allied with their congressional and interest group confreres. This fact of national political life, we suggest, will endure so long as Congress pursues the logic that has led to the solidification of subcommittee rule.

The importance of the agencies and bureaus as a force in the politics of the administrative process, however, is hardly a new phenomenon. The tenacity of power dispersion among agencies and bureaus has been, as we see in the next chapter, one of the major impulses behind executive branch reorganization, dating back at least to the Brownlow Committee in the 1930s; behind the creation and expansion of the Executive Office of the President; the development of the congressional liaison office; and other innovations designed to provide the president greater policy and administrative power over the bureaucracy. What has gone partly unnoticed, however, is that recent developments in the national legislature, especially the rise of subcommittee government, have tended by and large to perpetuate the natural tendency toward policy dispersion in the executive branch. And the downward drift of the locus of policymaking in Congress appears to be a prime force behind the dispersed and pluralistic nature of policy execution in the administrative state. So long as subcommittee government and subsystem politics endure, the executive branch may be best characterized as agency or bureau government rather than presidential government in the true sense of the word.

We would caution the reader against the assumption, however, that policy dispersion—either in Congress or in the executive branch—is necessarily an unmitigated evil. Policy pluralism is a reflection of the broader political system, and the decentralized way in which much of policy is made and implemented carries with it all the advantages of an incremental and cautious approach to policy development. But the issues of representativeness and responsiveness remain, and it is by no means clear that dispersed, incremental policy is appropriate for the range of issues and questions facing the American polity. The implications of subcommittee government in the legislature and bureau government in the administrative state, and as well the continuing problem of subsystem politics, bear close scrutiny. It is to these implications and to possible remedies that we finally turn.

8
Congress and the Administrative State: Executive Reorganization and Congressional Change

We have covered a good deal of ground in the preceding chapters, tracing historical developments and posing some general questions raised by them. In this final chapter, we recapitulate our basic themes and address what remedies, if any, may be in prospect for the excesses of subsystem government. In this connection, we examine the possible contributions of executive branch reorganization, congressional reform, and constitutional change. We also bring back into the larger picture some questions concerning presidential leadership and the position of the president in what increasingly appears to be a "post-imperial" era. First, a brief look backward to summarize some of our principal findings.

Themes Revisited

The emergence of a federal executive branch of vast scope and power is a phenomenon that owes its legitimation to the Congress. The federal bureaucracy, with its myriad of organizational forms, is the creature of our national legislature. Granted, there have been periods in which Congress has given the president

324

great latitude in the creation and organization of executive branch agencies, but these have generally been periods of national emergency. When they have ended, Congress has taken most of the power to create and reorganize back into its own hands.

The nature of Congress' response to the bureaucracy it has created has been conditioned both by the vagaries of history and by institutional changes within the Congress itself. The initial period of executive branch expansion, from the late 1800s until the end of World War I, roughly paralleled an era in which Congress was becoming more professional and more "institutional," and also a period in which it was undergoing a shift from strong party leadership to the emergence of committee government. Congress in this period paid relatively little attention to executive branch organization and structure—save for several investigations of the "economy-and-efficiency" variety. Nor was the notion of congressional control of administration through other than appropriations and occasional investigations much in evidence on the congressional agenda.

The second and major wave of executive branch expansion took place, as we have seen, in the decade and a half following the Great Depression of 1929–1932. By the depression era, committee government prevailed in Congress. The relationships among congressional committees and the agencies of a growing administrative state were forged in a number of separate crucibles, with ties between committees and agencies maintained in "whirlpools" of mutual interest.

As the rapid administrative growth of the New Deal period continued, Congress became increasingly aware that it was not enough to create (or assent to the creation of) federal agencies; surveillance of their activities and behavior began to emerge as a congressional concern. Indeed, it was in the New Deal period that the Congress, responding to the recommendations of the President's Committee on Administrative Management—to which it had initially given reluctant approval—came as close as it probably will in this century to a substantial restructuring of the federal executive branch.

The contemporary period of congressional-bureaucratic relations dates from the close of World War II. Though the Legislative Reorganization Act of 1946 wrote into law the outlines of congressional responsibility for surveillance of administration, the committee reorganization provided by the Act eventually led to the proliferation of subcommittees, to a downward drift in the power centers of the Congress from the committee to the subcommittee level. As power has shifted downwards in Congress, we have also witnessed a downwards drift in the executive branch from the department or agency to the bureau as the central focus of activity. We have seen as well the rise of "single interest" lobby groups—a decentralization of interest group politics. The result has been a proliferation of "mini-subsystems" in which the political process revolves around a subcommittee, a bureau and one or more single-interest lobbies.

As we have seen, the organizational development of Congress in this century has largely reinforced the decentralized nature of congressional interactions with the administrative state. In the early 1900s, as Congress became more professional, it moved from a system of party government to one of committee government. The move to committee government gave a wider range of members within Congress a taste of prestige and power, and instilled in others the hope that they, too, could gain power positions—if only power were spread more broadly. Once the move to power dispersion began, it was difficult to stop its spread until most members, or at least most members of the majority party, chaired a committee or subcommittee. And once power was widely spread, members of Congress who gained power positions wanted to maintain decentralization as a way of serving reelection interests, maintaining personal decision-making prerogatives in key policy arenas, of satisfying personal power drives, and of furthering their careers.

Because a decentralized system served the immediate interests of members of a professionalized Congress, committee government has dominated congressional organization for most of the twentieth century. The most significant widely-supported organizational changes in Congress, particularly during the post-war years, have been the moves to shift power from committees to subcommittees and to spread subcommittee positions more widely. With decentralization have come serious problems for Congress—problems that have inhibited its ability to perform its constitutional role as the legislative branch of government.

Increasingly, Congress has lacked the internal leadership necessary (a) to act in an independent fashion legislatively, and (b) to justify persuasively to the nation the legislative action that it has taken. As a result of the lack of leadership capacity, together with numerous specific problems associated with the committee and subcommittee system and procedural rules that grew up around them, Congress has often found it difficult to respond quickly and coherently to new problems. Congress has tended to make many of its decisions in an insulated and closed fashion, thereby undermining its legitimacy in the eyes of the public. In addition, it has until recently lacked centralized mechanisms to provide coordination of the budgetary process. Finally, committee and subcommittee government have made difficult rational, authoritative, coordinated, and independent oversight of the executive branch.

These problems that have emerged within Congress have tended to slow its decisionmaking process. With Congress partly immobilized, and with the problems of the nation growing ever greater, the country has turned to the executive branch, both to the presidency and the bureaucracy, to fill part of the vacuum left by congressional drift. Presidents increasingly have provided leadership by presenting presidential programs and by personally lobbying for them, using presidential resources to break congressional logjams. Bureaucratic agencies have come to provide legislative leadership by initiating many specific proposals for statutory changes and by extensive agency liaison operations in Congress in an effort to help pass agency proposals. Likewise, the presidency and bureaucracy together provide for budgetary coordination through extensive efforts every year to develop a national budget.

Both the increased involvement of the executive in policy formulation and legislation and its expanded budgetary role have occurred in this century *after* the rise of committee government. These shifts toward legislative leadership and budgetary control by the executive seriously threaten the ability of

Congress to play a forceful role in national policymaking. Faced
with the increased involvement of the presidency and bureaucratic agencies in the legislative sphere, Congress has responded
in part by attempts to move into the turf of the executive
branch—to influence the *implementation* of policy. Its reforms
have focused to a significant degree on attempts to improve its
oversight capacity by restructuring the committee system, improving its access to information, and decreasing its dependence
on interest groups. These reforms have fallen short of the
mark—largely because of the pull that subsystem politics exerts
on members and because of their fears that reform may undermine their personal power.

Aside from organizational and procedural reform, much of
the recent story of congressional-executive branch relations in
the modern period turns on congressional attempts to develop
and refine new methods and mechanisms of oversight. As innovative as some of these have seemed, however, we suggest
they have been clouded by their utilization for purposes other
than just oversight. It appears that quite often the development
of such devices reflects struggles inside the Congress—among
legislative subcommittees, between legislative and appropriations subcommittees, and so on—instead of pristine intentions to
monitor the bureaucracy more closely or bring it to heel. Oversight is at least partly a pawn used by elements of Congress in
their jockeying for position among one another and for
hegemony over the agencies of administration and benefits they
provide to congressional constituencies.

The modern period has also witnessed the development by
Congress of devices for *presidential* control over the departments
and agencies of the executive branch, especially the establishment of the Executive Office of the President and to some extent, as we discuss later, the granting of presidential authority to
reorganize executive branch structure to make its components
more responsive to presidential control. This effort, however,
has been accompanied by the rise of an institutionalized or "imperial" presidency, which has given Congress considerable pause
as to the further utilization of this technique for bureaucratic
surveillance—especially as it tends to contribute further to what

is seen as a growing constitutional imbalance between the Congress and the president. Recent attempts to restrict presidential flexibility in the structuring of the Executive Office, including the move to bring increasing numbers of its top level appointees under senatorial confirmation; restrictions on presidential prerogatives in the foreign affairs area; the congressional budget process; and increasing limitations placed on presidential reorganization authority, are evidence of this trend.

The abuse of presidential power by Nixon during the Watergate years reinforced congressional reluctance to augment the powers of the presidency over the organs of the executive branch. This tendency shows little sign of abating even in the present period when Congress and the president are both of the same party. It appears in our judgment unlikely that the conscious expansion of presidential powers over the bureaucracy, powers that can and have been turned against the Congress, continue to offer an attractive alternative to enhanced congressional surveillance of administration.

A basic problem is that Congress, thrust back on itself for control of administration, does not seem to be in a position to speak with one authoritative voice nor to develop institutional mechanisms of bureaucratic control that supercede the enduring bonds of subsystem politics and subcommittee government. It is true, as we have previously discussed, that institutional and leadership developments at the highest levels of Congress, and the endurance of the congressional budget process as well, offer Congress certain possiblities to enhance its capacity as an institution for monitoring the administrative state; but we are not sanguine that developments in this direction will be carried to the point where they compete effectively with the entrenched interests of subcommittee government.

As we have seen, the emergence of subcommittee government has enabled many if not most agencies to escape oversight of a severe or restrictive nature. More often the ramification of oversight devices has allowed the agencies to negate potential control by the staff agencies of Congress and in some cases to turn oversight mechanisms to their own advantage. These devices may appear to force executive agencies to pay more heed to

Congress, but their attention is directed largely to the substantive subcommittees and the appropriations process rather than to "Congress" as a whole. In the eyes of many agency officials, "the Congress" is increasingly an abstract notion.

Members of Congress are not unaware of the fact that committee and subcommittee government have generated problems. There have been periodic reform movements within Congress throughout the twentieth century to establish and strengthen centralized organs of party leadership, budgetary coordination, and executive oversight. These reform movements have peaked in rather cyclical fashion during this century—first in 1946 and later in the 1973–1976 period.[1] The problems with these centralizing reform efforts have been twofold: (1) as previous chapters have indicated, centralizing reforms normally are either defeated or are considerably weakened before passage, thus the reformers never achieve the centralized systems of party leadership, budgetary coordination or bureaucratic oversight that they deem necessary; and (2) judging from the experience of the 1946 Legislative Reorganization Act, those reforms that do pass have no guarantee of survival over the long run. Once the crisis atmosphere that generates centralizing reforms has passed, the pressure for decentralizing Congress reemerges.

Both with regard to passing centralizing reforms and sustaining them, the history of the twentieth century Congress is a testament to the tenacity of the long-term preoccupation of members of Congress with personal power. It also reflects the preference that many major political actors inside and outside Congress have for subsystem politics. It seems that members of Congress will allow congressional power to be recentralized only under the direst of circumstances; when crises that generate centralized reforms recede, members will attempt to spread power once again. The opposition to centralizing power is fueled by lobbyists and bureaucratic agencies with vested inter-

---

[1] For a theory arguing that this cyclical pattern of reform is inherent in the nature of the twentieth century Congress, see Lawrence C. Dodd, "Congress and the Quest for Power," in Lawrence C. Dodd and Bruce I. Oppenheimer, *Congress Reconsidered* (New York: Praeger, 1977.)

ests in the existence and persistence of a decentralized system of committee and subcommittee government. Efforts to break subsystem politics and control the administrative state that rely on internal, centralizing reforms of Congress have not proved fruitful or enduring.

Executive Branch Reorganization: An Historical Perspective

Partly because strengthening Congress through internal reform seems to hold little promise for improving the responsiveness and performance of the administrative state, reformers have often stressed another approach—reorganization of the executive branch itself. Reorganization of the executive branch is sometimes viewed as an effort that could have substantial potential for weakening the bonds of subsystem politics. The argument suggests that shaking up executive branch structure and creating new departments and agencies from the old would produce a freshness and organizational vitality as well as breaking up (or limiting the influence of) prevailing subsystem patterns.

A basic problem with this approach, of course, is that just as Congress is responsible for executive branch organization, so is it responsible ultimately for its *re*organization. Congress has, however, allowed both the president and agency heads considerable flexibility in matters of executive organization over the years. On the other hand, it has kept a rather short rein on substantial alterations in the existing structure, especially on the creation of new agencies and the abolition of old ones. Indeed, initiative for massive overhaul of executive structure has come almost without exception from the executive and from presidential commissions and study groups—not from the Congress.

Congress has given latitude to the executive in reorganization matters through a variety of procedures. One of these is the statutory delegation of reorganization powers to the president, whereby he may inaugurate structural changes (with certain limitations) through executive order. Such broad delegations have been used sparingly by the Congress, and have generally been granted only during times of national emergency. A prime example of this was the Overman Act of 1917, which gave the president the right to reorganize the executive branch in pursuit of war mobilization.

Even here, however, the Congress stipulated that the president's authority could not extend to the consolidation of the existing departments nor could whole bureaus be abolished. Further, organizational arrangements were to return to pre-war status within six months after the conclusion of the war.[2] Similar powers were also given the president under the Economy Act of 1932 and its amendments of 1933. This Act gave the president somewhat wider latitude than the Overman Act but contained the stipulation that he could not abolish any departments or agencies that had been created by statute. Moreover, as noted previously, here was applied for the first time the legislative veto device that required executive orders pertaining to reorganization to be laid before Congress for 60 days, subject to a concurrent resolution disapproving the reorganization. Again in 1941 under the War Powers Act, Congress gave the president substantial reorganization authority along the lines of the Overman Act of World War I. Powers were granted to the president to be exercised only "in matters relating to the conduct of the present war" and the Act required the president to submit proposals for abolition of statutory agencies to Congress for its approval.[3] As in the case of the Overman Act, the executive branch structure was to revert to the status quo ante after the cessation of hostilities. Such delegations of authority differ from the reorganization plan device (discussed below) in a number of respects and should not be confused with it.

A second reorganization procedure, also based on statutory delegation, runs directly to departmental and agency heads. Often in the organic act creating the agency, Congress will grant

[2]U.S. Congress, House of Representatives. Committee on Government Operations, *Executive Reorganization: A Summary Analysis,* 92nd Congress, 2nd Session (1972), p. 13; Herbert Emmerich, *Federal Organization and Administrative Management* (University Ala.: University of Alabama Press, 1971), pp. 42–43.
[3]Emmerich, *op. cit.*, p. 72.

its chief official certain powers to make structural adjustments internally on his own initiative (though these may be cleared informally with the legislative committee or subcommittee concerned). Such provisions are generally limited to minor adjustments, and statutory bureaus and functions may be exempt from reorganization. In terms of ongoing, incremental adjustment to the requirements of organizational change, this authority provided agency heads is probably the most common means of structural alteration—but in nearly all cases, such alterations are internal to the agency concerned.

These two types of reorganization authority are either an extraordinary response to a national emergency, as in the first instance, or relatively minor shifts in the internal workings of individual departments and agencies, as in the second. Much more important, however, in terms of their implications for Congressional-executive relations are the more salient and visible methods of reorganization: (1) those that take place under presidential reorganization plan and, (2) those that are enacted by statute ad hoc.

The reorganization plan approach to executive organization emerged on the scene in 1939, partly as an attempt to salvage for the president some additional "administrative management" powers from the ashes of the Brownlow Commission's report. The basic procedure allows the president to present plans for organizational changes. These plans are then laid before the Congress and after a certain period of time, go into effect if Congress has not moved to block them. Reorganization plan authority has been granted to all presidents since Franklin Roosevelt. The procedures stipulated and the extent of coverage permitted under such plans, however, have varied considerably, and the authority itself allowed to lapse on several occasions— the most recent case being the refusal of Congress to provide then-president Nixon with reorganization authority in reaction to the abuses uncovered in the Watergate scandals.

One interesting pattern in the scope and characteristics of the reorganization authority granted the president by Congress is that since 1939, the prerogatives of the president have been gradually circumscribed as Congress has moved to increase its control over reorganization under the plan approach. The original 1939 legislation had given the president the right to propose a wide variety of changes in executive branch structure (though it had exempted a few pet agencies such as the Corps of Engineers) and required that plans could be overturned only by a *concurrent* resolution of both houses, thus making it possible for a reorganization plan to go into effect should only one house fail to pass a resolution of disapproval.

The authority given the president in 1949 however, provided that a simple resolution of a majority of the membership of *either* house could kill a proposed reorganization. And though the 1949 Act provided for a four-year period of reorganization authority, renewals have gradually been provided for shorter periods of two or three years. In 1959, the Act was amended to make it even easier for a resolution of disapproval to be passed in either house. Under its provisions a simple majority of those present and voting was sufficient to disapprove a plan. Because of conflicts with President Kennedy over his attempts to create a Department of Housing and Urban Development through reorganization plan, Congress in 1964 stipulated that the reorganization authority of the president could no longer be used to propose the creation of new departments.[4]

The reorganization plan authority granted President Carter in 1977 contains several additional provisions that further restrict presidential initiative. The authority given Carter continues the proscription against formation of new executive departments and, further, prohibits any plan from abolishing or proposing substantial reorganization of the independent regulatory agencies, or from proposing the elimination of any agency or program that has been created by statute—a rather substantial restriction, given the overwhelming number of statutory agencies, departments, and programs. In justification of this provision, the House Committee on Government Opera-

---

[4]Committee on Government Operations, *Executive Reorganization,* pp. 14–15; U.S. Congress, House of Representatives, Committee on Government Operations, *Extension of Reorganization Authority of the President,* 95th Congress, 1st Session (1977), pp. 5–6.

tions argued that "if they [statutory programs and agencies] were created by Congressional legislation they should only be abolished in the same way."[5] The current authority also provides for the automatic introduction of a resolution of disapproval in each house, so that in nearly all cases, a floor vote on each reorganization plan will be forced. The current authority does, however, give the president the ability to amend a plan within the first thirty days of submission, a procedure that was not previously available to him.

From the perspective of our analysis it is significant that consideration of reorganization plans is lodged with the House Committee on Government Operations and the Senate Committee on Governmental Affairs—committees outside the subsystems of the legislative and appropriations committees. Thus one might suppose that here is a device for bypassing the provincial interests of the numerous subsystems and securing attention to reorganization plans by a "neutral" committee and eventually by the Congress as a whole.

An evaluation of the effect of reorganization plans to date, however, is somewhat mixed. First, one should note that major structural alteration of the executive branch is beyond the scope of the president's reorganization authority. Most major reorganizations, as we shall see, have been attempted through statutory enactments rather than plans. The majority of presidential plans have been accepted by the Congress (in that motions for disapproval have either been rejected or not offered); a substantial number of them, however, represent relatively minor modifications of executive branch structure that do not threaten subcommittee government. One major department, that of Health, Education and Welfare, was created through a reorganization plan in 1953. Other creations have included such independent agencies as the U.S. Information Agency and the Environmental Protection Agency, a number of units of the Executive Office of the President, and bureaus of major departments such as the National Oceanographic and Atmospheric Administration

---

[5]Committee on Government Operations, *Extension of Reorganization Authority*, p. 7.

(1970) in Commerce and the Drug Enforcement Administration (1973) in Justice.

The reorganization plan method does offer the potential for bypassing the legislative committees, getting a vote on a plan to the floor, and thus undercutting subgovernment politics. On a few occasions this has been successful, such as in the plan negotiated by President Johnson in 1967 to reorganize the District of Columbia Government—a plan that succeeded in spite of the hostile efforts of the House District of Columbia Committee. On other occasions, reorganization plans, though not themselves successful, have stimulated the introduction of statutory legislation on the part of the appropriate legislative committee. This occurred with a Truman plan of 1949, which spurred the Armed Services Committees to come up with a military unification bill.[6] Some plans have also had a limiting effect on subsystem government by reducing the power of bureau chiefs, often the primary actors on the executive side. A series of plans in the 1950s, urged by the recommendations of the Hoover Commission, were successful in transferring a number of statutory powers previously given bureau chiefs to the agency or department heads above them, a move that reduced somewhat the power of semiautonomous bureaus.[7] These efforts have, however, often paled before the power of legislative committees, which on occasion have been able to block a reorganization plan to protect the special position of a favored bureau. An example is the Office of the Comptroller of the Currency, which has been exempted in plans that have attempted to strengthen the power of the Secretary of the Treasury over the bureaus of that department.[8]

As a device for making inroads into subsystem politics, the reorganization plan approach has shown only moderate utility. Given the increasingly severe limitations placed on the *kinds* of reorganizations that may be introduced through this method, it

---

[6]Harvey C. Mansfield, Sr., "Federal Executive Reorganization: Thirty Years of Experience," *Public Administration Review*, Vol. 29, No. 4 (July/August, 1967), pp. 337, 341.

[7]Harold Seidman, *Politics, Position, and Power* (London and New York: Oxford University Press, 1975), p. 58, Mansfield, *op. cit.*, p. 339.

[8]Emmerich, *op. cit.*, p. 131.

nonetheless provides the president a chance to present to Congress a proposal that requires positive action on the part of Congress to block, and which flows not through the legislative committees but through the Government Operations Committees, whose ties are often less parochial. It also affords the president the possibility of mustering support in each house for a threatened disapproval resolution and to bring his case to Congress as a whole.

Harvey Mansfield, who has studied the history of reorganization plan efforts in detail, concludes that "the reorganization plan method has provided a compromise procedure for safeguarding congressional interests while permitting presidential initiatives on matters where considerable state power and prestige are at issue and in situations where deadlock might otherwise prevail. Reorganization plans have provided a serviceable device for shifting bureaus, realigning jurisdictions, regrouping activities, and upsetting some ties of influence."[9]

The last and most common method of making substantial alterations in executive branch structure is that which follows the normal process of legislation—statutory creation of new organizations or the realignment of old ones. This, indeed, appears to be the device Congress prefers for effecting organizational change in the federal bureaucracy. Even in the decade and a half after World War II, when use of the reorganization plan method was popular as a result of the numerous proposals of the two Hoover Commissions, the number of statutory reorganizations that took place were more than double the number of those accomplished by reorganization plan.[10]

With the single exception of the Department of Health, Education and Welfare, all departments of the executive branch have been created by statute, as have been the bulk of the independent agencies and regulatory commissions. This is hardly surprising. The creation of new agencies usually indicates congressional sanction for a new direction or substantial expansion of existing programs instead of a minor adjustment of ongoing activities.

[9]Mansfield, *op. cit.*, p. 341.
[10]*Ibid.*, p. 336.

From our perspective, the preference of Congress for the ad hoc statutory approach to reorganization is readily understandable. Statutory enactments of this sort run the normal legislative gamut and are handled by those legislative committees with jurisdiction over the agencies, policies, and programs in question. They are subject to the normal processes of amendment and reflect input from the various interests that may be affected. One can view the continuing limitations on the presidential reorganization plan method as consistent with the growth and influence of subcommittee government over the past decades. As Mansfield has pointed out, nearly all statutory reorganizations have one thing in common: "being subject to the jurisdictions of the respective legislative committees enroute to enactment, they maximize the influence of these committees on the outcome."[11] The congressional preference for the statutory route, which protects its legislative committees, is testimony that this approach to executive reorganization will generally not threaten existing ties and alliances.

Major reorganizations have nevertheless been attempted. And it is instructive to pause briefly to review the results of one effort to restructure radically the federal executive branch—the legislation stemming from the President's Committee on administrative Management (the Brownlow Commission) in 1937–1939. The legislative response to this attempted reform highlights the problems associated with securing congressional assent to any substantial alteration in existing executive branch structure and also the influence of parochial bureaucratic and private interests on the outcome.

Although the work of the Brownlow Commission covered a number of areas concerned with the president's managerial control over the executive branch, among the most controversial of its proposals was a complete restructuring of executive branch agencies—which the Commission members saw as chaotic and unmanageable. The Commission proposed taking the more than 100 independent agencies, boards, commissions, and administrations and placing them by executive order in twelve

[11]*Ibid.*

major executive departments, several of which were to be new creations. Reaction was swift. In addition to congressional concern at allowing the president such tremendous latitude in reorganization by executive order, strong protest was triggered by affected bureaus and agencies and a number of important interest groups, among them the American Legion, the Veterans of Foreign Wars and the Forest Service lobby. Feelings against the magnitude of additional powers that the legislation would give the president ran deep in the Senate when the reorganization bill was considered there in 1938. Senator Burton Wheeler of Montana, a chief opponent, offered the observation that should such authority be granted, the president himself could not possibly decide which agencies should be moved where, and he queried his colleagues

> So who is going to do it? Some professor or some clerk in the department is going to do it. They are going to be the boys who will do the work and they are going to say to my people in Montana, "we are going to abolish the Bureau of Indian Affairs" . . . although they have never set foot on an Indian reservation in their lives and have never seen an Indian, except in the moving picture in New York City, they are going to sit down in some office in Washington, prepare reports and tell the members of the Senate and of the House what ought to be done.[12]

What is striking is that in spite of the numerous objections to the reorganization bill, which included civil service and accounting reforms as well as executive restructuring, it actually passed the Senate in 1938 by a vote of 42 to 40 after several weakening amendments had been adopted. Polenberg attributes the Senate passage to the fact that "it found favor with a block of pro-Roosevelt New Dealers and a number of disinterested men to whom reorganization seemed urgent."[13]

After acrimonous debate in the House, however, the reor-

---

[12]Quoted in Richard Polenberg, *Reorganizing Roosevelt's Government: The Controversy Over Executive Reorganization 1936–1939* (Cambridge, Mass.: Harvard University Press, 1966), p. 130. The standard work on the Brownlow Commission is Barry D. Karl, *Executive Reorganization and Reform in the New Deal* (Cambridge, Mass.: Harvard University Press, 1963).

[13]*Ibid.,* p. 140.

ganization proposals were watered down even further, but not far enough to secure their passage. The bill was recommitted by a vote of 204–196. Defeat in the House was due to a series of factors, including fears that congressional independence would be diminished if it passed, objections to provisions not immediately germane to the proposed reorganization, a concern for special relationships between committees and bureaus, and the active opposition of various interest groups. In sum, Polenberg concluded, "the demise of the Reorganization Bill was brought about . . . by a combination of forces. Congressmen who wished to restrict the executive authority, protect pet bureaus, or inflict a defeat upon the President united against the measure. They were encouraged by powerful interest groups and ordinary citizens whose fear of dictatorship and resentment at the recession were exploited by opponents of the bill. The countervailing forces—Roosevelt's political skill, his influence over New Deal Democrats, the need for reorganization—were offset by lapses in political strategy. Even in a diluted form, reorganization could not overcome these obstacles."[14] (Congress did in the next year provide the president with the staff assistance requested by the Brownlow Committee and with the reorganization plan authority discussed above.)

Polenberg's analysis suggests that interest group pressures and those emanating from the bureaucratic establishment were perhaps as strong or stronger than hostility toward reorganization flowing directly from the various committees. Even after the concerns of many of the committees had been somewhat mitigated by the exclusion from reorganization of certain pet bureaus, the reforms failed, due partly to an ever-present problem—the lack of a constituency for reform per se.

Reorganization in the 1970s: The Nixon and Carter Administrations

Executive reorganization was high on the agenda of both Presidents Nixon and Carter. In planning for structural change,

[14]*Ibid.*, pp. 166–175.

Nixon adopted the study commission approach typical of most of his predecessors. The reform proposals of the Ash Committee, headed by Nixon's onetime Director of OMB, Roy Ash, aroused substantial opposition from various interest groups and especially in Congress—where concern over committee and subcommittee jurisdictions ran high. The congressional ire the Ash Committee proposals raised appears to reflect the increased dominance of subcommittee government that has developed in the post-war years.

The Nixon proposals for reorganization were considerably more modest in scope than those of Roosevelt. They would have created four new departments, blending into them the activities of six existing departments, which would have been abolished, plus some functions of certain independent agencies. The independent agencies, however, were for the most part left outside the proposed restructuring, as were the regulatory commissions. Introduced in 1971, the proposals would have created new departments for community development, natural resources, human resources, and economic affairs, organized around what the Nixon administration called "basic goals."[15] The core of the Nixon proposals were presented to Congress in the form of bills to establish each of the four new departments. Initial overview hearings were held by the Committees on Government Operations of the House and Senate.

There was something in the Nixon proposals to displease and alienate nearly every committee of the Congress. One facet that was alluded to several times in the hearings was the disruption of existing committee-agency relationships and the enhanced powers to be given the secretaries of the new supercabinets—powers in internal reorganization and allocation of appropriated funds among the various elements of the new departments. Many members of Congress feared that such provisions were aimed at the heart of existing subsystem ties. John Gardner, then head of Common Cause, suggested as much in a statement that was later

---

[15] A discussion of the Nixon-Ash proposals may be found in U.S. House of Representatives, Committee on Government Operations, *Executive Reorganization: A Summary Analysis* (Washington: U.S. Government Printing Office, 1972).

referred to on several occasions by members of the House and Senate.

> [S]ome elements in Congress and some special interest lobbies have never really wanted the departmental Secretaries to be strong. As everyone in this room knows but few people outside of Washington understand, questions of public policy nominally lodged with the Secretary are often decided far beyond the Secretary's reach by a trinity—not exactly a holy trinity—consisting of (1) representatives of an outside lobby, (2) middle-level bureaucrats, and (3) selected Members of Congress. . . .
>
> Participants in such durable alliances do not want the departmental Secretaries strengthened. And they oppose even more vigorously any reorganization that might shake up the alliance. If the subject matter is shifted to another congressional committee, the congressional leg of the trinity may be broken. If the departments are reorganized, a stranger may appear on the bureaucratic leg of the triangle. The outside special interests are particularly resistant to such change. It took them years to dig their particular tunnel into the public vault, and they don't want the vault moved.[16]

Gardner, of course, was describing classic subsystem politics. His analysis was echoed later by the staff director of the House Government Operations Committee who, referring to Gardner's remarks, suggested that "outside lobbyists, middle bureaucrats and selected congressmen are an unholy trinity, and it is against this kind of combination that the reorganization is pointed."[17]

Closely linked to the potential disruption of subsystem politics that the reorganization presented was the reshaping of committee jurisdictions. Concern for committee relationships with the new departments and the elements of other agencies that might be drawn into them was high. The chairman of the House Government Operations Committee, Chet Holifield (D-Calif.) cautioned an official of the OMB, "you are going to have to look at this thing in a practical way. If by this organization you affect

---

[16]U.S. Senate, Committee on Government Operations, *Executive Reorganization Proposals: Hearings* (Washington: U.S. Government Printing Office, 1971), pp. 57–58.

[17]U.S. House, Committee on Government Operations, *Reorganization of Executive Departments (Part I—Overview): Hearings* (Washington: U.S. Government Printing Office, 1971), p. 267.

in a major way the powers of the various committees in the Congress, you might as well forget it. The only way I know of to get one or more of these departments through is to allow the committees that now have the programs within their jurisdiction to follow their programs, just as they are followed now, and authorize those programs wherever those programs are distributed. If you don't do that, we are in practical trouble on Capitol Hill."[18]

Moreover, the proposals would have changed the way in which appropriated funds were handled in executive departments, and would have substantially changed the subcommittee structure of the appropriations committees. Since appropriations subcommittees are organized around departments and agencies rather than by program or policy areas (the usual case with the legislative committees), alterations in departmental structure would have meant a shift in appropriations subcommittee organizations as well. But the legislative committees were equally concerned with the disruption that the reorganization would have implied, for the plan would have challenged traditional ties between agencies and committees. A study done by the Congressional Research Service found that 31 of 39 congressional committees authorized to report legislation would have their jurisdictions affected by the reorganization—16 of them rather extensively. What appeared especially controversial and threatening was not the loss of jurisdiction over programs (it was a fact that no legislative committee or subcommittee would *lose* jurisdiction over a program) but rather that those programs would be placed in different organizational locations in the executive branch, thus threatening to disrupt the established ties of the subsystem. As the House Government Operations Committee report put it rather diplomatically:

> *For certain committees, jurisdictional influence and control over a single department would be eliminated or reduced, but they would have jurisdictional fingers, so to speak, in more departmental pies. To the extent that they retained established working relationships with bureaucracies inside departments and interest groups outside, their effect on specific programs*

[18]*Ibid.*, p. 324.

would not necessarily be changed. On the other hand, disestablishment of historic departments and program dispersion could affect the ability of committees to influence departmental policy and program direction. [19]

Throughout the hearings on the Nixon proposals there is evidence that members of Congress were concerned with the disruption of established ties, including the possibility that a given bureau or program might occupy a lower hierarchical position and thus less status and prestige in a "super department" than in its present location. Members could not be assured that the established lines of communication, personal relationships, and knowledge of the departmental context in which a program or agency operated would be maintained intact.

As did the Brownlow recommendations, the Nixon proposals triggered interest group reaction. Indeed, Nixon's original intention to dismantle the Department of Agriculture and merge it with one of the new departments was scuttled because of pressure from agrarian interests. One of the arguments of the executive branch proponents of reorganization had been that the new super-departments would be above special interests and the "narrow missions" of the departments to be abolished. Fear that interest group access to executive agencies and congressional committees might be limited by the reorganization proposals also gave pause.

Another issue that caused concern was the emphasis on decentralization of a number of functions of the new departments from Washington to the field and the granting of greater authority to regional officials. Such decentralization, it was feared, would make it more difficult for members of Congress to process constituent requests and complaints, for it would shift the locus of power away from Washington, where they were most happy and comfortable in dealing with established agencies in constituent matters. As the committee report put it rather delicately:

All Members of Congress, in principle, would favor better regional organization and making Government more responsive. In practice, Members of Congress would be greatly interested in a shift of authority, patronage, and

[19]House Committee on Government Operations, *Executive Reorganization: Summary Analysis*, pp. 41–42.

money-disbursing privileges to regional offices for their political as well as administrative implications. For those Members who now have established points of contact and channels of communication with the various departments and agencies of the executive branch, reorganization undoubtedly would entail extended periods of readjustment.[20]

Finally, the Nixon proposals also threatened the security of a number of organizational units (mostly bureaus) below the departmental level, by requesting that the statutory basis for these bureaus be "lapsed." The legislation requested the lapsing of 63 bureaus created by statute, including such congressional favorites as the National Park Service, the Bureau of Reclamation, the Federal Highway Administration, the Office of Education, and others.[21]

One has the feeling that the reorganization proposals of the Ash Committee, extensive as they were, had not been designed with a view to congressional realities, certainly not the reality of subcommittee government as it has emerged over the past several decades. Ash himself came from a business background and received some grilling for his lack of knowledge of the congressional scene during testimony.

MR. HORTON (R-New York). I do not know whether you are familiar with the process, but we have authorizing committees and Appropriations Committees. The Department of Agriculture comes up to Congress now and gets authorization for its programs, and then it goes before the Appropriations Committee to get appropriations for that authorization.

Now, when you transfer, for example, from the Department of Agriculture all of its functions and it goes into all four of these new departments, there is a very serious question as to whether or not you need a realignment of the committees of the Congress. I do not know whether you have gotten into that or not, but do you have any comment on it?

MR. ASH. Mr. Horton, I will have to defer that to OMB who is clearly more expert than I on such a matter.

MR. HORTON. In other words, your Council did not go into the problems that you might have with regard to presenting the programs to the Congress?

MR. ASH. That is right. We did not.[22]

[20]*Ibid.,* p. 33.
[21]House Committee on Government Operations, *Reorganization of Executive Departments: Hearings,* p. 744.
[22]*Ibid.,* p. 220.

Given their impact on the Congress, it is not surprising that the Nixon proposals made little progress on the Hill—though the effect of Watergate on presidential-congressional relations probably sealed their doom. After the overview hearings, only one of the bills, that to create a Department of Community Development, was reported. It was killed in the Rules Committee by the chairmen of a number of committees that would have been most affected by it—including Interior and Insular Affairs, Education and Labor, Public Works, Banking and Currency, Agriculture, and, last but not least, the Appropriations Committee.[23]

The approach to reorganization taken by the Carter administration appears to differ both in scope and concept from that of its predecessors. Rather than working from some grand design or immutable organizational principles, the Carter effort attempts to analyze problems or deficiencies in government services and, based on this analysis, to propose organizational improvements or realignments. In the words of Harrison Wellford, associate director of OMB for reorganization, the approach rejects "the assumption that government is so simple that it can be reorganized according to one or two basic principles."[24]

The Carter effort, moreover, has shied from the study comission model of planning for reorganization. Instead, there has been created a permanent reorganization staff that is the locus for coordinating reform efforts. Housed in the OMB, the staff conducts organizational studies and makes recommendations for legislation or presidential reorganization plans. It is divided into functional divisions—natural resources, economic resources, national security, and so on—and also includes a group responsible for management and regulatory affairs. Moreover, a position of Special Assistant for Reorganization has been created in the White House Office, testimony to the symbolic closeness Mr. Carter feels to the problem.

The Carter approach also differs in its relative openness and the inclusion in the study process itself of affected agencies,

[23]Seidman, *op. cit.,* p. 45.
[24]*National Journal Reports,* December 3, 1977, p. 1872.

interest groups, and members and staffs of Congress. The OMB staff is supplemented by consultants and civil service careerists seconded to it from other agencies, and attempts are made to keep open the lines of communication to affected parties.

Given its limited ambitions, it is unlikely that the Carter approach will develop proposals so all-encompassing (and thus so controversial in Congress) as earlier efforts. Incremental adjustments, rather than the massive overhaul originally promised the electorate by candidate Carter, appear to be the order of the day. But judged against its rather modest claims, the Carter effort, at least at this writing, has proved relatively productive—partly because of its very modesty. The first years of the Carter administration have produced a new Department of Energy, the reorganization of the civil service system into two separate components (the Office of Personnel Management and the Merit System Protection Board); the amalgamation of the cultural affairs activities of the Department of State into the U.S. Information Agency, now renamed the International Communication Agency; consolidation of various equal employment opportunity enforcement programs; and a restructuring of the Executive Office of the President.

Although some aspects of these reforms have met resistance in Congress (the defeated proposal to modify veterans' preference in federal hiring, for example), few have made serious inroads into the political or jurisdictional turf of agencies, interest groups, and committees. More substantial proposals, such as the creation of a new Department of Education, which would take over educational programs conducted by various other agencies, have encountered serious opposition in Congress and in the executive branch. And like previous departmental creations, these more ambitious reform proposals will have to run the gauntlet of congressional authorizing committees.

In sum, our analysis suggests that the potential of executive branch reorganization as a counterweight to subcommittee government is minimal. Congress and its committees create the organizations of the executive branch, and have over the years proved generally reticent to allow major modifications in its structure. Congress has given certain agency heads the right to make minor internal adjustments and the president the right to make somewhat broader modifications subject to its veto. But it has reserved for itself, through statute, the ability to pass on most reorganizations that would seriously affect the way in which the committees and subcommittees of Congress go about their business with the federal bureaucracy. Executive branch architects of major reform proposals have often used efficient administration and good management practice as criteria for reform efforts. Congress, on the other hand, has been more interested in preserving the pluralism of the political system within which the federal executive branch operates and places greater emphasis on responsiveness than on efficiency or neatness of organizational structure. Although the Congress has given the president substantial controls of an "administrative management" nature, it has not been willing to extend these controls to a point where they would seriously affect its ability to maintain its special relationships with the bureaus, agencies, and departments of the federal bureaucracy. Given this demonstrated antipathy toward major executive reform, it is likely that incremental amendments to executive branch structure will continue to be the way in which the administration of public policy at the national level is adjusted.

Strengthening Congress Through Reform

The general theme of our analysis in this and the preceding chapters leads us to return to some questions concerning representative government posed by the endurance of congressional ties with the administrative state. One set of questions concerns the extent to which the federal bureaucracy is responsive to "overhead democracy" through its institutional ties to the president and to the Congress, that is, whether it is ultimately responsible to officials who themselves occupy positions by virtue of the electoral process. These ties, as Redford and others have suggested, are crucial to the maintenance of democratic control of administration.[25] Is, for example, the federal bureau-

---

[25]See, for example, the discussion of these themes in Emmette Redford, *Democracy in the Administrative State* (New York: Oxford University Press, 1969), pp. 70–82.

cracy really "out of control" or at least in a position where it is able continually to play one of its masters off against the other? The answer to this question, in our view, is not clear-cut.

In many instances, executive branch agencies appear to stand suspended between the elective institutions who are their reputed masters. That they may on occasion play one element of Congress off against another or Congress against the president does not necessarily mean that they have escaped the controls exercised by these institutions. It does demonstrate the bargaining, negotiation, and elaboration of the bureaucratic dynamic that is endemic to the setting of public organizations. The administrative state is not a fully autonomous, independent fourth branch of government, but its crucial position in the struggle between executive and legislative over who shall determine its directions allows it considerable leverage that can affect the balance of power between the president and Congress. The growth of the federal bureaucracy has not, in our judgment, destroyed our constitutional system of government. It *has* produced problems for representative government that have taken the nation far beyond the constitutional scenario projected by the framers.

Related to the question of the position of the administrative state in the overall constitutional system and to its control by its democratic superiors is the issue of the effectiveness of congressional oversight of the executive branch. We have traced in some detail the evolution and application of a variety of forms and techniques by which Congress attempts to ride herd on the activities of federal agencies and have also attempted to assess, in a preliminary way, the impact many of the newer techniques have had on the federal bureaucracy.

As we have suggested, there may be more form than substance to a number of these techniques, especially with those associated with those elements of the Congress that appear at the periphery of congressional activity—the Committees on Government Operations, the General Accounting Office, and the other congressional staff agencies. We have also suggested that even those devices developed by the legislative and appropriations committees, which are at the vortex of bureaucratic surveillance, may on occasion reflect internecine struggles within Congress rather than a desire for better policy surveillance per se.

Moreover, oversight appears to us to be somewhat more sporadic and transitory than is commonly assumed. Further, it may "meddle" more in the details of administration than address the substantive problems of policy surveillance—producing a thorn in the side of agencies but rarely holding a dagger to their hearts.

We conclude that the range of techniques developed over the years that have arisen with subcommittee government have improved only marginally the ability of Congress to conduct meaningful oversight of the administrative state. In addressing its own problems of the distribution of institutional power over the past few decades, Congress has largely neglected its responsibilities in exercising that power in terms of constructive oversight of the federal bureaucracy. And in spite of recent attempts by the Congress to provide greater incentives for the conduct of oversight, its present norms and structure mitigate against its elevation as a congressional function equal to those of law making and representation.

We come to a crucial question. Is there any way to strengthen Congress sufficiently to ensure that its reliance on the administrative state will not continue to erode its ability to formulate public policy and to oversee policy implementation? The answer to this question is not an easy one, but we hope the analysis in this book has suggested some directions. We would argue that the central problem lies not in the administrative state itself—neither with malevolent presidents nor insensitive bureaucrats. The root causes for the decline of congressional authority lie neither with the bureaucracy nor the presidency, but within Congress—with the inability of Congress to organize itself in a rational, coherent way that allows it to provide legislative leadership and authoritative oversight. If the executive branch has assumed leadership of legislative policymaking, control of the national budget, and unprecedented independence in policy implementation, it has gained these powers not because it has met Congress in a dramatic duel and won. Instead, the decentralized system of committee and subcommittee government has kept Congress so immobilized that it has often acquiesced in the leadership and strong role of the administrative state.

If Congress is to increase its capacity to play a strong policymaking role in the face of a growing administrative state, it must address far more earnestly than it has to date the problems caused by decentralization. To increase its leadership and coordination capacity, it must strengthen the party leaders in both houses, simplify the jurisdictional structure of its committee systems and provide continued support for its new budget process. Moreover, maintenance of popular support and institutional legitimacy requires that it be an open, accountable, responsive institution. In part this means that its elections must be fairer and that members have fewer advantages as incumbents. Thus reform of campaign laws and of congressional perquisites would seem in order. Likewise, it is critical that the remaining institutional barriers to responsiveness and openness—such as closed conference committee meetings—be eliminated.

Further, Congress must devote far more attention than it has thus far to systematic oversight reforms. To increase its capacity for serious oversight and control of the administrative state, Congress must address the problems of agency dependence, information capacity, and lobby power. A *proximate* solution to the inadequacy of congressional oversight lies along the lines of reforms attempted in the 1970s, but rejected. To decrease its dependence on agencies, Congress must take most oversight responsibility out of the hands of the appropriations and authorizations committees that are enmeshed in subsystem politics and place it in an independent, centralized oversight committee. The Government Operations Committees offer vehicles for such reforms, and could be given the extensive powers debated by the Bolling Committee. In addition, Congress might be well advised to consider the experiments of state governments with sunset legislation. Should Congress choose to adopt such legislation, the Government Operation Committees would be the natural ones to exercise responsibility for its implementation.

An increase in the information capacity of Congress requires that it reconsider the approach it has used thus far in this area. In the past thirty years, Congress has been successful in increasing its staff. But the staff has been dispersed among the members in ways that encourage repetitive activity, of which casework is a major illustration. Congress should give more attention to how best to coordinate and use the staff it has, perhaps through centralized casework efforts, pooling of casework staff, and so forth. In addition, Congress must focus more on developing a truly professional staff capable of analyzing the information that is available. The creation of the Congressional Budget Office, the expansion of the General Accounting Office, and the adoption of computer facilities, are illustrations of the types of changes that might better allow Congress to maximize its information capacity.

Finally, Congress must break the hold of lobby groups if it is seriously to oversee executive agencies. In fact, controlling the power of lobbies is probably a prerequisite to any serious reform of the committee system itself. During the 1970s, Congress shied away from lobby reform, actually choosing to pass more stringent ethics legislation for its members than for the lobbyists—an eloquent testament to the power of interest groups on Capitol Hill. Apparently members believed that so long as the lobbies maintained their power and access, they could protect members in their quest for reelection, even if that quest took place in a highly visible arena. Given the continued concern of members with reelection and personal power, we see little reason to believe that Congress will soon be willing to risk serious reform of lobby groups.

Our judgment is that efforts to strengthen congressional oversight of the executive by such proximate solutions as the reforms discussed here will be very slow in coming and probably are doomed to failure. The fundamental reason for this lies neither with Congress nor with its members. It lies, rather, in the Constitution. The congressional dilemma is, at its heart, a constitutional dilemma.

The Constitutional Dilemma

A basic problem facing Congress is that the writers of the U.S. Constitution never conceived of the possibility of a highly professionalized Congress composed of members who approached congressional service as a career. The founding fathers, particularly Madison, assumed that Congress would be a representative assembly in which most members served for only short periods of time and then returned to state or local politics or to private life.[26] They believed that Congress would experience high turnover because of the difficulty that existed in developing a national political career in an agrarian age in which travel was difficult and long absences from one's farm or business were costly; because the existence of federalism and a strong ethic of state's rights made service in state and local government seem relatively attractive; and because the low level of interstate and foreign commerce and the isolation of the nation from foreign entanglements made the national government seem of only moderate significance. For all of these reasons, the founding fathers assumed that Congress would have only a few members of great expertise and commitment, and that congressional power would be centralized in the hands of these members. In fact, a primary concern of the founding fathers was not that Congress would be too decentralized but that it would be too *centralized*—that a demogogue would be able to arise, collect the support of a majority of its members, and abuse its substantial legislative powers. Because of this worry, the authors of the Constitution concentrated their attention on building division into Congress rather than unity and cohesion, among other ways through the establishment of a bicameral legislature.[27]

Little thought was given to establishing constitutional provisions that would nurture cohesion, centralization, coordination, and leadership within Congress. While a single executive was created (to ensure centralized executive decisionmaking) and while the president was given the authority to nominate department heads (an authority viewed as critical to a cohesive executive branch), neither the Speaker of the House nor the President *pro tem* of the Senate was given authority to nominate committee

[26]See James Madison, *Federalist #53* in Alexander Hamilton, James Madison, and John Jay, *The Federalist Papers,* edited by Clinton Rosster (New York: New American Library), pp. 334–35.

[27]Madison, *Federalist #48,* p. 309.

chairs. The founding fathers simply assumed that a cohesive legislature would necessarily emerge by the very nature of legislative politics in an agrarian age where few politicians would want to develop long-term congressional careers.

Our government of separation of powers rests on this critical assumption of the founding fathers. In our separation of powers system, legislative, judicial, and executive authority is divided among three different branches. In addition, each branch is given certain checks that it can use against encroachment by the other branch, resulting in an ultimate system of shared powers. Explicit in this conception of government is the expectation that tension will exist among the branches of government, a tension deriving in part from the natural ambitions of political leaders within each institution. Ambition will naturally lead to the assertion by these leaders of a broad political role for their institutions. Inherent in this Madisonian conception is the expectation of thrust and counter-thrust between the institutions, particularly Congress and the presidency, with one branch asserting itself only to be constrained by the other.[28]

From a Madisonian perspective, itself based on the agrarian nature of the times, Congress should have no problem in knowing and asserting its "will" against executive aggrandizement. As we have seen throughout this book, however, that expectation no longer holds. Ours is no longer an agrarian society isolated from the main currents of international politics. Instead, dramatic alterations in our national and international life beginning in the late nineteenth century have made service in national political life, and thus in Congress, much more attractive.

These developments have tempered the Madisonian assumption that Congress would experience high turnover, would necessarily be able to act in a cohesive, authoritative manner to carry out its legislative responsibility and protect itself from executive encroachment. The move to a powerful national government has attracted those interested in the exercise of power and brought large numbers of them to Congress in search of long-term careers and influence over national policymaking.

[28]Madison, *Federalist #51*, pp. 321–327.

These members gradually united with lobbyists and bureaucratic agencies to develop mutually self-serving relationships that helped make Congressmembers electorally secure. In the process, Congress was transformed from a highly unprofessional and centralized institution into a professionalized and decentralized one.

In the twentieth century, the separation-of-powers system has eroded, partly as a result of the growth of an administrative state that appears often to overpower Congress. Another factor weakening Congress, and thus the separation of powers, is the fact that no provisions exist within the Constitution that inhibit career-oriented members of a highly professionalized Congress from decentralizing congressional power and thereby producing what often appears to be a leaderless and uncoordinated legislature that is at a distinct disadvantage vis-à-vis the executive branch. The responsibility for this phenomenon does not lie solely with the individual members of Congress. In seeking power, they are only acting as politicians are expected to act. Were politicians not to seek power, our separation of powers system would certainly dissolve. Likewise, the fault does not lie with presidents or bureaucrats. In filling the partial vacuum left by Congress, they are helping ensure that major policy decisions get made, decisions that in economic depression or wartime will often be critical to the very survival of the nation. Rather, much of the problem lies with the structure within which all of the actors are operating—the Constitution itself.

Having been written for a very different age, the U.S. Constitution does not really address the question of how best to structure institutional politics in an era when national government will be so strong as to attract a professional class of politicians to Washington, as well as support a professional bureaucracy and a professional lobby. Assuming the desirability of maintaining a separation of powers form of government, we feel that certain reforms may be in order, reforms that would nurture the growth of a more cohesive and truly democratic Congress, one that could maintain its institutional integrity vis-à-vis the other branches. To weaken the hold of subcommittee government, to reduce the appeal of subsystem politics, and thus to strengthen Congress against the administrative state, one must attempt to redress the problems that were not foreseen by the founding fathers. In part, this could be accomplished by reforms or statutes that would provide for a Congress closer to the one envisioned by the framers, and in part by modification of the Constitution itself.

One reform, which could be accomplished through legislation, would be to ensure a more responsive and fluid congressional membership by providing for truly competitive elections. Such a reform would severely limit candidates' use of personal wealth and reduce the power of incumbency by providing for government financing of primary and general election campaigns for House and Senate seats. Such reforms, coupled with other provisions that assured equal access to the electoral marketplace would produce more competitive elections and thus greater turnover within Congress. This increased fluidity, in turn, might lead in the direction of a more powerful and centralized leadership.

Another approach, which would initially involve a modification of the rules of both houses, would be to augment the renascent power of the leadership. For example, the Speaker of the House and President *pro tem* of the Senate could be given the authority to nominate committee chairs. Such a measure would give the party leadership incentives to create and maintain substantial leadership structures as well as a greater say in policy direction and coordination. Indeed, recent reforms, especially in the House, may provide a foundation on which to build further.

To the extent that congressional malaise, however, is a symptom of the growing imbalance between Congress and the presidency, constitutional reforms may be required. And to the extent that power dispersion in Congress is a function of the swelling of the presidency, such reforms could go hand in hand with the measures outlined above. One area for attention could be the national security and war-making prerogatives of the Congress, which have been vitiated by the ability of recent presidents to wage war without declarng it. And though the War Powers Act goes some way in the restoration of Congress' constitutional rights in this area, a revised enumeration of these rights might be helpful. Similarly, the presidential tendency to resort to executive agreements rather than treaties, in an attempt to avoid senatorial scrutiny, might be discouraged by more inclusive constitutional language. And the mandating of some kind of congressional security council might be considered.

Revision of the presidential veto, by reducing the extraordinary majority required to override, might help bolster moves toward more coherent congressional policymaking and centralized leadership. And explicit authorization of the congressional veto technique, though probably not its committee variant, would remove this device from the fog of debate as to its constitutionality. Lastly, specific reference in the Constitution to congressional responsibilities in the oversight as well as the authorization of legislation might give added legitimacy and weight to this vital but neglected legislative function.

We make these observations and suggestions with the full understanding of the difficulty of passing legislation and amending the Constitution in an attempt to correct the current deficiencies of Congress. Nor are we so egg-headed as to believe they will achieve fruition in the near future. But we are convinced that Congress faces a serious problem in monitoring and influencing the administrative state under existing institutional and constitutional arrangements. We are also convinced that the problems of Congress cannot be solved by Congress alone. The power motive is simply too strong to allow career-oriented members of a professionalized Congress to accept long-term centralization of Congress without the pressure of constitutional provisions that encourage and reinforce centralization. The efficacy of our separation of powers system of government and the ability of the nation to adjust successfully to the existence of the administrative state both suggest reforms not only of Congress but also of the Constitution.

359